| DATE | | | |
|---|---|---|---|
|  |  |  |  |
|  |  |  |  |
|  |  |  |  |
|  |  |  |  |
|  |  |  |  |
|  |  |  |  |
|  |  |  |  |
|  |  |  |  |
|  |  |  |  |
|  |  |  |  |
|  |  |  |  |
|  |  |  |  |
|  |  |  |  |
|  |  |  |  |

# MARKETING

## IN THE HOSPITALITY INDUSTRY

### SECOND EDITION

**Ronald A. Nykiel,** *Ph.D., CHA*

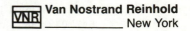

**Van Nostrand Reinhold**
New York

**Van Nostrand Reinhold**
115 Fifth Avenue
New York, New York 10003

**Van Nostrand Reinhold International Company Limited**
11 New Fetter Lane
London EC4P 4EE, England

**Van Nostrand Reinhold**
480 La Trobe Street
Melbourne, Victoria 3000, Australia

**Macmillan of Canada**
Division of Canada Publishing Corporation
164 Commander Boulevard
Agincourt, Ontario M1S 3C7, Canada

16 15 14 13 12 11 10 9 8 7 6 5 4 3 2

**Library of Congress Cataloging in Publication Data**

Nykiel, Ronald A.
  Marketing in the hospitality industry / Ronald A. Nykiel. — 2nd ed.

    p.    cm.
  Bibliography:  p.
  Includes index.
  ISBN 0-442-26697-9
  1. Hotels, taverns, etc. — Marketing.    2. Motels — Marketing.
3. Food service — Marketing.    4. Tourist trade — Marketing.
I. Title.
TX911.3.M3N94 1989
647'.94'0688 — dc19                                        88-5645
                                                              CIP

*To my wife, Karen, our son Ron, Jr.,
and my friends in the hospitality industry.
A special thanks to Irene and Marge
for all their help in this endeavor.*

# Contents

# Preface

*I*n order to understand marketing in the hospitality industry today, one must have a thorough understanding of the marketplace. The consumers of the lodging, food and beverage, and other travel-related products and services have changed. A look at the demographics, psychographics, user characteristics, or any other measure of the market will demonstrate that marketing hospitality products and services is no longer a simple sales call or a good advertising message. The key to marketing in the hospitality industry today is understanding that there is no *one* consumer; there are many, even within the same individual, as defined by the particular set of needs associated with that purpose. Comprehending this concept, understanding the needs of the consumers, knowing the segmentations of the market, and selecting the best weapon from the arsenal of marketing tools to reach your consumers is what this book is all about.

Let us think about the consumer for a moment, be it Mr. Jones, Mrs. Jones, or Ms. Jones. When this individual travels or makes use of the products and services offered by the hospitality industry there is a response to a marketing message that can trigger a decision to purchase from you. This purchase translates into market share, sales, occupancy, average check, rate, profit, passenger miles, or whatever your measure of success is for your marketing program. The key to marketing today is to find the right marketing messages. When this individual travels for business purposes and dines out with clients, his or her needs may be very different than when traveling or dining out with family or friends.

The hospitality industry has responded to the consumer and his changing wants and needs. In the food and beverage sector of the industry we have seen the all-purpose, all-occasion restaurant come and go — and come again. We have seen numerous fast-food concepts, themed restaurants, and even new dining environments emerge. In air travel, the results of deregulation have led to everything from specialized segmentation or carriers offering all one type or class of service to a plethora of discount and advance-purchase fares. In air travel the response has also included frequent flyer programs, consolidations, the "hub" concept, and new automated technologies. In lodging, a proliferation of segmented product specialties ranging from budget to all-suite concepts has emerged. Major downtown mega-hotels arrived, departed, and returned. The motor inn replaced the motel, and concepts such as club floors, all-women floors, and concierge floors emerged. While new chains popped up weekly in the mid-1980s, consolidation began to accelerate in the late 1980s.

This great number of changes in products and services offered represented an effort to begin addressing the needs of different market segments. Now, where is marketing? But more important, where should marketing be and what should it be doing? These questions will surface throughout this book, as will some case examples. We will examine and dissect marketing ideas and techniques — some that have failed and some that have succeeded.

An instructor's manual is available from the publisher.

# *Acknowledgments*

*W*orking in the hospitality industry is perhaps one of the greatest learning experiences an individual can have. Over the years I have learned from each person I have met and worked with or for, and from every travel experience. The contents of this book were influenced by the exposure I have had to a number of people within the industry and in other professions.

I would like to acknowledge the contributions of the following reviewers to the development of this book: Bob Halverson, Iowa Lakes Community College; Kenneth Crocker, Bowling Green State University; James Downey, University of New Haven; Robert Johnson, Cape Cod Community College; William Jaffe, Iowa State University; Dr. John Palmer, James Madison University; and Ralph Tellone, Middlesex County College. A specific acknowledgment is due Dr. Jim Myers, author of *Market Structure Analysis,* for sharing his knowledge on market positioning and brand preference. To my good friend, Bob Aronin, thanks for the many discussions on travel market intermediaries. To Eric Orkin, inventor of the HOTMAMA (Hotel Marketing Management) Training Program, a sincere thanks for the healthy discussions on setting rates and flexible break-even analyses. My special appreciation to Bill Marriott, Jr., of Marriott Corporation, Mike Rose of Holiday Corp., Juergen Bartels of Carlson Companies, Bill Hulett of The Stouffer Hotel Company, and Jim Biggar of Nestle Enterprises, Inc. for the opportunities they provided me to learn about the industry and the knowledge gained from exposure to their leadership. Finally, a special acknowledgment to my father for sharing with me his wisdom of 40 years in sales and marketing at Colgate Palmolive Co.

# Understanding the Hospitality Industry

1

---

## PURPOSE

This chapter emphasizes the consumers' perspective of the hospitality industry. The purpose and motivation of travel are discussed, focusing on the consumers' needs. This overview perspective of the industry provides the key definitions of the major components of the industry. How these industry components market their services and products will also be discussed. Finally, this chapter looks at "brand preference," which is coming of age in the hospitality industry.

---

## OBJECTIVES

1. Relate to the consumers' perspective of the hospitality industry.

2. Provide an understanding of how the industry has evolved in terms of its approach to marketing.

3. Understand the products and services offered to the consumer by today's firms, and the marketing approaches employed by these firms to "sell" the consumer.

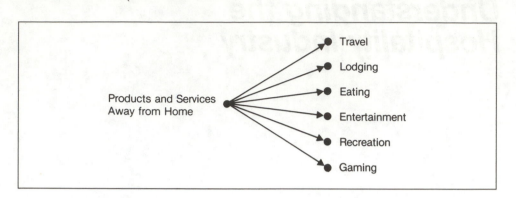

**Figure 1.1**　The Hospitality Industry

For any business that has experienced rapid development, a concise definition of the industry is virtually impossible. Moreover, the definition depends on the perspective of the individual. A hotelier might believe the industry is defined as rooms, food and beverage. A restauranteur might define it as a quality dining experience with the focus on food and beverage offerings. An airline's definition of the industry would be providing travel to people for business and pleasure. This chapter will present these different perspectives, beginning with the traditional or historic perspective and ending with the consumers' perspective. All of these viewpoints can fit under one umbrella definition of the hospitality industry: that is, products and services offered to the consumer away from home. The industry encompasses travel, lodging, eating, entertainment, recreation, and gaming (Figure 1.1).

## HISTORIC PERSPECTIVE

Restaurants with white tablecloths, hotels with grand ballrooms, and the business executive being pampered by a favorite airline with personalized matches and a reserved seat are both traditional and, to some extent, obsolete. Although the airplane, hotel, and gourmet meal are still with us today — all but the matches — the difference lies in how they are developed and marketed to the consumer. Historically the industry's focus was on the full-service hotel, the business traveler, and the "glory" of travel. Then a new concept in lodging evolved, synonymous with the word *motel* — Holiday Inns. Kemmons Wilson founded more than the world's largest lodging chain — he founded a product based on a marketing premise. Holiday Inns, as they existed in the 1950s and 1960s, carved out a market segment, and the consumer responded to that product. The continued success of the Holiday Corporation can be attributed to its ability to change that product and associated levels of service to reach many market segments and fulfill many different consumer segment needs.

**Table 1.1**   Historic Perspective and Trends

| | |
|---|---|
| 1800s | Private rooms become the norm in hotels. |
| 1859 | First hotel elevator is installed in New York's Fifth Avenue Hotel. |
| 1860 | The Manhattan cocktail is invented. |
| to | The Tremont House in Boston becomes the first hotel to have indoor plumbing, free soap, and guestroom doors with locks. |
| 1900 | The Waiters and Bartenders National Union is formed. |
| 1900 | The American Hotel Association is formed. |
| | Print advertising for hotels appears in newspapers. |
| 1920 | More new hotels built (1920–1930) than during any other ten-year period before or since, resulting in lowest occupancy rate of 51% in 1933. |
| 1929 | The first airport hotel opens in Oakland, California. |
| 1935 | Howard Johnson initiates the first hospitality industry franchise. |
| | Heated pools, air cooling, radios and TVs appear. |
| 1940 | The first hotel management contract is signed by Inter-Continental Hotels (1940). |
| 1946 | The hotel industry experiences it highest occupancy ever—95%. |
| 1950s | Holiday Inns' roadside motels begin the motel era. |
| 1960s | Market segmentation and product segmentation begin in earnest in the hotel industry. |
| | Motor hotels, roadside inns, develop along the interstates. |
| 1970s | Spectacular design and architecture exemplified by the Hyatt Hotel in Atlanta establish the "new" era of the hotel. |
| 1980s | Major developments in computers, telecommunications, etc., result in sophisticated reservations systems. |
| | Deregulation occurs. |
| | Full product segmentation in progress from econo-budgets to motels to motor hotels to hotels to all-suites to resorts to mega-hotels. |
| 1990s | Travel-related companies emerge as multi-billion-dollar forces in lodging and air transportation. |
| | Travel Purchasing Systems emerge, as the marketing giants step in on the purchasing process. |
| 2000s | |

Bill Marriott did the same when he opened the Hot Shoppe Cafeteria; he developed a food service concept that met a market segment's needs. McDonald's and Kentucky Fried Chicken went beyond just food concepts — they were delivery systems that specifically addressed the needs of consumers. So, despite the comfort one receives from the nostalgia of the Grand Old Hotel or the excitement of a new restaurant theme, marketing and the consumers were responding to their needs being met by products and services. As the needs and the consumers changed, so did the hospitality industry. Table 1.1 shows the evolution in the industry over the past 200 years and predicts trends into the year 2000.

## WHO'S WHO TODAY

Holiday and Marriott are multi-billion-dollar companies today, but are very different from 20 years ago. For that matter, most of the growth firms in the hospitality industry today are different than they were even 10 years ago. Their products and services have evolved, their creativity has resulted in new businesses, and their profits from products and services have grown. Today there are many chains, airlines, restaurant franchises, rent-a-car companies, and even gaming companies. More important, the consumers' needs are being met by the variety and level of services offered. These services are offered with an increasingly sophisticated arsenal of marketing weaponry.

Who's Who in the hospitality industry merits its own volume. The purpose of looking briefly at a select number of hospitality industry firms is to appreciate the integration and evolutionary process that has occurred. As the hospitality industry grew, so did interest in the industry on the part of the business and financial communities. Interest was not only from within the United States but had an international scope as well. The industry had its base in notables such as Baron Hilton, Bill Marriott, Kemmons Wilson, and Colonel Sanders, to name a few founding fathers. These individuals conceived of a product or service and, through their ambition and drive, developed their products or services. The keys to their success vary, but the common denominator was meeting the market's needs.

There are the lodging firms like Holiday, Best Western, Hilton, Sheraton, Ramada, Hyatt, Stouffer and Westin Hotels — their products relate to a variety of market segments, and their success is due to marketing and meeting the market's needs. There are the food service leaders, too, such as McDonald's, Burger King, Wendy's, Red Lobster, and Kentucky Fried Chicken. Each may offer a food product with its own identification, but each has grown and developed, based on meeting the market's needs and through marketing. There are the major air carriers like United, American, Northwest, Texas Air Corporation, and Delta, all of which offer a flying service — the difference between them is their marketing.

Since deregulation, the industry has seen many acquisitions and mergers, a trend which continues as the strong grow stronger and swallow the weak. Likewise, tax reforms of the late 1980s and the sorting out of financially weak companies (not able to survive times of weak demand) continue to result in absorption or acquisition of chains, with many going out of business. Therefore, while the tables which follow may not reflect all of the changes, they provide the reader with a scope of the hotel, airline, rent-a-car, and cruise-line firms. One should recognize that in the period 1980 through 1988, over 75 new brands emerged in the lodging industry with over 35 either going out of business or being absorbed by others. The airline industry dominated the headlines during this same eight-year period as mega-carriers emerged and under-capitalized upstart carriers were either absorbed or just disappeared. (Tables 1.2 through 1.6 list some of the major players in the industry.)

**Table 1.2**   Top U.S. Lodging Chains

| *Luxury/First Class/Full Service* | *All Suites* |
|---|---|
| Hyatt | Embassy Suites |
| Westin | Lexington Hotel Suites |
| Stouffer | Hotel Corp. of Pacific |
| Ritz Carlton | Guest Quarters |
| Four Seasons | InnSuites International |
| Omni | Park Suite Hotels |
| Loews | Residence Inns |
| Helmsley | |
| | |
| *Major Multi-Product Chains\** | *Inns/Motels/Budgets* |
| Holiday* | Days Inns* |
| Marriott* | Motel 6 |
| Radisson* | Best Value Inns |
| Ramada | Econo-Travel Motels |
| Quality* | Super 8 Motels |
| Trusthouse Forte | Red Carpet/Master Host |
| Hilton | Rodeway Inns |
| Sheraton | La Quinta |
| Best Western | Treadway |
| Doubletree*-Compri | Magic Key |
| Prime/Howard Johnson's | |

| *Other (and Non-U.S. in U.S. Market\*)* | | |
|---|---|---|
| Downtowner/Passport | Meridien** | Royce Hotels |
| Thunderbird/Red Lion | Sofitel** | Rock Resorts |
| Americana | Hotel Ibis** | Colony Resorts |

*Multiple products/brand chains.

**Chains based/headquarter outside of U.S. now in U.S. market.

**Table 1.3** Major Restaurant Chains*

| | |
|---|---|
| Arby's[1] | Howard Johnson's[3] |
| Baker's Square[4] | Jack-in-the-Box[1] |
| Baskin-Robbins[2] | Kentucky Fried Chicken[1] |
| Bennigans[7] | Long John Silver's[1] |
| Big Boy[3] | Magic Pan[7] |
| Bob Evans Farms[4] | McDonald's[1] |
| Bonanza[4] | Pizza Hut[6] |
| Brown Derby[4] | Ponderosa[4] |
| Burger Chef[1] | Red Lobster[7] |
| Burger King[1] | Roy Rogers[1] |
| Church's Fried Chicken[1] | Sam's[3+] |
| Dairy Queen[1] | Sizzler Steak Houses[4] |
| Denny's[3] | Sonic Drive Inns[1] |
| Domino's Pizza[6] | Taco Bell[1] |
| Dunkin' Donuts[5] | TGI Friday's[7] |
| Friendly's[3] | Wendy's[1] |
| Hardees[1] | |

*Sales in excess of $250 million
+Formerly Sambo's
[1]Fast food; [2]ice cream; [3]coffee shop; [4]family restaurant;
[5]donuts; [6]pizza; [7]dinner house.

**Table 1.4** Major U.S. Air Carriers

Texas Air Corporation* (Continental/Eastern)
United*
American*
Delta*
Northwest*
TWA
Pan Am
*US Air (including PSA and Piedmont)

*These top six, as a group, control over 75% of the total market.

**Table 1.5**  Major Rent-A-Car Firms

| | | |
|---|---|---|
| Hertz | Dollar | Alamo |
| Avis | American International | Ajax |
| Budget | Agency | Value |
| National | Thrifty | General |
| Rent-A-Wreck | Snappy | |

**Table 1.6**  Major Cruise Ship Operators

| | *Registry:* |
|---|---|
| American Hawaii Cruises | United States |
| American President Lines | United States |
| Carnival Cruises | Liberia |
| Chandris, Inc. | Greece |
| Commodore Cruise Lines | West Germany |
| Costa Cruises | Greece |
| Cunard Line | Britain |
| Delta Line Cruises | United States |
| Eastern Steamship Lines | Panama |
| Epirotiki Lines | Greece |
| Holland America Cruises | Netherlands Antilles |
| Home Lines | Liberia |
| Italian Line Cruises | Italy |
| "K" Lines | Greece |
| Karageorgis Lines | Greece |
| Lauro Lines | Italy |
| Moore-McCormack Lines | United States |
| Norwegian American Cruises | Norway |
| Paquet French Cruises | France |
| Princes Cruises | Britain |
| Royal Caribbean Lines | Norway |
| Royal Viking Lines | Norway |
| Sitmar Cruises | Liberia |
| Sun Lines | Greece |
| United States Cruises | United States |
| Western Cruises | Panama |

The Who's Who of the hospitality industry now offers the consumer everything from a budget motel to a motel, a motor hotel, or a full-service luxury hotel. The Who's Who offers the consumer a means to get to a destination, be it by air, auto, train, bus, or ship, as well as dining experiences ranging from a Big Mac to a gourmet meal by candlelight. Recreational needs are met by offerings ranging from campgrounds to ocean-front condominiums to spectacular entertainment and gaming facilities. How these products and services are marketed to the consumer is what this book is all about.

## A MARKETING PERSPECTIVE OF THE INDUSTRY

As products and services offered by the hospitality industry have evolved, so has the marketing of these products and services. *Marketing focuses on the needs of the buyer in today's hospitality industry.* The audience of buyers has also become complex. Not only do the firms' products or services have buyers, but so do the firms themselves. Marketing must be aware of and relate to the total audience, including the firms' buyers, such as the shareholders, investment community, investors, and franchisees (Figure 1.2).

To explain these multiple purposes of marketing, it is necessary to briefly touch upon how the hospitality industry functions to achieve its growth and vitality. In order to function, sources of capital are required for investment. These sources come from the internal profits generated by the firm and from a variety of investors. To emphasize this point, one hotel executive was asked who owned the most hotels in the United States today. His response was quick — the insurance companies who hold the mortgages. In the food sector it could be the banks, local investors, and so on. This point is important as one tries to understand why hospitality industry firms spend marketing dollars on everything from image and awareness advertising to painting stripes on their aircraft.

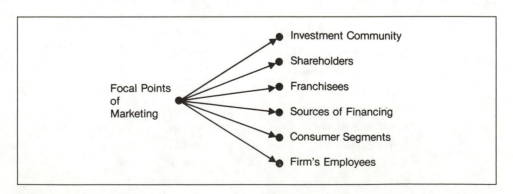

**Figure 1.2** Marketing Perspective

This full awareness of the total audience for marketing is perhaps even clearer when one looks at the effort that goes into the firm's annual reports to shareholders. After all, this document represents a principal marketing vehicle to those who purchase pieces of the firm. Even more illustrative is the next tier of marketing to the franchise section of the audience. Annual franchise conferences often rival the best of a Broadway production. The reason is simple. They are marketing to a very important audience — those who make the company grow.

To summarize, the hospitality industry marketing perspective is multipurpose and must relate to many different audiences. The overall goal is not only the sale of the product or service, but the sale of the firm's image to its total audience.

## A CONSUMER PERSPECTIVE OF THE INDUSTRY

How consumers view the industry is one of the major focuses of this book. It is the understanding of the consumers' perspective that creates a marketing message that sells the product or service. As a matter of fact, if marketing is thorough in its research and analysis, then it can perform even another service to a firm. This is to influence product development or recommend changes to services being offered to be in line with what the consumers express as their needs. Marketing cannot succeed if the product or service offering is not in line with its consumers' needs.

The consumer's perspective centers around the needs a product or service satisfies or fulfills. As will be discussed in the next chapter, not all consumers have the same needs. Much depends on a consumer's purpose — the reason for utilizing the product or service. For example, when an executive travels for business purposes, his or her needs may well relate to first-class air travel, an upscale lodging facility, and a gourmet dining experience. The executive, therefore, may have a set of needs that is best served by a Hyatt, Stouffer, Embassy Suites, or Westin hotel and their more expensive dining facilities. This same executive, when traveling with his or her family for purposes of pleasure, may have a set of needs that correspond to economy-rate air travel, a budget motel, and a nearby fast-food restaurant. For this trip the executive's needs may be best served by a package deal on air, rooms, and food, or a Day's Inn and nearby McDonald's or Burger King. The point to remember is that *a consumer's perspective of the industry and its products and services will change based upon the reason or purpose of his or her away-from-home venture.*

## BRAND PREFERENCE COMING OF AGE

To some extent the hospitality industry lags behind the consumer goods industry in that preference for a brand or brand identification is just now coming of age in the services industry. Ten years ago people could tell you their favorite brand of cigarette or auto, and some would even swear a loyalty to that brand. Think of good old Camels — "I'd walk a mile for a Camel" — or the loyal Volvo owner who's on his or her sixth Volvo. That type of brand loyalty is hard to recall in the hospitality industry 10 years ago; however, it is not so hard to envision 10 years from now. Even today there is an awareness among consumers of what the Hyatt "brand" or Day's Inn "brand" represents. Today, there are Big Mac loyalists, Kentucky Fried Chicken loyalists, and those who prefer to fly American or United. No longer are people saying, "Get me a room and rent-a-car along with a seat to L.A." Today's consumer of the hospitality industry's products and services more and more frequently is saying, "I want the 6:00 p.m. American flight to L.A., a room at the Marriott and a Hertz car — make it a T-bird." The message is getting clearer as brand preference comes of age. Marketing is one key to the consumers' preferences, but so must the product or service meet those consumers' needs in order to turn the lock on the sale. How marketing views the consumer becomes increasingly important, and is the focal point of the next chapter.

## KEY WORDS AND CONCEPTS

**Away-from-Home Products and Services** The scope of the hospitality industry.

**Marketing** Selling a service or product by focusing on the needs of the buyer.

**Focal Points of Marketing** Targets of marketing that extend beyond offering the product or service and include shareholders, investors, franchises, and employees.

**Consumer's Perspective** The consumer's attitude toward a product or service that centers around the needs that it satisfies.

## ASSIGNMENTS

1. Describe how your needs as a consumer change as your purpose of travel changes.

2. Explain what you look for in a hospitality industry product or service and who best meets those needs.

3. Have you developed a brand preference, be it for an airline, hotel/motel company, or food service, and are you a loyalist?

4. Who is doing the best job of meeting your needs? Describe those needs and why they are, or are not, being fulfilled.

# Segmentation and the Industry

**2**

---

### PURPOSE

Markets can be segmented or subdivided in many different ways. This chapter briefly describes the traditional territorial concepts, as well as contemporary segmentation methods, and how each can be applied to the hospitality industry.

---

### OBJECTIVES

1. Understand the ways in which markets can be segmented.

2. Develop an understanding of how consumers of hospitality industry products and services can be viewed in manageable methods of segmentation for the purposes of marketing.

3. Comprehend key markets for the hospitality industry, including the strategic feeder city market concepts.

Segmentation can be a very complex subject. Very simply, however, a segment is a portion of the total market that has customers with common needs.

The 1980 census provides a number of examples of segmentation, such as geographic segmentation (where people reside) and demographic segmentation (age, sex, race, and income). These breakdowns have been widely used as methods of subdividing a total population or market. Besides these customary examples from the census, marketing employs other classifications to segment the market. This chapter will focus on a number of the elements of segmentation as they relate to the hospitality industry.

## GEOGRAPHIC SEGMENTATION

Geographic segmentation is the division of a market by region, zone, state, district, county, city, Standard Metropolitan Statistical Area (SMSA), and zip code zones. There are many purposes and applications of this type of segmentation within the hospitality industry today. Our discussion will focus on marketing's use of geographic segmentation.

### REGIONS, ZONES, AND DISTRICTS

*Regions and zones* are used primarily to establish subdivisions of a country and, in the case of zones of the international marketplace, the world. Frequently, natural borders, such as the Rockies, define a region. (For example, in the United States, the region west of the Rockies is known as the western region.) The regional subdivision is very useful to the industry. For instance, the bulk of the travel of a corporate sales force is within a region. In fact, travel between cities within regions accounts for over 65 percent of all travel in the United States.

Quite often, principal cities of a region tend to "feed" each other. For example, in the Western Region, Los Angeles feeds such markets as Palm Springs, Las Vegas, Phoenix, and San Francisco, and vice versa. Marketing efforts within a region may, therefore, concentrate on both the primary feeder market, say, Los Angeles, as well as the markets that feed Los Angeles, for instance, San Francisco. Likewise, regional advertising, sales efforts, public relations, and promotions can be concentrated on where the business comes from and goes to in terms of geographic markets. This is known as the *feeder market concept*. It is important for the travel sectors of the hospitality industry to recognize intraregional travel.

Travel *zones* are areas similar to regions but are usually, especially on a domestic basis, smaller than a region. (In some hospitality industry organizations with international operations, a zone may designate a section of the world; for example, the Southeast Asian Zone or the Northern European Zone.) Zones designate a sales or marketing area for management purposes. For example, the area from Albany to Syracuse to Rochester might be classified as a zone. Zones frequently are synonymous with, or can be added together to form marketing districts.

A *district* encompasses a geographic area with a concentration of customers or products. For example, the Midwest Regional Office located in Chicago may have a district manager for the Milwaukee area, while Milwaukee and La Crosse, Wisconsin may fall under the Wisconsin zone.

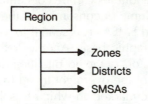

## COUNTIES AND SMSAs

Counties and Standard Metropolitan Statistical Areas are another type of geographic segmentation. SMSAs tend to be the core of population within one large county or a number of small counties. For example, the New York City SMSA, which is a huge market in terms of population, encompasses counties in three states and Long Island.

*Examples of Key Strategic SMSAs*

| | |
|---|---|
| Los Angeles | Denver |
| Atlanta | Dallas |
| Chicago | Minneapolis-St. Paul |
| New York | Boston |
| Washington, D.C. | San Francisco |
| Houston | Seattle |
| Detroit | Pittsburgh |
| St. Louis | Miami/Dade County |
| Phoenix | Cleveland |

Counties and SMSAs play an important role in marketing for a variety of reasons.

1. Frequently, both print and broadcast media exposure will relate to SMSA markets.

2. In many places within the United States, laws concerning operating businesses will vary by county with respect to liquor licenses, hours of restaurant operations, food service regulations, and so on.

3. There are direct correlations between SMSA size and the number and type of food service outlets such markets can absorb.

For the travel sectors of the hospitality market, such as airlines, bus companies, rail service, and lodging, SMSAs serve as a major marketing research tool. For example, *city pairs* such as Boston and New York, or Washington, D.C. and New York represent pairs of cities between which a *heavy travel pattern* exists. The importance of city pairs to marketing is that marketing expenditures can be concentrated on the city pairs that generate the highest possible volume of consumers of the product or service. Understanding the major city pairs and SMSAs is essential to assessing the best use of marketing expenditures on a geographic basis. Another reason for the importance of cities and SMSAs to the travel sectors of the hospitality industry is that 24 SMSAs generate approximately 50 percent of the overnight travel in the United States. These SMSAs then become *key strategic markets* in which to sell the travel product or service. The travel between key strategic markets and city pairs is referred to as *traffic flow* (Figure 2.1).

On a worldwide geographic basis there are major traffic flow patterns of great significance to the marketing of travel products and services.

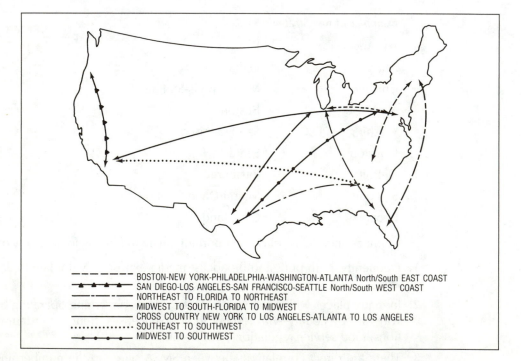

| | |
|---|---|
| – – – – – | BOSTON-NEW YORK-PHILADELPHIA-WASHINGTON-ATLANTA North/South EAST COAST |
| ▲▲▲▲ | SAN DIEGO-LOS ANGELES-SAN FRANCISCO-SEATTLE North/South WEST COAST |
| – · – · – | NORTHEAST TO FLORIDA TO NORTHEAST |
| — — — | MIDWEST TO SOUTH-FLORIDA TO MIDWEST |
| ——— | CROSS COUNTRY NEW YORK TO LOS ANGELES-ATLANTA TO LOS ANGELES |
| ·········· | SOUTHEAST TO SOUTHWEST |
| –•–•–•– | MIDWEST TO SOUTHWEST |

**Figure 2.1** Map of Major Traffic Flows in the United States

*Examples of Major World Market Traffic Flows*

East Coast of North America to Europe

Europe to East Coast of North America

Northern Europe to Southern Europe and the Mediterranean

Northeastern United States to Florida and Southeast

Midwest United States to Florida

North and South on West Coast of United States

Japan to Hawaii and West Coast of United States

Japan to Asia and South Pacific

United Kingdom to Germany, France, and Spain

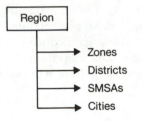

## CITIES

The core of a Standard Metropolitan Statistical Area is usually a major city. Cities tend to be ranked in some order, be it by population, affluence, industry base, or other criterion. However, cities carry an even greater significance within the hospitality industry. As mentioned earlier, the heavy travel patterns between two sets of city pairs — Boston and New York, and New York and Washington, D.C. — have created the need for air shuttle and rail services. In addition to city pairs, another important categorization of cities exists in many sectors of the hospitality industry; the *destination city*. Destination cities have attractions unto themselves that create demand for that spot on the map. For example, in the last 50 years such major destination cities as Orlando, Las Vegas, Acapulco, West Palm Beach, Lake Tahoe, and Atlantic City have emerged or reemerged as significant travel markets. While Las Vegas and Acapulco may represent examples of "pure" destination cities, many major cities are also viewed as "destination markets" because of their attractions. A "destination market" is simply a large metropolis with business and commerce in a structure, for example, New York City versus a pure destination city such as Las Vegas.

*Examples of Destination Cities and Markets*

| | |
|---|---|
| Las Vegas | Washington, D.C. |
| Atlantic City | New Orleans |
| Orlando | Palm Springs |
| San Francisco | Acapulco |
| Lake Tahoe | Miami-Ft. Lauderdale |
| West Palm Beach* | Tampa-St. Petersburg |
| San Diego | New York City |

## ZIP CODES

Zip codes, currently five-digit United States Postal Service designations, correspond to some extent with city and SMSA areas; however, zip codes further refine the area into smaller pieces (square blocks within a city). As a finite geographic marketing tool, zip codes and the first three digits of the zip, known as a sectional center, have special significance for marketing by direct mail. This significance has been greatly enhanced through the correlation of demographic data from the U.S. census tapes over the past 10 years. More will be said about this as we look at the second element of segmentation — demographics.

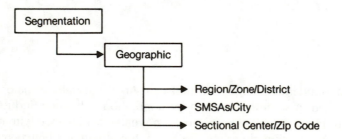

## DEMOGRAPHIC SEGMENTATION

Demographic segmentation is the division of the market by like characteristics such as sex, age, income, home ownership, marital status, occupation, and education.

Within each region, state, district, zone, SMSA, city, and even sectional center and zip code reside demographically different consumers (Figure 2.2). As a result of

*Palm Beach County

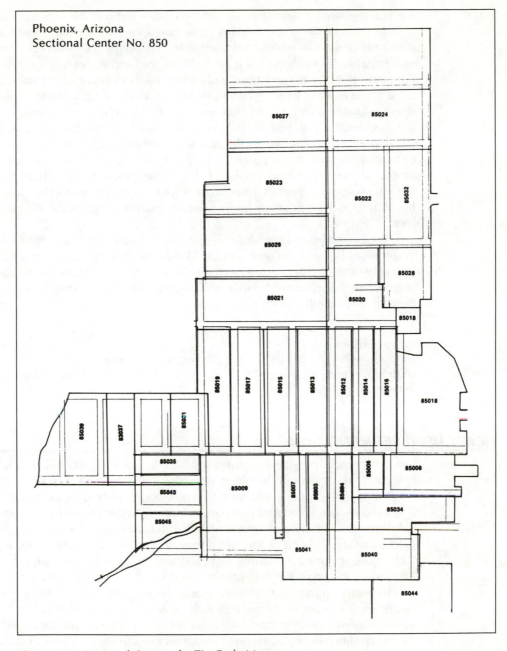

**Figure 2.2** Sectional Center of a Zip Code Map

the comprehensive demographic data available through the U.S. census tapes and private research firms specializing in demographic market data, there are virtually hundreds of ways in which to demographically segment the market. The hospitality industry is just now recognizing the sophisticated applications of such research data. For years, direct mail operations, publishers, retailers of consumer goods, and others have made extensive use of demographics by developing a *demographic profile* of the consumers of their products or services. This profile varies by product or service, but in general is matched against geographic markets that contain large percentages of people who correspond to the profile. To demonstrate how cost effective a good demographic profile and purchase pattern correlation can be, we can use the example of the direct mail publisher. For some products, less than 35 percent of the zip codes can generate more than 80 percent of the sales. Thus a good mailing list eliminates 65 percent of nonrespondent market areas for the direct mail marketeer.

Looking more closely at the hospitality industry one finds that there are direct correlations between income and the likelihood of using travel services. To a point, the higher the income, the greater the frequency of travel. Likewise, for the restaurant segment of the industry, demographic profiles exist for criteria for fast-food restaurants, bars, and full-service restaurants.

| Characteristics of Consumers of Products and Services | + | Demographic Profile | = | Targets for Marketing |
|---|---|---|---|---|

## HEAVY USER SEGMENTATION

Just as zip codes provide a useful demographic tool for direct mail marketing in that one can find correlations between zip codes and consumer profiles, so too does the hospitality industry have a method to profile and market to its most valued customer — the *heavy user*. Frequent purchases of airline tickets, hotel rooms, and restaurant meals (even fast food) can be correlated. The heavy user, a recurrent consumer of a product or service, can be identified through demographics and other segmentation techniques (Figure 2.3). To the fast-food industry, the heavy user is the regular at McDonald's, Burger King, Kentucky Fried Chicken, and Wendy's. To the airlines and lodging companies, the heavy user is the frequent traveler and often the repeat customer. For example, of the 225 million Americans counted in the 1980 census, approximately 5 to 7 million are heavy users of the travel products and services of the hospitality industry. Thus one can appreciate the effectiveness of such marketing tools as the American Express Card mailing lists and in-flight magazines, and the appeal of advertising to the recurrent business traveler.

| Age: | 25 to 44 years old | |
|---|---|---|
| Income: | $25,000 plus | |
| Education: | College degree plus | |
| Occupations: | Administration | Technicians |
| | Sales | Business Executives |
| | Marketing | Buyers |
| | Engineers | Consultants |
| Industry Origins: | Electronics | Manufacturing |
| | Pharmaceuticals | Publishing |
| | Chemicals | Banking/Finance |
| | Service | Energy-Related |
| Travel Habits: | Ten business trips plus per year | |
| | Heavy air travel | |
| | Intra- and interregional travel | |
| | Two pleasure trips plus per year | |
| Location: | Suburban and center city | |
| | Corresponding sectional centers/Zips to above | |
| | High income geodemographic census tracks | |

**Figure 2.3**   Frequent Traveler Profile

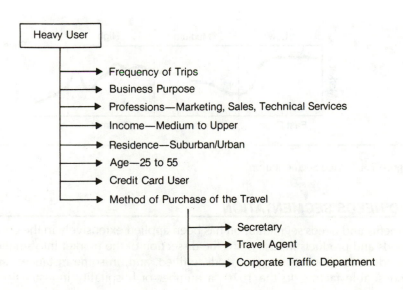

## PRICE SEGMENTATION

Price segmentation is the identification of sectors of the market whose purchase of the product or service is within the limits of certain dollar amounts. Such identification has always been important to the hospitality industry. In times of high inflation, business recessions, and economic turmoil price segmentation becomes even more significant. Markets or groups of consumers are often segmented by price as a result of per diem allowances for travel, lodging, and meals. For example, government employees, sales people, and military personnel are usually price-sensitive market segments because they have limited per diem allowances. Price sensitivity and related segmentation extends to virtually every area of the hospitality industry, ranging from the family who goes out for an inexpensive fast meal at the local fast-food restaurant, to the salesperson who wants a comfortable but inexpensive room within the per diem allowance of his or her firm, to the executive whose need to impress a client supersedes any interest in economizing. Awareness of the price segmentation and sensitivity points of the market for the product or service offered is another key marketing tool (Figure 2.4).

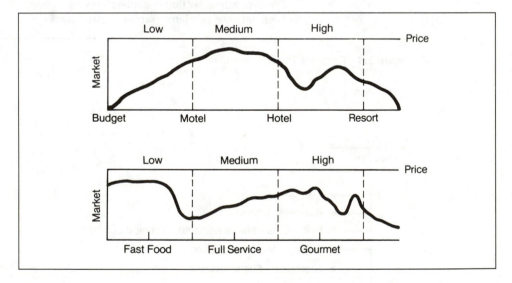

**Figure 2.4**   Price Segmentation

## BENEFITS AND NEEDS SEGMENTATION

Benefits and needs segmentation has been applied extensively in the consumer hard goods and products industry. It is the dissection of the market into smaller segments based on the benefits sought, needs fulfilled, and, in some instances, avoidance of undesirable factors. In the 1970s a number of hospitality industry firms began to make use of this research technique to help relate their products or services more closely to the consumers' needs or benefits desired. For example, the airline shuttles between New York and Boston and/or Washington, D.C. serves a large group of consumers whose single largest need is convenience of no-reservation multiple-departure-time transportation. The schedule of shuttles on the hour or on the half hour from early morning to late night fulfills the need of these consumers. Likewise, a fast-food restaurant may satisfy a number of needs or benefits such as low price, convenience, location, and fast service. Another example of this concept, and one frequently related to travel services, combines benefits sought and the avoidance of undesirable aspects. The couple escaping for the weekend to a hotel seeks a memorable experience in a relaxed atmosphere. Further, they try to avoid a child-oriented facility or one full of business meetings. In this case, the successful lodging facility must recognize what this couple on an "escape weekend" wishes to avoid, as well as the benefits sought. It is in this area of segmentation that marketing and product research must closely relate to operations and product development. We discuss this relationship in Chapter 17.

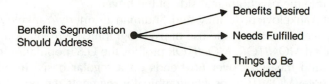

Benefit and need segmentation presents a challenge to the hospitality industry since each market segment frequently seeks different benefits from or has different needs in a product or service. The business executive who is trying to impress a client and close a major contract needs an atmosphere conducive to a business discussion and impressive to the client. Obviously, an upscale hotel with a special table in the dining room can fulfill the need. But that same environment where the executive's need is being met while negotiating a business deal is exactly what he or she wants to avoid when traveling for pleasure with his or her family.

During the 1970s, a leading hotel company hired the firm of Yankelovich, Skelly and White to examine the needs of the different segments in the lodging sector of the hospitality industry. The firm determined that a specific hotel was promoting two types of "escape weekend" programs that differed in kinds of benefits offered and needs satisfied. One was the "second honeymoon" concept, and the other was a "family escape" weekend. The "honeymooners" were fleeing from the children for peace, relaxation, and a memorable experience. The "family escapers" were out to have fun with the children and were looking for activities, excitement, and a different kind of experience. Yankelovich identified these different needs and explained the conflict of benefits between the two segment groups. The hotel's marketing team came up with the solution. All families on an escape weekend were located in the wings of the property surrounding the pool, game room, and coffee shop. The hotel lodged all "second honeymooners" in rooms high up in the tower section of the hotel or near the indoor pool and bar; it also served them breakfast in bed and made their dining reservations in the upscale food facility far removed from the coffee shop. Marketing and operations were working together, applying the research on benefits and needs segmentation to maximize the sale of the product or services while satisfying the guests' different needs.

## PSYCHOGRAPHIC SEGMENTATION

The marketing objective in the hospitality industry is to satisfy customers with its products and services. While each of the previously described methods or elements of segmentation has merit in that each describes and narrows the market, they do not provide an in-depth understanding of *why* customers respond to products and services the way they do. Psychographic segmentation is a method of subdividing the market based on like needs and psychological motivations of groups of consumers. Psychographics, along with beneficial needs segmentation, does provide certain insights into the psychological side of the buyer.

The firm of Yankelovich, Clancy and Shulman (formerly Yankelovich, Skelly and White) has been a leader in the use of psychographic segmentation through its research tool called *MONITOR. MONITOR* profiles the U.S. population over a time period of years and measures over 60 trends on a regular basis. In addition, for participating clients, *MONITOR* psychographically segments the population based on the value groupings. Both trends and value groupings may change as new ones come in and old ones disappear. For example, the *MONITOR* program measures the percentage of the U.S. population holding traditional Protestant-work-ethic-type values. It also measures and profiles other population groups holding common values, such as forerunners, new conformists, and conservatives, to name a few. Many industries apply the output from *MONITOR* to product development, advertising, promotions, and brand image (Figure 2.5).

There are many examples of the successful application of psychographic segmentation to the hospitality industry. In the late 1960s United Airlines was losing passengers whereas its competitors were gaining passengers on the same routes. Examination of aircraft, complaints, and scheduling revealed no major differences. The airline contacted a psychological research firm to interview current and former passengers to see if it could uncover the "problem." Through the use of a research technique called focus groups, passengers and former passengers were asked a series of questions under the general topic of travel. Then the interviewer asked more specific questions about passengers' likes and dislikes of air travel, but was as yet unable to identify the airline's particular problem. The interviewer took another approach, asking those interviewed to rank airlines from favorite to least favorite and to explain their ratings. Although some interviewees said this particular air carrier was average, others said the air carrier was too cold and militaristic. This was the first break-

*Examples of "Value Segments"\**

Autonomous
New Conformists
Forerunners
Moralists
Aimless

○ Each "value segment" is profiled demographically and geographically

*Examples of "Trends" Measured\**

Economizing on food purchases
Dining out more/less often
Planning more/less vacations
Planning shorter/more frequent vacations
Postponing major purchases
Not concerned about credit usage/or luxury
Desire for more/less materialistic purchases

○ More than sixty trends are profiled with specific implications for marketing behavior tailed by industry impact

**Figure 2.5** Psychographic Trend Categories
*\*Reprinted with permission of Yankelovich, Skelly and White, Inc.*

through for the interviewer. Skillfully, the interviewer shifted the focus group onto a discussion of issues facing the United States at the point in time. The result was a very outspoken negative attitude toward the military as a result of the then current controversy about U.S. involvement in Vietnam. The problem was identified: the air carrier had a very militaristic image — from the aircraft paint job, to the flight attendants' uniforms, to its superefficient service. The survey convinced the carrier's management that the company needs an image change. The airline did just that — it added new, warm colors to the exterior and interior of the aircraft and implemented a more friendly approach to service. The result was a recovery of load factors and greater market share.

A more recent case is that of US Air, formerly Allegheny Airlines. US Air fashioned its image change around new colors, new planes, new routes, and, most important of all, a new image in line with a swing in psychographics toward "feeling good about the U.S.A."

Psychographics thus is a valuable marketing research tool, especially in the decade of the 1980s. Life styles change constantly, and new values and beliefs continue to evolve; hence, understanding how the consumer thinks and why the consumer purchases becomes increasingly important.

## THE PENDULUM SWINGS TOWARD VALUE

The mainstay of customer satisfaction is providing a "value," regardless of the market segment; that is, offering a quality product or service at a fair price.

One very interesting response to a research question demonstrates how emphasis on value cuts across every segment of the market. The same question was asked of buyers of two automobiles, Volvo and Mercedes Benz: "Why did you buy this car?" The response was the same: "Its quality" and "Its value." The same type of question was posed to a family eating at McDonald's: "Why do you buy your family dinner at McDonald's?" The response from an entirely different geographic, demographic, heavy user, price, and psychographic segment than the Mercedes consumer was the same: "It's a value — good quality at a fair price." Every demographic, psychographic, and economic indicator points to *value* as the key need that marketing must fulfill in the decade ahead.

## KEY WORDS AND CONCEPTS

**Segmentation** A portion of the total market that has customers with common needs.

**Geographic Segmentation** The arbitrary division of a market by region, state, zone, district, SMSA, city, sectional center, or zip code.

**Feeder City** A city that generates major travel to another city. Example: Los Angeles to Las Vegas.

**City Pairs** Two or more cities that share intercity travel as a major proportion of their total travel. Example: Boston and New York.

**SMSA** (Standard Metropolitan Statistical Area) A census definition for a large concentration of people.

**Strategic Market** One of 24 major U.S. markets that generate, in total, over 50 percent of the overnight travel in the United States.

**Traffic Flow** A term used to describe the flow of travelers between destinations.

**Destination City** A city or area with one or more attractions unto itself that creates a demand for the specific area. It is the ultimate stopping place or a place offering at least 1,500 rooms to tourists.

**Sectional Centers** The first three digits of a zip code that signify a specific geographic area; used widely by the direct mail industry.

**Demographic Segmentation** The division of a market by like characteristics such as age, sex, income, home ownership, marital status, occupation, education, and so on.

**Heavy User Segmentation** A method of segmenting the market by identifying the most frequent customers of the product or service.

**Price Segmentation** The identification of sectors of the total market whose purchase of a product or service is within the limits of certain dollar amounts.

**Price Sensitivity** The point at which product or service price begins to affect the same of that good or service.

**Benefits or Needs Segmentation** The dissection of the market into smaller segments based on the benefits sought, needs fulfilled, and, in some instances, avoidance of certain things.

**Psychographic Segmentation** A method of subdividing the market based on like needs and psychological motivations and values of groups of consumers.

**Value** A quality product or service at a fair price.

## ASSIGNMENTS

1. Define the market segments you fall into as a consumer in the hospitality industry.
2. Identify three destination cities that have emerged over the past 50 years, and state why they are destination cities.
3. Name three sets of city pairs based on the intercity traffic flow.
4. What are the demographic characteristics of the sectional center and zip code area in which you reside?
5. What benefits do you seek and needs must you have satisfied in a restaurant or food service facility, and how do these compare to what your parents seek?
6. Based on the Yankelovich psychographic divisions of the population, how would you categorize yourself and why?

# Positioning in Line with Consumer Preferences

# 3

## PURPOSE

Up to this point we have discussed a number of ways of segmenting the market in order to better understand the consumer of the hospitality industry's products and services. This chapter focuses on further refining our understanding of the consumer marketplace and the decision-making process within the marketplace. We divide consumers into the broad categories of *end users* of the product or service and *intermediaries* who frequently make the decisions for end users. Each end user and each intermediary has his or her own needs or benefits which must be satisfied by a product. In addition, there are many things each broad category of consumer seeks to avoid in a product or service offering. These consumer perceptions and preferences are important if you are to properly position your product or service for effective marketing.

## OBJECTIVES

1. Understand who actually makes the decision to purchase your product or service and who influences that decision.

2. Categorize your customers by identifying them as end users or intermediaries within the hospitality industry marketplace.

3. Compare the specific needs or benefits sought by each consumer group and identify specific things each group seeks to avoid in a product or service.

4. Present specific customer perceptions and preferences so they relate to the product or service and the marketing message.

5. Provide an understanding of how to use this valuable marketing tool to ensure that your dollars are not wasted by ineffectively or improperly conveying your product or service offering to the marketplace.

In Chapter 1 we learned that the hospitality industry, specifically lodging, travel services, airlines, and food and beverage operations is maturing. With this maturation comes the need for segmentation. In Chapter 2, a number of segmentation methods were examined, such as geographic market segmentation, demographic consumer segmentation, psychographic segmentation, benefit segmentation, and heavy user segmentation. Historically, most industry marketing organizations were set up on a geographic market basis for sales-related activities. Then research found that certain demographic characteristics correlated to a greater frequency of travel. Thus, a heavy user segment was identified as to geographic origin, reading habits, and travel directions for marketing purposes. This level of segmentation, which is still prevalent today in many hospitality industry organizations, might be compared with the automobile industry's marketing efforts of the late 1950s.

While it is important to know *where* your marketing must be targeted, very little has been done within the industry to help target *what* the marketing message should be. For years the consumer products industry has applied benefit segmentation to determine what consumers look for in a product and what they avoid. This research is applied to everything from the color, smell, size, shape, and appearance of the product and package to the advertising message. Granted, a hotel, restaurant, or aircraft does not lend itself to this same level of refinement as far as the physical product is concerned, but each can be packaged and marketed using the same principles of benefit segmentation.

Before we focus on applying benefit segmentation, we must understand the consumer segments that purchase the hospitality industry's products and services.

## DEFINING THE MARKET SEGMENTS

The first step — identifying the major geographical markets yielding the greatest number of consumers for your product or service — is undeniably most important. There are many methods of self-analysis and competitive analysis that can provide you with this answer. If you are a nationwide airline or hotel chain, the fact that there are probably less than two dozen major markets that provide you with over 50 percent of your business becomes a real marketing tool. You know where to apply your resources for maximum benefit. But knowing where to apply your resources is not going to maximize your marketing effort unless you understand how your marketing message(s) should address your consumer segment(s). Therefore, the second step is to determine the needs of your market segments. This can be achieved through research that looks at the psychographics of the market. Simply stated, psychographic segmentation categorizes consumers into a *need segment* with common interests in and desires of benefits from a product or service. It is important to note that these needs or interests do not always follow demographic lines.

There are two broad consumer categories for the hospitality industry's products: the end user and the intermediary (or the person who influences the buying decision). Different types of end users and intermediaries relate to different benefits or needs.

# END USERS

The purpose of travel, for example, may be further clarified by determining the motivation and needs of the consumer. We can subdivide end users into business-oriented travelers and those whose purpose of travel is pleasure. Figure 3.1 graphically presents the major type of end users.

### BUSINESS

In the business segment there are three major subsegments of travelers. These are:

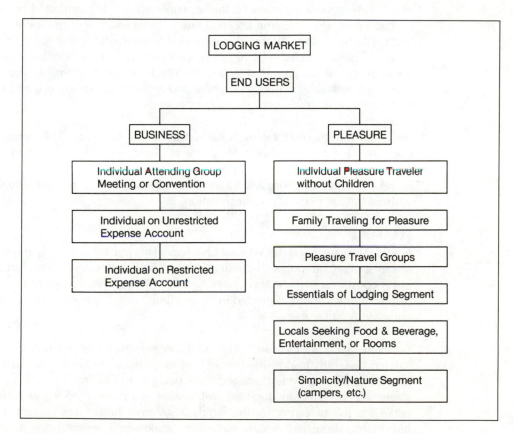

**Figure 3.1**   End Users

**Individual Attending a Group Meeting or Convention.**   The selection of the hotel or motel usually has not been this individual's choice, nor does he or she have much control over the price of room accommodations. The only choice the individual has is whether to attend the convention or meeting (although in some cases, attendance may be mandated). As an association member or individual, there may be some concern with price. As a corporate representative, there may be little or no concern with price. This subsegment's needs include comfort, service, entertainment, and relaxation as an escape from the structure of the meetings. This individual is also interested in being comfortable *during* the meetings. Almost always, the individuals in this subsegment make a prior reservation.

**Individual Traveling on a Relatively Unrestricted Expense Account.**   This person seeks comfortable, dependable, full-service accommodations and has little concern for cost. He or she almost always books in advance and has a secretary make the room and travel reservations. It is important to point out that the woman business traveler in this subsegment represents a further subsegment, as manifested by a distinct set of specific needs, including acceptability without exasperation on check-in; respect and credit treatment equal to that extended to men within this subsegment; specific room amenities, including large towels, mirror, and ample electrical outlets; and a sense of security as provided by secure door locks or other visible signs of security. This is a very fast-growing subsegment and a major marketing opportunity for those who know how to address the segment's needs.

**Individual Traveling on a Relatively Restricted Expense Account.**   This person is possibly traveling on a per diem basis. He or she is conscious of how much things cost, but still wants as much comfort and service as his or her money will buy. Usually a secretary makes the room and travel reservations, although the individual may arrive without having made a prior reservation.

## PLEASURE

**Individual Pleasure Traveler Without Children.**   This person is usually traveling with his or her spouse, but not with children. He or she is interested in comfort and service, but is conscious of price and is seeking value. This traveler is not restricted by family responsibilities and is interested in "living it up" and enjoying various restaurant and entertainment facilities.

**Family Traveling for Pleasure.**   The adult members of the family are somewhat restricted by family responsibilities and are more interested in providing the essentials of getting the family fed, lodged, and occupied than in "living it up." They are interested in restaurant facilities, televisions, swimming pools, and so on, which make the job of caring for the family away-from-home less complicated. Price is important. These individuals sometimes make their reservations in advance, but often do not. (There are two or more subsegments here that are differentiated by income.)

**Couple or Family Interested Only in Essentials of Lodging.**   They need a place to eat and sleep and nothing more. They are very conscious of price and are not interested in paying for extras.

**Couple or Family Seeking to Avoid the Service, Tipping, High Costs, Semi-Rigidity, etc., of Hotels, Motels, and Resorts.**   They seek simplicity, outdoor recreation, and freedom in their pleasure travel experience. Such people are particularly interested in camping, beach and mountain cottages, and so on, and shy away from hotels, motels, and resorts to fulfill their pleasure travel or vacation needs. (There are possibly several subsegments here, especially if condominium renters are considered, but basically none in this segment are interested in hotel services. They are seeking an unstructured, do-it-all-yourself vacation.)

## INTERMEDIARIES

Intermediaries are depicted graphically in Figure 3.2. This grouping may also be further segmented between business-oriented and pleasure travel. Intermediaries are generally a "buying influence," not the actual user of the product or service. Let's briefly look at some key intermediaries.

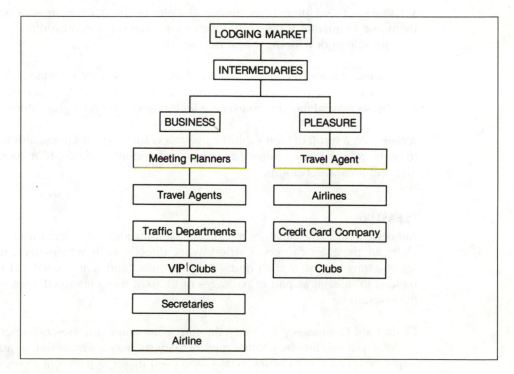

**Figure 3.2**   Intermediaries

## BUSINESS

**Meeting Planner.**   He or she is an association executive, a corporate executive, or a training company executive, whose major concern is to run a successful meeting. Meeting room facilities, services on demand in these facilities, and group feeding facilities are of primary importance. Individual restaurants, room accommodations, and so on, are important, but they are usually secondary to the meeting room facilities and service. This person is usually price-conscious, although this varies with his or her association's or company's policies.

**Travel Agents.**   They act as individuals or as representatives of small companies and may or may not be familiar with booking facilities. The travel agent is interested in booking clients into lodging facilities that are dependable in honoring the booking and in providing consistent services. He or she seeks to make the reservation with a minimum of complication and is very interested in receiving prompt payment of his or her commission.

**Traffic Departments of Major Corporations.**   Within a number of major corporations, travel has reached a point where volume dictates setting up a department to "manage and schedule" company travel.

**VIP Clubs.**   There are certain customers every business recognizes as important to them and frequently addresses through some method of expression. VIP clubs play a major role in developing repeat business.

**Secretaries.**   One of the largest groups of intermediaries are secretaries. While some entrust the total travel purchase decision (air, hotel, etc.) to their secretaries, others use the secretarial function to execute their predetermined flights, hotels, etc.

**Airline.**   As a result of their sophisticated reservation systems, most airlines may perform the role of a travel intermediary by also handling individuals' requests for hotel and rent-a-car reservations.

## PLEASURE

**Airlines.**   Selling the pleasure market segment through intermediaries is also a specialty of most air carriers. Carriers work directly with wholesalers, retail travel agents, travel clubs, and so on by offering flights and seat capacities to key destinations to be sold as part of packages or to assist these intermediaries in selling to the consumer.

**Credit Card Companies.**   Many credit card companies sell the consumer the travel package put together by another intermediary such as a wholesaler. In addition, the larger credit card companies, banks, and even major department stores often have an in-house travel division to promote travel and travel packages to their customer lists.

**Clubs.**   As the travel market has become more sophisticated, travel clubs have emerged to meet both general and specific needs of consumers. These travel clubs, such as Club Universe and Club Med, target the frequent pleasure traveler by offering club members special packages to desirable destinations. In addition, these packages are frequently tailored to specific pleasure interests, such as golf, tennis, visiting historic sites, and getting away from civilization.

## EATING AWAY FROM HOME

To this previous segmentation of the consumer as defined by purpose of travel we need to add the banquet customer and local restaurant customer. Figure 3.3 illustrates a similar conceptual segmentation of the restaurant or eating-away-from-home market. Segmenting this market can be accomplished by purpose or experience desired, price sensitivity, locational convenience, and user characteristics. Let's briefly examine each and look at the market's needs by segment.

### PURPOSE

In this segment the overall dining experience is to fulfill a specific purpose, such as to provide a location for a business meeting, to impress a client, to renew a marriage, to get out of the house, and so on. Food quality and level of services sought will vary with purpose. Specific needs and marketing messages will require a tailored or pointed approach.

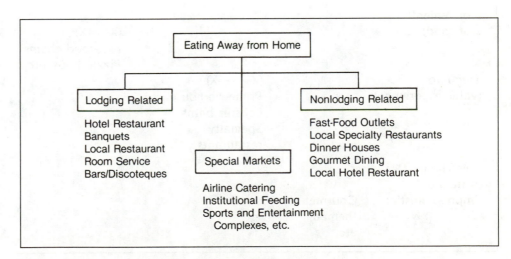

**Figure 3.3**   Eating-away-from-home Market Segmentation

## PRICE SENSITIVITY

A segmentation by price and related demographic consumer characteristics has been the topic of many studies. Usually the higher the income (up to a certain point), the greater the propensity to dine out and spend. The one exception is consumption of fast food or convenience food. In this regard, the key today is not only convenience but value, value being a quality (for convenience/fast food) product at a fair market price. Examples include the major fast-food chains (McDonald's, Burger King, Wendy's, etc.) and the local convenience food operations (such as the pizza shop owned and operated locally).

The first tier of the three-tiered price-related market is fast food. Figure 3.4 further breaks down the multitiered price market segments. The second tier is the medium-priced segment seeking to step up from fast food (and also a change of pace) and "experience" good food at a fair price. This tier is also value-oriented within the preceding definition. The choice might range from the prime-rib house to the lobster barn. Again, occasion and food type preference are key determining factors. Tier three is the least price sensitive. This tier or subsegment represents two need groups. The first is the special occasion group, exemplified by the anniversary cou-

<br/>

**Price Sensitivity**

| | Low | Medium | High | Cost per Meal |
|---|---|---|---|---|
| Tier One (convenient/ fast food) | | | (X——X) Fast-food chains Pizza shops, etc. | $ 5 |
| Tier Two (value/experience) | | (X——X) Prime-rib house Lobster barns Specialty restaurants | | $10 |
| Tier Three (X) (affluent/ impressionistic) | | | | $15 |
| | Gourmet- themed, etc. | | | $20+ |
| | | | | $25+ |

**Figure 3.4**   Price Segment Sensitivity

ple going to the best restaurant in town — again, purpose overrides price sensitivity. The second is categorized as affluence/impression giving. This subgroup has the means and specifically chooses to impress. This becomes the primary motivational reason for selecting the "best" (which equates with most expensive) restaurant. In fact, as long as the food is good (not necessarily outstanding) and the service is appealing to the ego (impression), the dining experience will be rated high by this subsegment regardless of the price.

## LOCATIONAL CONVENIENCE

When time becomes a critical factor (which may apply in any of the three tiers in Figure 3.4) locational convenience takes over in the needs area. However, this does not mean solely geographic location or proximity. In fact, it more often implies quickness of service. This is often the *one* dominant decision factor for any subsegment when time is involved in the equation.

## USER CHARACTERISTICS

You can read voluminous studies on the quantitative statistical comparisons of restaurant users and their demographic characteristics. They are important to help place your marketing in the ballpark, but may not help you score unless you consider the qualitative needs segmentation and related characteristics as part of your marketing message.

## SEGMENTATION AND OTHER TRAVEL INDUSTRY BUSINESSES

The segmentation process may be applied to any away-from-home service business: airline, bus tour company, credit card company, gaming operation, retail travel agent, wholesaler, hotel/motel, rent-a-car firm, or restaurant. The same individual we have described under needs segmentation in this chapter is probably your customer if your business is any one of these. Needs may vary slightly, but overall market segment characteristics hold special meaning for you.

## KEY WORDS AND CONCEPTS

**Hospitality Industry** Away-from-home services including the travel industry, lodging, and food and beverage industry.

**End User** Ultimate user of the service.

**Intermediary** One who makes the decision to purchase for the end user; comes between end user and service.

**Needs** Specific benefits or things sought from a product or service offering.

**Things to be Avoided** Specific turn-offs in the product or service offering or in the marketing message.

## ASSIGNMENTS

1. Rank your most important to least important end user.

2. Rank your most important to least important intermediary.

3. What is the primary need each market segment perceives your service or product to be offering?

4. Does your marketing message relate to this need?

5. Does your product or service need improvements to really address the needs?

6. Is your service or product priced right for the market segment your quality level or offering attracts?

7. How price sensitive are each of your market segments?

# The Channels of Distribution

**4**

## PURPOSE

In Chapter 3 we defined some basic categories of consumers and discussed the needs and benefits each segment seeks in a product or service offering. Because the hospitality industry serves many consumer segments, it has established *channels of distribution* through which it markets its products and services. The industry is also becoming increasingly more complex in that very often a variety of products and services is offered by the same firm or interrelated firms. The purpose of this chapter is to describe the channels of distribution and discuss the evolution of integrated hospitality industry firms and their relationship to marketing.

## OBJECTIVES

1. Identify the channels of distribution through which the hospitality industry's products and services reach the consumer.

2. Understand the complexity of the industry by providing an assessment of the vertical and horizontal relationships of industry firms, their products and services, and marketing of these products and services.

Up to this point we have been looking at the consumer and segments of consumers who make up the market for the products and services of the hospitality industry. At the end of the last chapter we briefly looked at another type of decision maker or facilitator who functions as the travel intermediary. As with most industries, the hospitality industry offers its travel product and service to its customers in a variety of ways. This chapter focuses on channels of distribution, that is, the various entities through which all or parts of the travel product or services may be purchased directly or indirectly by the consumer.

## PURPOSE OF TRAVEL

In order to understand the complexity of how the travel product can be purchased and marketed, let's return briefly to the consumer. At the outset the consumer must determine which travel-related products and services to use. Often the *purpose* of the trip corresponds to the selection of the entity, or channel of distribution, that will bring the trip to the consumer. Consumers may travel to visit friends and relatives, for business, for recreation, for sightseeing and entertainment, for personal or family reasons, to gamble, or to visit a specific destination or attraction (Figure 4.1). The industry can market to the consumer the travel product and services that best relate to the purpose of travel through a variety of channels.

The travel product or service can be purchased directly and usually in its entirety (from flight to lodging to meals) by the individual consumer, be it for business or pleasure. However, today there is a much greater inclination among consumers to seek and use the services of either a *captive* or *commercial intermediary.*

A captive intermediary is an individual who does not receive a commission for handling travel arrangements for others. Examples include secretaries, office managers, and company travel departments. A commercial intermediary is an individual

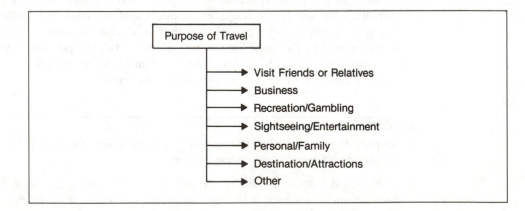

**Figure 4.1**   The Purpose of Travel

(or entity) who works for a commission from a supplier of travel for handling the travel arrangements of individual or group consumers. Examples include travel agents, commercial convention and meeting planners, and group tour operators.

Whether commercial or captive, the intermediary obtains the travel product and services through specific channels of distribution.

**Retail Travel Agents (RTAs).** These people sell tours, hotel rooms, airline tickets, steamship tickets, and so forth for wholesalers and tour operators. Retail agents are actually subagents who earn all or most of their gross revenue from commissions. Travel agent commissions from suppliers vary by supplier and by country, but usually range from 10 to 40 percent.

**Tour Operator/Retailers.** These firms create tourist "packages" that may include air, lodging, and ground services, and then offer them to consumers through a variety of marketing tools such as print media, broadcast media, storefront operations, travel agents, direct mail, and other techniques. In some markets, such as Germany and the United Kingdom, these travel packages are sold through retail outlets directly to the consumer on a large-scale basis.

**Tour Operator/Wholesalers.** These individuals create a tourist package of their own by buying the transportation, accommodations, and attraction components and retailing their packages through travel agents. Some tour operators now have over 500,000 clients per year. Wholesalers service retail travel agents by preparing tour packages, ordering, billing, and advertising. Wholesalers pay commissions and may sell through retail travel agents.

**Packager/Retailers.** Some packagers of tourist products and services have now integrated vertically into retailing through their own outlets, after having moved into ownership of their own accommodations and/or transport. One example is Club Med.

**Incentive Travel Company.** This type of company specializes in putting together and selling awards, prizes, gifts, premiums, and so forth for groups, companies, associations, and individuals. The incentive travel trip or tour is usually sold to the user organization as part of a complete motivational package. Incentive travel is often used in a sales or marketing area to raise money for a group such as a church or other association or to stimulate interest in a new product. Incentive travel companies supply the tour, as well as other administrative and creative capabilities, to the user.

**Convention Movers.** These individuals specialize in moving people to and from conventions. They may offer post- or pre-convention tours, and they usually use scheduled carriers.

**Travel Clubs.**  A newer merchandising method in group travel is the *travel club*. A travel club usually offers a group travel plan whereby a membership in the club makes possible travel opportunities and vacation destination facilities at a price below that which would be paid by a nonmember at a similar facility. The accommodations offered by clubs range from deluxe to very modest. Usually clubs offer a wide choice of locations, climate, terrain, and other vacation features. Unique atmospheres and sometimes specialized areas, events, and activities are often selling points of travel clubs. The best known example, again, is Club Med.

**Charter Travel Company.**  This type of company specializes in putting together groups of people with common interests. The individuals are then eligible for charter flights, which are governed by specific regulations. A charter travel company also aids groups in payment and operation of tours.

**Direct Mail.**  Today, travel is also marketed directly to the consumer through the mail. Domestically, credit card mailing lists frequently offer travel purchase opportunities. Internationally, travel is sold through the mails even more successfully than in the United States by the extensive use of "travel catalogs" sent directly to the home of the consumer.

## TRAVEL MARKETING

While the channels of distribution just described represent methods of marketing the travel product in the United States, they also exist in others parts of the world. In fact, the European and Japanese approaches to selling mass travel (including marketing and distribution services) is geared to a mature mass travel market. In Europe and Japan there is usually a more defined "holiday" period, meaning that large portions of the population take their vacations at the same time of the year. The industry markets to these masses in every imaginable way — both by the media and directly through sales outlets. Tourism retains a high level of recognition in European countries. In addition to the operations of the national tourist offices, travel is marketed by the following techniques:

1. Mass media (through catalogs, newspapers, magazines, direct mail promotion, radio, and TV).

2. Merchandising (through travel and recreational clubs).

3. Direct sales outlets (through storefront operations, tour operators, wholesalers selling directly to the public, banks, and, in Germany and Switzerland, sales in department stores).

Travel is marketed by airlines, travel companies (retail and wholesale), banks, department stores, tour organizers, tour operators, hotels, tourist ministries and departments, local tourist authorities, and other travel organizations. Low-cost holidays are made available to the public through the use of charter airlines and tour operators or wholesalers who purchase seats, rooms, beds, food, and so on in bulk.

Travel marketing in the United States, to some extent, is initiating aspects of travel marketing that have proved successful in Europe and Japan. These tactics include innovations in promotion and advertising, pricing, packaging, and selling. In the area of promotion and advertising, carriers are making greater user of direct mail and special promotions aimed directly at the consumer. The industry has become much more aggressive about luring consumers with attractive prices, using special promotional fares, excursion tours, and discount rates. Advertising is putting more emphasis on travel packages, which include air fare, lodging, meals, rent-a-car, and other services. There are also many new developments in merchandising such as selling travel more directly to the consumer through travel clubs, department stores, and bank credit card companies. In addition, there is a movement toward consolidation in the retail and wholesale areas that is resulting in changes in the traditional roles of wholesalers and retailers.

In addition to these outlets for the travel product, there are many others through which a consumer may purchase travel. These include, but are not limited to, credit card companies, auto clubs, travel clubs, vacation clubs, time-sharing resort condominiums, and holiday club plans.

## GROUND OPERATORS

*Ground operators* are those who provide services at destinations. They are specialists in providing all of the ground services (rooms, meals, and so on) related to the tour at the destination. The ground operator may be independent, part of a larger tour operator, or have some other direct or indirect relationship with the tour operator. In the case of larger and some specialized (by destination) tour operators, a tour conductor, who is an individual in charge of or who personally escorts a group of passengers for all or part of an itinerary, may have the expertise to provide most of the functions of the ground operator.

## CARRIERS

A major method of travel today is the aircraft, which has helped to develop the entire hospitality industry. There are two types of air carriers that transport people.

*Scheduled carriers* provide air transportation at specified times over specified routes and have published schedules. Until the mid-1980s the fares and routes of U.S. scheduled carriers were regulated by the Civil Aeronautics Board (CAB). In an effort to streamline government, the president and congress eliminated the CAB. While some jurisdictional functions were transferred to the Department of Transportation and the Department of Justice, most were reduced to allow for what is referred to as *deregulation*. Under deregulation, mergers and acquisitions have prevailed as the combined pressures of fare wars, lack of capitalization, and extensive route competition weed out the weaker companies. Under deregulation the Federal Aviation Administration (FAA), the Department of Transportation (DOT), and in cases of mergers and acquisitions, the Department of Justice are the major government entities involved in regulating the carriers. The FAA and DOT still closely monitor routes, safety, air traffic control, airport development, and other aspects of the industry. The laissez-faire marketplace was, and is, primarily in the rate area. DOT must approve participation of U.S.-flag carriers serving international routes. In addition, agreement must be reached with the International Air Transport Association (IATA). IATA is the trade and service organization for most of the world's scheduled airlines serving international routes. ATA, the Air Transport Association of America, is the trade and service organization representing U.S. scheduled carriers.

*Supplemental carriers* are a class of nonscheduled air carriers that hold certificates to supplement the regular service provided by scheduled carriers. Supplemental carriers are authorized to operate over broad areas. The National Air Carrier Association (NACA) is the trade and service organization that represents the U.S. supplemental carriers.

## GOVERNMENT AND REGULATION

With the travel component of the hospitality industry so complex, there are numerous domestic U.S. and international entities who influence or regulate travel.

### UNITED STATES

Interstate Commerce Commission (ICC), which has jurisdiction over railroads and motor coaches.

Federal Maritime Commission (FMC), which has jurisdiction over U.S. flag carriers.

Department of Transportation (DOT), which has jurisdiction over the Federal Aviation Administration (FAA).

Department of State, which negotiates bilateral agreements and handles matters of diplomatic concern.

Department of Justice, whose antitrust division sometimes participates in cases involving mergers and acquisitions, and expansion efforts. DOJ enforces antitrust laws.

Department of Commerce, whose United States Travel Service (USTS) is designed to promote travel to and within the United States.

Department of the Treasury, which concerns itself with the balance of payments.

Congress, whose Senate Commerce Committee's Subcommittee on Aviation and Subcommittee on Foreign Commerce and Tourism have jurisdiction over legislation related to international travel.

## FOREIGN GOVERNMENTS

Virtually all foreign governments tend to play a major role in shaping policy on internal and external tourism. The degree of such involvement, which is substantially greater than in the United States, flows from several factors. One is that most foreign governments have a higher appreciation for the importance of tourism, particularly in an economic sense, than does the United States. Also, with very few exceptions, the flag carriers of foreign countries are owned and controlled by their governments.

The ministries of tourism in the various countries exert a great deal of influence on government policy. Most foreign governments, particularly in Europe, tend to be more involved than the U.S. government in guiding or dictating the direction of the tourism industry. European governments also tend to participate more in intergovernmental organizations, such as the International Civil Aviation Organization (ICA), the European Civil Aviation Conference (ECAC), and the International Union of Official Travel Organizations (IUOTO).

Most of the countries that are prominent in the tourism field encourage travel to their countries, particularly from the United States, but discourage travel by their own citizens to other countries. This attitude is prompted by economic and financial motives.

## VERTICAL AND HORIZONTAL INTEGRATION

Vertical and horizontal integration is the interrelationship between two or more hospitality industry products or services performed or offered by the same firm or through a joint relationship with another firm within the industry. It may involve one or many of the channels of distribution.

The hospitality industry is unique in that a large number of firms within the industry engage in more than one function from a product, service, and marketing perspective. For example, United Airlines offers airline passenger service, freight shipping, and reservation services. Airlines and hotels have marketing agreements with rent-a-car firms, resorts have agreements with airlines, rent-a-car firms with resorts, and so on.

The integration of more than one product, service, and/or marketing arrangement may be formal, in that there is a parent or holding company, or informal via an agreement. For example, Marriott offers Hertz rent-a-cars at many of its locations through a joint marketing agreement with Hertz. Another example is Marriott, which has integrated products and services as well as marketing agreements. Marriott offers hotels and resorts accessible by cruise ships or through their own travel operation. In essence, the firm is both vertically integrated in that it offers the products and services through its wholly-owned travel service company, and horizontally integrated in that it has hotels, cruise ships, and restaurants. It can be even more complex in that one hotel chain also has marketing agreements with multiple rent-a-car firms, a variety of airlines, tour operators, and so forth.

It is important to recognize that the U.S. travel industry is becoming more integrated both vertically and horizontally. Marketing reflects this integration and has multifaceted jobs to perform. In Europe the integration is much more complete as a result of more permissive government regulations. As we move toward the year 2000, the integration of products and services will, in all likelihood, continue on either a formal basis, or on an informal basis through marketing agreements.

## KEY WORDS AND CONCEPTS

**Channels of Distribution** Vehicles through which travel-related products and services may be marketed by suppliers and/or purchased by consumers.

**Intermediary** An individual or firm that comes between the consumer of the travel product or service and the supplier of these services. Intermediaries frequently make decisions for the consumers. There are two types: commercial (those earning commissions) and captive (those whose salaried job it is to make travel plans for others).

**Incentive Travel** A trip offered as an incentive for performance or as an award.

**Carrier** A public transportation company such as an air or steamship line, railroad, trucking company, or bus line.

**Charter** The bulk purchase of any carrier's equipment (or part thereof) for passengers. Legally, charter transportation is arranged for time, voyage, or mileage.

**Package Tours** Inclusive travel arrangements designed to fit the requirements of a particular group of travelers. Some tours cater to special interest groups such as gourmets, accountants, students, or art lovers. Package tours may be either escorted or unescorted. They are advertised in brochures that contain the cost, terms, and conditions of the offered package.

**Retail Travel Agency** A company that sells carriers' tickets and wholesalers' or operators' tours to consumers. Retail agents are subagents. Usually, all or most of a retail travel agency's gross revenue is from commissions from carriers, wholesalers, or operators.

**Tour Operator** A company that specializes in the planning and operation of prepaid, preplanned vacations, and makes these available to the public through travel agents. Most of America's leading tour operators belong to the Creative Tour Operators' Association, which seeks to maintain the highest ethical standards.

**Tour Organizer** An individual, usually not professionally connected with the travel industry, who organizes tours for special groups of people — teachers, lawyers, etc.

**Travel Wholesaler** A company that services retail travel agents in the preparation of tour packages, ordering, billing, and advertising. In theory the levels are retail travel agent, travel wholesalers (whose customers are retail travel agents), and tour operators. It is possible for travel agents, travel wholesalers, and tour operators to perform each other's functions. Sometimes travel wholesalers and tour operators have their own retail company and their wholesaling is a specialty in one area.

## ASSIGNMENTS

1. During the purchase of your last trip, with how many channels of distribution did you use ?

2. Select a major hospitality industry firm, and through their annual reports and other information available about the firm, determine all the vertical and/or horizontal aspects of the hospitality industry in which the firm is involved.

3. If you were asked to call on your local travel agent to sell your firm's travel services or package, what would you emphasize in your sales pitch?

4. How many channels of distribution and/or roles (i.e., retailer, packager, etc.) does your local travel agent play?

# Marketing in Perspective

# 5

## PURPOSE

For many years marketing in the hospitality industry was dominated by one weapon as represented by the sales function. As chains began to expand from coast to coast, brand awareness dictated that some marketing dollars be allocated to other functions such as advertising, public relations, promotions, and the other marketing weapons. The purpose of this chapter is to place marketing in the hospitality industry in perspective.

## OBJECTIVES

1. Understand how marketing has evolved to its current state of using full weaponry.

2. Develop your thoughts on which marketing techniques are most applicable for your product or service.

3. Gain a perspective on the research and methodologies behind various marketing techniques.

4. Understand better the role of brand image and awareness in the hospitality industry.

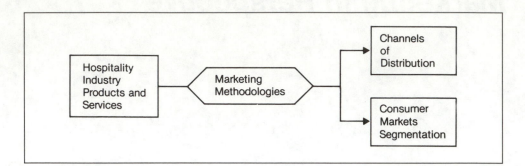

**Figure 5.1**    Product to Market Flowchart

Up to this point we have discussed the products and services offered by the hospitality industry. We have dissected the market into consumer segments and reviewed some of the channels of distribution — the ways by which travel product is sold (Figure 5.1).

We must now focus on how the travel and other industry products and services are marketed to the consumer segments. Obviously, the methodology or techniques selected will depend upon some overriding factors: (1) the product or service itself, (2) the targeted consumer audience or segments, and (3) the motivational factors of the audience purchasing the goods or services.

## THE PRODUCT OR SERVICE BEING MARKETED

How do I go about marketing and making best use of my limited budget? This is a very familiar question for marketing personnel in the hospitality industry. On the surface it is a very simple question, but in reality there are many decisions to make as to how best to spend those precious marketing dollars. First, one should think about *what* it is that is to be sold. For example, if you have 1,000 rooms to be sold, your response to this question is quite different than if your objective is to increase your restaurant volume. You must begin by identifying *what* your product or service is and *when* you need the business. Let's assume you have a 1,000-room property or hotel. The first step is to recognize when you do *not* have to spend those precious dollars. If an analysis of your occupancy revealed the hotel ran 100 percent capacity on Monday and Tuesday nights right off the reservation system, you probably do not need to budget a cent toward Monday and Tuesday nights, other than to pay your fee for the reservation system. Likewise, if your restaurant sells out at lunch, you need not concentrate your efforts on increasing lunch hour volume. Perhaps this sounds too logical and simple, but time and time again marketing budgets are put together based on the previous year's budget, which was based on the budget the year before that. Therefore, think "new" each time you begin to market your product or service. It is a new budget based on need — the need is "when I *need* business." Later on in Chapter 15 we will discuss the "Total Marketing Plan," but the key premise in deciding when and how you spend your marketing dollars is start with a zero-based budgeting concept.

In its most simple definition, zero-based budgeting states: no expenditure is justified just because it was spent last year. Every expense is reanalyzed and justified each year on the basis that its expenditure will yield more favorable results than spending the same amount another way. Chapter 15 will go into more detail concerning this concept.

First you define the product or service to be marketed. Then you identify the "core" dollars needed to maintain the business. You analyze the periods of need for the remaining dollars. Now comes the next step.

## THE TARGETED CONSUMER AUDIENCE OR SEGMENTS

Having identified when you need the business, it is now time to review all the market segments to determine which can provide the business you need at those times. Continuing with the example of the 1,000-room hotel that sells out on Monday and Tuesday nights, further analysis reveals that only 330 rooms sell on Friday, and only 250 rooms sell on Saturday. Hence, one target becomes the Friday and Saturday nights when your occupancy is only 33 percent and 25 percent. You can eliminate most of the business market segments because they do not travel or stay in hotels on Fridays or Saturdays — that's why the occupancy is so low. You must therefore look at the pleasure market segments, through both internal analysis and external analysis. On the internal side, ask yourself what types of pleasure travel segments this property has attracted without marketing expenditures and why. On the external side, look around at your competition and determine which market segments they are attracting Friday and Saturday nights and why. With the answers to these questions you are ready to determine what you can do to attract more weekend business and how you should do it.

At this point you should prioritize your targeted pleasure market segments based on the internal and external analysis. Put these in rank order, for example, (1) second honeymooners, (2) family escapes, (3) sightseeing groups. However, do not allocate a cent until you look at one more aspect of analysis, *segment profitability*.

### SEGMENT PROFITABILITY

Segment profitability is a concept of analyzing revenue and profit generated by each type of consumer and/or market segment for your product or service. As in any business, not all customers are worth the same. For example, analyze your guest folios and find out who is your most profitable guest. While each property may be different or unique, in general you may find the following rank order applicable:

*Rank Order of Market Segment Profitability for a Hotel*

(Most Profitable to Least Profitable)

1. Individual attending a group meeting (corporate).
2. Executive on an unrestricted expense account.
3. Individual attending a group meeting (association).
4. Second-honeymoon couple.
5. Family traveling for pleasure.
6. Individual on a restricted expense account (such as a government worker or salesperson on a per diem allowance).

Assuming you need business from the pleasure travel segments, your target might now become the second-honeymoon escape couples, since they appear to be the most profitable segment you can attract on a Friday or Saturday night. Ready? Not yet! You need to ask one more question before looking at how to spend those precious marketing dollars: Is there anywhere I can get a multiple sale for the same price or cost of a single sale? Can I attract a group that fills many rooms versus only one room with a like effort and/or expenditure? It just may be the Second-Honeymooners Club of America wants to meet for the weekend, or there is a National Football League team having their victory banquet. This raises the next two key questions: What are the key motivational factors for people to purchase my product or service? and How do I best reach those customers?

## REACHING YOUR MARKET

In the next few chapters we will be addressing the arsenal of marketing methods you can employ to reach your market. Before you can select the proper or most efficient marketing weapon, you must consider a few more steps. Up to this point, if you have answered all the questions you now know what your product or service needs from marketing and which market segments can produce the desired results. The remainder of this text is dedicated to producing results by presenting the marketing arsenal of weapons and providing insights as to how to get maximum effect from each weapon. It's appropriate to comment on the fact that not all consumers will run to buy your product or service just because you aim your weapon at them. As a matter of fact, the wrong weapon or wrong message may well be counterproductive. *Different consumer segments respond to different marketing approaches.* The reason for this is based on each segment's motivation and its specific set of needs.

For any person who is interested in marketing hospitality industry products and services, it is equally important to understand the motivations, significance, and their overall importance as it is to know the market segments, the channels of dis-

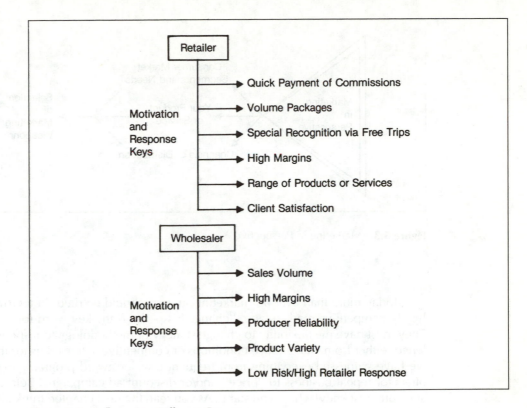

**Figure 5.2** Influencing Different Groups

tribution, and the arsenal of marketing weaponry. Examples of the wants and needs — motivational factors — that influence different groups in the distribution chain are depicted in Figure 5.2.

Figure 5.2 is only one example of how two different distribution channels are motivated. For each market segment and for each consumer, depending on the purpose of their trip or purchase, there are like sets of motivational factors or response keys. We will discuss these after we examine the arsenal of marketing weaponry we can employ to elicit positive responses.

Marketing should be viewed within the perspective of what your product or service is and where it needs help. It should also be seen as the relationship of that product or service to the market segments and the motivational response keys of each segment. Finally, understanding the role and function of the channels of distribution and selection of the appropriate marketing tool to reach the respective consumer market segments is essential to placing marketing in perspective (Figure 5.3).

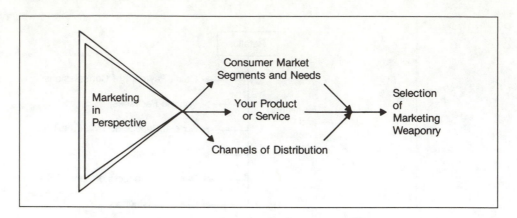

**Figure 5.3**   Marketing in Perspective

Today more than ever no marketing strategy should be rigid. In a crowded and highly competitive marketplace, "change" is perhaps the key word for marketeers. They must have the flexibility to change strategy or methodology to respond to challenges either from marketplace conditions or competitive actions. It is for this reason we have witnessed everything from frequent traveler award programs to incentive offers for repeat business to "price" and/or discount ad campaigns. Before you can act, you must know where you stand. As you read the next chapter, think about what changes or strategies you would select to respond to the challenges of the market and competition.

## KEY WORDS AND CONCEPTS

**Zero-Based Budgeting** Budgeting based on the belief that no expenditure is justified just because it was made last year. Every expense is reanalyzed and justified each year on the basis that its expenditure will yield more favorable results than spending the same amount another way.

**Segment Profitability** Analysis of revenue and profit generated by each type of consumer and/or market segment for your product or service.

**Competition** Any business concern, product, or concept that competes for customers in your own market. It may be a product or concept completely different from your product or service.

**Core Market** Represents a core of consumers who are vital to your product or service and who form the largest consistent segment of purchasers.

## *ASSIGNMENTS*

1. Select a hotel, restaurant, airline, or other hospitality industry product or service and identify its marketing needs.

2. Select one marketing need of a product or service and identify which consumer market segments can best fill that need if targeted.

3. Identify a market segment for your product or service and identify the key motivational responses and needs that segment wants from your product or service. Are you expressing those needs in your marketing message and meeting those needs with your product or service offering?

4. Analyze your product's or service's market segments and determine what your core market is. Which segments are most profitable? Which are least profitable?

# Your Product or Service in Perspective: Marketing Strategy Grid Concept

# 6

## PURPOSE

In the last two chapters the question of what and how you need to market arose a number of times. One of the most difficult tasks in developing a marketing strategy is understanding objectively what your product or service really is in relation to your competition and the marketplace. The purpose of this chapter is to provide you with an analytical tool that will help you place your product or service in perspective. Once this objective is accomplished, you can begin selecting marketing strategies that produce results. In the chapters that follow a look at each marketing weapon or methodology will be presented.

## OBJECTIVES

1. Identify your marketing problem and related objectives.

2. Understand your product or service in relation to the market and competition.

3. Stimulate your ability to select marketing strategies that produce results.

4. Acquire an analytical tool to help relate your product or service to the proper marketing and operational approaches.

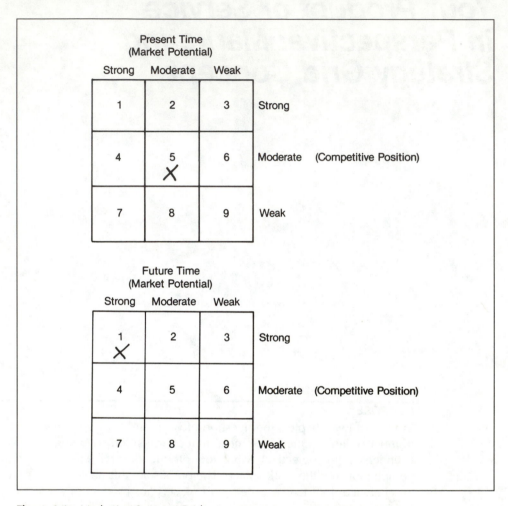

**Figure 6.1**  Marketing Strategy Grid

Placing your own product or service in perspective is a task in honesty and frank objective evaluation. In order to objectively evaluate your product or service you must understand the market you are in, where it is going, and how your product relates to both the current and future market as well as competition. This can be achieved by using an analytical tool called a Marketing Strategy Grid (Figure 6.1).

## MARKETING STRATEGY GRID

The Marketing Strategy Grid profiles the success of your product or service and is a function of both the potential of the market and the competitive position within the market of your product or service. The horizontal axis of the grid denotes the potential of the market sector, while the vertical axis represents the competitive position of the subject property within that market sector. Ranking on both axes ranges from strong to weak. Competitive position is a function of both quantitative and qualitative considerations, such as the following: (1) amount and quality of competition; (2) competitive advantages as to location, access, image, facilities, size, rate, and so on; and (3) ability to meet the needs of available market segments. Whereas present competitive position is an input on this evaluation, the time period under consideration is usually five years.

Obviously, there is a meaning to the position on the grid in which a particular product or service is placed. In order to explain these meanings more easily, we will make use of a number code:

Numbers 1, 2, and 4 denote a favorable, advantageous, or "go" situation. It occurs when one or both factors are strong and neither factor is below the moderate level.

Numbers 3, 5, and 7 denote a less favorable, less advantageous, or "caution" situation. It occurs when one factor is weak and one is strong, or both factors are moderate.

Numbers 6, 8, and 9 denote an unfavorable, disadvantageous, or "no go" situation. It occurs when one or both factors are weak and neither factor is above the moderate level.

Given these definitions, the optimum position on the grid is the upper-left corner, where a strong market potential combines with a strong competitive position within the market. The worst position on the grid is the bottom-right corner, where a weak market potential combines with a weak competitive position within the market.

Since both factors being evaluated are dynamic, movement can take place within the grid framework. The position of a particular product or service can vary over time. Horizontal movement involves changes in the potential of a market. Such changes are due to pressures in both the overall and local external economic and social forces.

Vertical movement on the grid is possible from the lower six positions. These positions can be considered "action squares." Such vertical movement denotes changes in the competitive position within the market and can be accomplished through the upgrading of management, marketing, product, facilities, or services.

Movement on the grid can also be related to the numerical sequence. In addition to denoting the strength of a particular position on the grid, the numerical code also denotes the profitability and cost of favorable movement. Thus, the profitability of favorable movement from the action squares is lowest from the 6, 8, and 9 positions and highest from the 1, 2, and 4 positions, with the 3, 5, and 7 positions between these two extremes.

The use of the grid concept is based on two key assumptions as follows:

1. In order to best meet the needs of each market segment, as well as maintain a strong image and market share, we can assume that the 1, 2, and 4 positions (favorable positions) on the grid will be sought whenever possible.

2. The position on the grid in which you place your product or service assumes that no major capital improvement programs or other changes are undertaken, and few, if any, major changes are made in the quality of management or the direction of expenditures for marketing. The position characterizes your product or service within a five-year period.

Let's review one example of how to apply this Marketing Strategy Grid to a product or service in the hospitality market. The first step is to objectively evaluate what your product or service is and where it is located within the grid. Let's assume you own a restaurant and its position on the grid is #1. This means your restaurant is in a strong market and is the best restaurant in that market. So, what should be some marketing strategies to employ?

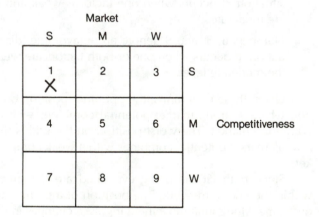

One plan of action is to do everything possible to protect your position by maintaining not only the quality of your food and operation but also the core clientele who put you in that position. Special recognition programs for this core clientele could be developed. Another strategy that could be considered in view of a very solid #1 position would be to raise your prices to take advantage of your market positioning and to maximize profits.

Not everyone is situated in the #1 position on the grid. Let's take another example of a hotel that is currently in the #4 position on the Strategy Grid.

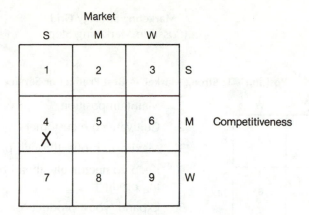

This positioning denotes an average property in a very strong market. If the market movement is to remain strong in future years, there are several steps or marketing strategies that may be implemented. One example is that of an average hotel located in San Francisco — a #1 strong market and a #4 competitive position on the grid. The competition across the street is in a #1 position — the best product in a strong market. What do you do if you are second, third, or fourth best in this situation? Let's explore this example a little more and look at what this average San Francisco property did to maximize profitability. At this time the market was running an 87-percent average occupancy, which is a very strong market. Demand was projected to continue strong with a minimal amount of new rooms coming into the market. The hotel in position #1 on the grid was charging $70 to $95 per night with an average rate of $81.75. Our theoretical average hotel across the street in a #4 position was charging $40 to $48 with an average rate of $44.85. Both properties were running an occupancy factor of 87 percent.

The ingenious hotel marketing department in the #4 position came up with the following strategy: (1) change our image by adding a canopy, doorman, and refurbishment of the public space, and (2) revise the rate structure to $60 to $75 per night. The result was no loss in occupancy (because of the strength of the market) and a bulge in profitability.

Depending on your product's or service's position on the Strategy Grid, there are many different marketing strategies that can assist your product or service. Upgrading (refurbishing) and pricing represent two that worked in the preceding example; there are many others to consider based on your position on the Strategy Grid. The following is a simple listing of the grid positions and some sample marketing strategies you might consider.

**Marketing Strategy Grid**
(Possible Marketing Steps)

**Position #1: Strong Market — Best Product or Service**

| S | M | W | |
|---|---|---|---|
| 1 X | 2 | 3 | S |
| 4 | 5 | 6 | M |
| 7 | 8 | 9 | W |

1. Maintain position.
2. Cultivate core customers.
3. Maximize profits through pricing.
4. Keep competitively ahead by adding services or upgrading product.
5. Expand your product or service (for example, more rooms, more restaurant seats, more flights, more gaming devices, etc.).

**Position #2: Moderate Market — Strong Product or Service**

| S | M | W | |
|---|---|---|---|
| 1 | 2 X | 3 | S |
| 4 | 5 | 6 | M |
| 7 | 8 | 9 | W |

1. Go for market share via competitive pricing.
2. If the market movement tends to be strong in future years, improve to a #1 position.
3. If the market movement tends to be weak, go after additional market segments (for example, build core market, consider alternate pricing strategy, etc.).
4. Become the "only" place in town to stay or eat, or become the "only" airline to take.

**Position #3: Strong Product — Weak Market**

| S | M | W | |
|---|---|---|---|
| 1 | 2 | 3 X | S |
| 4 | 5 | 6 | M |
| 7 | 8 | 9 | W |

1. If the market movement tends to be moderate or strong, build market core now and retain loyalty of consumers.
2. Go after all market segments with multiple pricing strategies and/or product and service offerings.
3. Strongly emphasize cost control and targeted promotions.

### Position #4: Strong Market — Moderate/Average Product or Service

| S | M | W | |
|---|---|---|---|
| 1 | 2 | 3 | S |
| 4 ✗ | 5 | 6 | M |
| 7 | 8 | 9 | W |

1. Maximize profits through pricing slightly below the #1 competitor.

2. Consider upgrading your product or service to move closer to or into the #1 position if the future markets look strong.

3. Go after the "value-oriented" market segments.

4. Distinguish your product or service as an acceptable replacement for the #1 competitor.

### Position #5: Moderate Market — Average Product or Service

| S | M | W | |
|---|---|---|---|
| 1 | 2 | 3 | S |
| 4 | 5 ✗ | 6 | M |
| 7 | 8 | 9 | W |

1. If the direction is toward a stronger market, put the product or service in a stronger position with upgrading.

2. Expand the number of market segments you are attracting with specialized promotions.

3. Go after the market share through competitive pricing.

### Position #6: Weak Market — Average Product or Service

| S | M | W | |
|---|---|---|---|
| 1 | 2 | 3 | S |
| 4 | 5 | 6 ✗ | M |
| 7 | 8 | 9 | W |

1. If the market movement is too moderate or strong in the future, maintain your core market through recognition programs and go after your weakest competitors with special pricing to gain share.

2. If the market movement is stagnant, and it appears that it will remain weak in the foreseeable future, gear your marketing programs to capture as many segments as possible.

3. Create your own markets via specialized promotions and programs.

### Position #7: Strong Market — Weak Product or Service

| | S | M | W | |
|---|---|---|---|---|
| | 1 | 2 | 3 | S |
| | 4 | 5 | 6 | M |
| | 7 ✗ | 8 | 9 | W |

1. Upgrade the most visible aspects of your product or service.
2. Once the upgrading is completed, increase your rates or prices to take advantage of overflow or strong sell-out times or periods.
3. Become the best at servicing the market segments your stronger competitors are not paying attention to.
4. Theme your promotions toward special functions and go for volume.

### Position #8: Moderate Market — Weak Product or Service

| | S | M | W | |
|---|---|---|---|---|
| | 1 | 2 | 3 | S |
| | 4 | 5 | 6 | M |
| | 7 | 8 ✗ | 9 | W |

1. If the market is not moving toward being strong, look at special rate or price schemes to build share.
2. If the market is moving toward strong, make every effort to upgrade the product or service offering to move along with the market.
3. If the above is true, work promotions, sales, and advertising to convey your product's or service's availability and value orientation.
4. Consider marketing your product or service around a theme such that you serve segments but obtain greater volume from competition by this specialization.

### Position #9: Weak Market — Weak Product or Service

| | S | M | W | |
|---|---|---|---|---|
| | 1 | 2 | 3 | S |
| | 4 | 5 | 6 | M |
| | 7 | 8 | 9 ✗ | W |

1. It is time to dispose of your product or service.
2. Consider alternate uses for your product or service that make sense in this poor environment.

These possible marketing strategies are only suggestions. There are many variables to consider and each product or service may have a uniqueness unto itself that needs to be taken into consideration prior to selecting a strategy. The Marketing Strategy Grid is a tool designed to help you think about how to maximize your marketing strategies for the most productive results. In the final analysis, it is management's judgment that will dictate the strategy selected; the grid tool should help sharpen that judgment.

During the next series of chapters we will focus on the weapons or methodologies that can be employed to improve your product's or service's market position and take market share from competition.

## KEY WORDS AND CONCEPTS

**Marketing Position Strategy Grid** An analytical tool designed to help select strategies to improve your market share and gain on competition.

**Market Share** Your product's or service's piece of the total market for that product or service. Usually expressed in a percentage basis or on a point scale.

## ASSIGNMENTS

1. Select a product or service you are familiar with and locate it on a current Marketing Strategy Grid and on a projected (60 months) grid. State the condition of the market and the competitive position of your product or service.

2. Place a product or service in one of the nine positions on the grid and develop marketing strategies to improve your product's or service's position.

3. Analyze your number 1, 2, and 3 competitors by locating each of them in a grid position, and try to determine their next marketing strategy.

4. Locate your own product or service on the same grid as your number 1, 2, and 3 competitors and develop a series of marketing strategies to take one of their positions that is better than your own.

# Applying Key Marketing Methodologies: Sales

# 7

## PURPOSE

In the last six chapters we discussed the relationship of different marketing methodologies to the consumer segments. In Chapters 7 through 14 we will examine the application of each marketing method or approach. The purpose of this chapter is to examine the *sales method*. We will discuss organization of the sales function, direct face-to-face sales, over-the-phone sales, sales through direct mail, reservations, and sales techniques. The hotel sector of the hospitality industry is used in this chapter as it encompasses more ''sales functions'' than in most other sectors.

## OBJECTIVES

1. Determine the best way to organize your sales effort for maximum results.

2. Understand the various methods of direct selling used in the hospitality industry.

3. Identify which sales methods are most applicable to your firm, product, or service sales organization.

4. Develop techniques to increase the yield from your sales effort in both productivity and the bottom line.

This section of the chapter addresses "getting back to basics" in the hospitality industry. We will discuss the basic tools with which a sales department should work, and provide a sales and marketing audit checklist.

## ORGANIZING THE SALES EFFORT

Earlier we discussed identifying *what* your product or service is and *how* it is conveyed to the consumer. By going through this sample audit checklist for a hotel, you will have a checklist of the tools required to sell.

_____ Brochures. Is there a brochure that includes the following: a description of the meeting rooms, including seating fashion and capacity; a listing of the property's amenities; services available; directions; map; transportation services; phone number; address; and sales personnel to contact?

*Comment:* There are many examples today of beautiful four-color brochures. Look them over and you may find nice pictures, but if any of the above elements are missing, these are not *sales* brochures.

_____ Activities and Amenities. Is there a guide that describes what activities are available at or near the property? Does the guide address what there is to do for the spouse and children? Is there a listing of shops, recreational offerings, and nearby attractions?

*Comment:* No one wants to meet in or bring his or her family to a sterile oasis. Tell what is offered, not only at your facility, but also nearby. *Maximize* your market.

_____ Tentative Confirmation Letter. Is there a model tentative confirmation letter and does it include the following: date of proposed meeting; dates of arrival and departure; rates clearly stated; number of rooms and type being held; an understanding of the meeting requirements, including set-up of the room, meal functions, equipment reserved, and coffee-break information; suggested times; statement on billing and payment procedures; a brochure on the property and amenities; and the method for changes and confirmations? (See Figure 7.1 for a sample confirmation letter.)

*Comment:* Cover all the facts, and don't forget to say "thank you."

_____ Sales Checklist. This is a working document that should be stapled to the file folder. It provides room for changes and recording of all arrangements so that anyone in the sales department knows exactly what the customer wants, with whom the customer has spoken, and what has been said to date. Included on the sales checklist should be: salesperson's name and date; date confirmation letter was mailed; dates for the meeting; rates agreed to; front office instructions, including copy of the confirmation letter, contract; rate confirmation; housing

October 11, 19___

Mr. Phil Jackson
Vice President of Marketing
Michigan Insurance Co.
811 Anchor Way
Lansing, Michigan

Dear Phil:

It certainly was a pleasure speaking with you yesterday concerning the possibility of the Grand Plaza Park Hotel hosting the Michigan Insurance Company in February of 19___.

I'm now holding 120 rooms on a tentative basis for arrival on Wednesday, February 4th and departure on Saturday, February 7, 19___.

The following rates will be in effect for your meeting:

| | |
|---|---|
| Singles: | $65.00 |
| Doubles or Twins: | $72.00 |
| Junior Suites: | $85.00 |
| Parkside Suites: | $95.00 |
| Skyline Suites: | $115.00 |

The following is my understanding of your meeting requirements. On February 4th you will need a reception/dinner for 120 guests. On February 5th, 6th, and 7th you will need a meeting room set for 120 guests, from 8:00 A.M. until 3:00 P.M.

Bill Robinson, our Director of Banquets and Convention Services, will be in touch with you to further finalize all details such as coffee breaks, audio visual equipment, etc.

It is my understanding that all room, tax, and incidental charges will be charged directly to the Master Account.

Phil, it is my further understanding that you will be forwarding a rooming list; we need to be in receipt of this rooming list no later than January 6, 19___ to insure proper confirmation. After that time, rooms will be on a space-available basis.

I've enclosed detailed brochures on both the meeting facilities and property amenities that we have available, and we will make every effort to have your meeting a success.

Phil, enclosed is an additional copy of this letter which can be signed and returned as definite confirmation.

Again, thank you for calling and we look forward to working with you and Michigan Insurance Company in 19___.

Sincerely,

Paul J. Winslow
Director of Marketing

PJW:ms
#432

APPROVED BY:

_____
Phil Jackson, V.P. Marketing

_____
Date

**Figure 7.1**   Sample of a Confirmation Letter

requests and billing procedures; reservation reply cards; references to any complimentary rooms; billing instructions; overflow housing requirements, if necessary; catering department instructions, including dates, times, menus, seating, etc.; research data on arrival times, flights, and listing of key people; and miscellaneous comments such as special rooms, amenities, etc. (Figure 7.2 is a sample sales checklist.)

*Comment:* Leave no stone unturned. Ensure personal contact is made by sales with every other area in the property.

____ Convention Booking Form. This form is designed to provide a permanent record of a definite booking of a convention or meeting, and it should be cross-referenced with the firm's or organization's file number. On the form are: group name, person contact and title; address and phone number; attendance anticipated and past history, if available; rooms promised and past rooms picked up; main and early arrival dates and times; main and late departure dates; room blocks identified and cut-off date for holding; final decision date; single and double rates; suites and rates required; billing instructions; complimentary rooms; person's name booking business; and special instructions, if any. (Figure 7.3 is a sample booking form.)

____ Contact Report. This is a simple chronological listing of the contacts made to the firm or organization. It contains: organization name and address, anticipated attendance, phone numbers, executive officers, whom to contact, and a chronological list of contacts in the form of brief sentence recaps. (See Figure 7.4 for a sample contact report.)

*Comment:* This simple listing not only helps avoid overkill, but it also serves as a tickler to record last contact and next required.

____ Post-meeting Report. This is a report for accurate billing and to ensure satisfied customers. This report contains: name of organization; arrival date(s); departure date(s); contact's name, title, address, and phone number; brief history; action steps for follow-up regarding future business; reference file number; guest rooms actually used, including day-by-day count, rates, and complimentary rooms; meeting room and exhibit charges; history of catering functions; and special comments, complaints, or important non-routine requests which occurred. (See Figure 7.5 for a sample post-convention report.)

____ VIP Reservation Request Form. This important sales tool is designed to record: arrival and departure dates; key VIP names, address, and affiliations; reason for visit; detail on accommodations; detail on special requests, such as wine, flowers, etc.; special rates or complimentary room information; key person to see if all of above occurs; and appropriate approval. (See Figure 7.6 for a sample VIP request form.)

Salesperson Responsible_____ Date_____

Confirmation Letter Sent_____ Date_____

Key Dates:  CONFIRMED ___ YES ___ NO  If Yes, when:_____To_____

    If No, Tentative_____To_____

                 Logged in Master Book _____Yes _____No

Room Data:  _____To Front Office with Confirmation Letter

              _____To Front Office with type, number, and special require-
ments.

              _____Specified rates for all room types to front office and
bookkeeping.

              _____Special Housing Procedures—list, VIP's, etc.

              _____Complementary rooms—numbers, location, list match

              _____Final confirmation _____date _____initials

              _____Final log in Master Book

              _____Reservation cards _____reply required

Billing Instructions:  _____Individual

              _____Master Account Number _____

              _____Other (Specify) _____

Catering:        _____Program listing confirmed with client

                  Date confirmed_____ Copy sent_____

        _____Rates per person or meal confirmed

        _____Liquor/Beverage special arrangements

Exhibit Requirements:

        _____Yes _____No   (If Yes, dates and schedule recorded)

        _____Rates      _____Move in   _____Move out

        _____Special needs list _____.
                                    _____.

Key Data:    _____Arrival time/flights recorded

        _____Departure time/flights recorded

        _____Van/limo pick-up/drop required

Comments:    _____Special people requirements, i.e., handicapped,
children, etc.

                  Specify_____
                  _____

        _____Anticipated problems (if any, identify problem
and who is responsible to pre-resolve)_____
                  _____

**Figure 7.2** Sample of a Sales Checklist

File #_____

Definite_____     Date_____        Approval_____

Booking group name and address_____

_____

_____

_____

_____

Key contact name, title,      _____
address, and phone:           _____

_____

_____

_____

Key Data: Attendance          _____
          Rooms Committed     _____
          Main Arrival Date       _____    Time_____
          Main Departure Date     _____    Time_____
          Hold Rooms Until        _____    Contact_____
          Rates Promised:     $_____Singles  $_____Doubles
                              $_____Jr. Suites  $_____Suites

          Billing:            _____Individual  _____Master Account
                              _____Special instructions—Detail_____
                              _____

          Reservation Process:  _____List by sales office
                              _____Other

          Comps               _____#  _____Names
                              _____Approved

| Sun. | Mon. | Tues. | Weds. | Thurs. | Fri. | Sat. | Auth.<br>Sign._____ | |
|------|------|-------|-------|--------|------|------|------|------|
|      |      |       |       |        |      |      | Room<br>Req. | Date: |
| Check In _____.<br>Check Out _____. | | | | | | | | |

**Figure 7.3**   Sample of a Definite Confirmation Booking Form for Meetings and Conventions

```
Date:_____ Organization_____
                                        Key Contact _____
                                        Title        _____
                                        Address      _____
                                        Phone No.    _____
                                        Sec't Name   _____
Interview and Comments:_____
     Date: _____
           _____
     Date: _____ _ _ __
           _____-- __
     Date: _____
           _____
     Date: _____
           _____
     Date: _____
           _____
Do's_____   Don't's_____
     _____         _____
     _____         _____
     _____         _____
     _____         _____
```

**Figure 7.4**   Sample of a Contact Report

*Comment:*   Take your time to ensure that this form is filled out entirely and correctly. If at all possible, personally review requirements with the manager on duty at projected time of arrival of your VIP guests.

____ Events Timetable/Workplan Program. This is an action document to be clearly reviewed by all and posted. It should contain: firm name and address, signing officers for billing and approval purposes, billing instructions, room block information, rate information, special instructions on complimentary items, audiovisual and equipment requirements, listing of key events in chronological order and by the hour during the day and evening, specific descriptions on set-up, cocktails, bar service, menu, and other required details. (See Figure 7.7 for a sample events timetable/workplan form.)

*Comment:*   The workplan or instructions to which the entire property or operation is to march will make for a successful meeting and satisfied customers.

____ Reminder and Final Confirmation Letter. This letter should contain all the final details and include all items listed in the original contract letter of agreement.

```
                                        File #_____
Organization_____
Arrival_____   Departure_____
Contact_____   Title_____
Address_____   Phone_____
History_____

          _____
          _____

Action Steps 1._____   Person Resp._____
           2._____   Person Resp._____
           3._____   Person Resp._____

Follow-Up: Dates:_____Steps:_____   Call _____
           _____        _____   Letter_____
           _____        _____   Visit _____

Rooms Booked_____   Rooms Used_____  _____Comps.
Early Arrivals_____  Late Checkouts_____
Rate History _____S _____D _____JS _____S _____Other
Meeting Room _____Charge _____Set-Up
Catering Functions _____No.
                   _____Menu Ref. # for File

Special Remarks_____
               _____
Booked By_____
```

**Figure 7.5**    Post-meeting or Post-convention Report

It serves as both a reminder to the customer and as another opportunity to ensure all details, requests, and requirements are in order. It also helps to prevent the surprise of a late cancellation or no-show.

_____ Telephone Assurance Procedures. This is a follow-up phone call to ensure that the reminder and final confirmation letter is accurate and mutually agreed upon. This is one final chance to change items or even sell up.

_____ Key Contact Assignment. For the duration of the meeting or convention, one person, preferably the salesperson who made the arrangements, should be available at all times to handle any and all problems. This is perhaps the single greatest key to a successful customer experience.

*Comment:*    When something goes wrong, make sure you are there to personally handle it. This is the one place you cannot risk a referral to "call mainte-

```
Name:_____        Arrival Date:_____
Title:_____        Time:_____
Organization:_____        Departure Date:_____
Address:_____        Time:_____
Phone:_____        No. in Party_____

Purpose of Visit:          Personal
                           Inspection
                           Other (State):_____

Accommodations Requested:  Single                           Queen
                           Double                           King
                           Double/Double                    Jr. Suite
                           View                             Suite

Rate Instructions:         Comp.
                           Special (State):_____
                           Billing Instructions:_____

Instructions:              Wine & Cheese                    Std. Fruit
                           Std. Liquor Tray                 Wine Only
                           Champagne                        Other (State)_____
                                                            _____

Requested by:_____     Date:_____
Approved by: _____     Date:_____
```

**Figure 7.6**  VIP Reservation

nance or call catering." *Do it yourself*. Remember, you work for the customers, they don't work for the property!

____ Billing Procedures. Billing should be clear, concise, accurate, and to the letter of the agreement — with no variations or surprises. Clear and accurate billing ensures not only a satisfied customer but quick payment.

____ Thank You Letter. The thank you letter should take on two specific formats and include a personal letter from the individual who actually booked and handled the business. In addition, a phone call should be placed to express personal thanks, which also provides an opportunity to clear up any problems on a personal basis.

____ "We Want You" Letter. This is the letter that closes the loop and just may bring you that valuable repeat business. It is a friendly reminder of thanks and a request to please allow you to satisfy your customer's meeting needs again. Don't forget to ask and note when!

Group/Party Name:_____

Key Person(s):        _____    _____

Telephone Number(s):    _____

 

☐   Do above have signature authorization for account?
☐   Master Account/Billing Ref. #_____
☐   Individual Account/Instructions_____
_____

 

Event:_____

Rooms Assigned:_____

A-V Requirements:_____ ☐ _____ ☐ _____ ☐ _____ ☐

Special Instructions:_____

Comp. on Meeting Room: ☐

Charge on Meeting Room: ☐ If Yes, state agreement_____

| Day | Time | Event | Description (All details specified) | Person Resp. |
|-----|------|-------|-------------------------------------|--------------|
|     |      |       |                                     |              |
|     |      |       |                                     |              |
|     |      |       |                                     |              |
|     |      |       |                                     |              |

**Figure 7.7**   Sample of a Timetable or Workplan Format

If you have all of the above items in place and believe you are organized to sell, you're wrong! What happens when you are not at your desk and Mr. VIP calls? Are your phone operators and secretaries trained? Let's make sure they are, and consider a sales and marketing audit or checklist for your sales office secretary. Just as the salesperson needs a manual or workplan, so does the secretary. This secretary's manual should contain:

____ Telephone Answering Instructions. This is perhaps the most important, yet overlooked, step for any sales department. Secretaries should be provided with a fill-in sheet pad on which he or she may record the person's name, address, title, company, and phone number; basic meeting dates and general requirements; a clear statement that rates are either negotiable or a very broad range to quote; the general property brochure descriptive data; and a specific sales representative's name that can be provided to the caller and a time at which a return call can be made to this individual.

*Comment:* Untold amounts of business are lost because these instructions do not exist or are not followed. It should be made clear that such instructions are to be followed and are part of the job.

____ Greeting Procedure for Walk-in Customers. A warm, friendly but businesslike greeting procedure should be rehearsed for all personnel who greet walk-in guests. If no sales representative is immediately available, provide the walk-in with a brochure on the property or other collateral material along with coffee. Keep the walk-in "warm!"

____ Desk Manual. A desk-top notebook/manual should be part of every secretary's or receptionist's office equipment. Included in this manual should be a number of key items, all of which the secretary should know how to use. These key items should include: telephone answering instructions; greeting procedures for walk-ins; tentative convention booking forms; convention booking forms; change notices to convention booking forms; cancellation forms; VIP reservation forms; and brochure request forms.

____ Instructions Guide. All clerical and secretarial personnel, as well as the sales staff, should be trained and provided with an instructions guide that contains: requisition and purchase order forms; brochure request forms; reader file instructions; and instructions on how to make a file, how to trace a file, and how to kill a file.

Organizing for the sales effort is an important and essential step. The materials listed on the previous pages are the sales office's tools to see that the job gets done properly and the business is booked. The procedures are summarized in Figure 7.8. The results of using these procedures religiously will be an organized office, maximum efficiency, and a satisfied repeat customer.

_____I.      Brochure
                                          _____Meeting rooms—seating fashion and
                                                  capacity
                                          _____Amenities
                                          _____Services available
                                          _____Directions/map/transportation
                                          _____Phone/address
                                          _____Sales personnel
_____II.     Activities and Amenities Brochure or Guide
                                          _____Spouse activities
                                          _____Children's activities
                                          _____Recreational
                                          _____Nearby attractions
                                          _____Shopping
_____III.    Tentative Confirmation—Letter 1
_____IV.     Sales Checklist
_____V.      Convention Booking Form
_____VI.     Contact Report
_____VII.    Post-Convention Report
_____VIII.   VIP Reservation Request Form
_____IX.     Events Timetable/Workplan Program
               _____Is it posted and circulated?
_____X.      The Reminder and Final Confirmation—Letter 2
_____XI.     Telephone Assurance Procedures
_____XII.    Key Contact Assignment (One Person—YOU!)
_____XIII.   Billing Procedures
_____XIV.    The Thank You—Letter 3 (Call also)
_____XV.     Come on Back!!—Letter 4

Sales Secretary's Manual

_____Requisition and Purchase Order Forms and Instructions
_____Brochure Request Form
_____VIP Reservations Forms
_____Tentative Convention Booking Forms
_____Convention Book Forms—Definite
_____Change Convention Booking Form
_____Cancellation Forms
_____Telephone Answering Instructions
_____Greeting Customers Who Walk In
_____Reader Files
_____How to Make a File
_____How to Trace a File
_____How to Kill a File

**Figure 7.8**  Sales and Marketing Audit Checklist

## DIRECT FACE-TO-FACE SALES

There is a plethora of literature on the sales call or personal selling. Some of the literature expounds the values of appearance, other literature goes into the psychology to use, and still others suggest using biorhythms and positive strokes. Each has its own merits, gives some good ingredients for the successful sales approach, and may even help you sell. Obviously, looking good, feeling good, and conveying a positive attitude are all helpful. Equally important is knowing your product or service and knowing how to identify your client's needs, and then performing the logical match-up of the two — with the result being the sale.

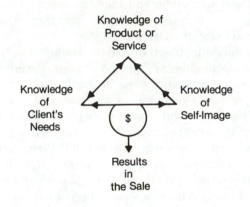

Can it really be that simple? The theory is simple, but it takes careful study and a lot of hard work to put it into practice. Let's look a little closer at these three keys of face-to-face sales.

### KEY 1: KNOWLEDGE OF YOUR PRODUCT OR SERVICE

This means you know every aspect of your product or service and that you seldom, if ever, have to look up a fact or get back to a client. For example, you are selling group business for a major hotel and calling on Ms. Haskell, the National Sales Manager for EBM Corporation. Can you readily state your hotel's meeting room sizes, set-ups, capacities, ceiling heights, audiovisual equipment, room prices, recommendations from the banquet menu, amenities of the property, and so on? If so, you have knowledge of your product or service.

### KEY 2: KNOWLEDGE OF YOUR CLIENT'S NEEDS

This means you have done your homework — you know what EBM Corporation does, who Ms. Haskell is, what type of meetings she usually holds, and how much she usually spends. Even if you do not know all of this, you will within the first few minutes of conversation with Ms. Haskell's secretary or Ms. Haskell herself. You need to identify the client's requirements before you try to sell him or her your services. Even more important than this is to understand that Ms. Haskell has more on the line than you might think. A successful meeting within the stated budget makes Ms. Haskell look good to Mr. Big — remember that when you sell. The old expression, "We know you want a successful meeting; our success and yours are one in the same," is to be remembered and stated at some point.

## KEY 3: KNOWLEDGE OF YOUR SELF-IMAGE

This is a tough thing to learn, especially if you are not looking closely at yourself. What image do you convey in your dress, speech, mannerisms, and so forth? To what image do you think Ms. Haskell will respond during a sales call? If the answers are not the same, you need to adjust yourself to fit Ms. Haskell's image. Yes, it may even mean getting a haircut and shoeshine. You may be very well prepared with knowledge of your product (Key 1), knowledge of your client (Key 2), and still lose the sale because you lack knowledge of yourself (Key 3).

Direct face-to-face sales should be based on the marketing premise of meeting the customer's needs, not on meeting the salesperson's needs. Recently a text was published with many sales articles written by key hospitality industry executives, and it contained many pieces of advice on the successful sales call. There were such statements as: "If you're well-groomed and wear a meticulous suit or dress, you're more than likely going to land the sale"; or my favorite, "Convey yourself as a real swinger; most men like to be with people who are with it!" Well, you and I both know many different attitudes and beliefs exist among prospective clients and the sale does not totally hinge on your being a "swinger" or "the best-dressed kid."

All these pages of advice reminded me of a recent observation I made on a flight between Boston and New York. A few rows up on the other side of the curtain was Mr. Hospitality Sales Executive — going first class all the way. It really hurt. He not only was wining and dining a decision-maker for a big medical group meeting, but he even had a better property than Ms. Tryharder in the coach section. So there sat that swinging Mr. Hospitality, sipping his second scotch — the entertainment of the cabin — and the clients were just eating it up. His grand finale in impressing his new "buddies" (no longer clients) was the old third drink trick. As the flight attendant went past him, he extended his arm with a just-about-empty glass right out against her back, dropped the glass, and said, "Good grief, woman, you've spilled my drink all over." The embarrassed flight attendant apologized and quickly gave Mr. Hospitality a complimentary third drink. This really impressed his buddies — by this point booking the business was a mere formality. Mr. Hospitality sprayed his mouth with a breath spray, popped in a piece of gum, and headed for his hotel to further impress his buddies. Poor Ms. Tryharder had to wait until later that day to meet these same clients and try to convince them that her slightly inferior property at a slightly higher rate is where they should bring their meeting.

As the afternoon arrived, so did the potential clients. Ms. Tryharder did her best by answering every question, displaying thorough knowledge of her product and thorough knowledge of her clients' needs. Ms. Tryharder really did her homework and now it was going to pay off. As the clients retreated to Ms. Tryharder's office for a cup of coffee (which was really needed after the liquid lunch with good old Mr. Hospitality), she began to apply her three keys to success.

"Ladies and gentlemen," she said, "obviously Mr. Hospitality has a better hotel and a slightly better rate; let me call him for you and save you the trouble. We do it all the time in our business, you know." She dialed Mr. Hospitality and learned that he was gone for the afternoon. Ms. Tryharder told the clients not to worry; she would be sure to call Mr. Hospitality for them in the late morning when Mr. Hospitality usually arrived at work. Ms. Tryharder then sat back and said in a casual manner, "Your group will be bringing their spouses, won't they?" The clients said, "Definitely." Ms. Tryharder reached into her desk and laid out a map of the city with the shopping areas clearly marked. The clients thanked Ms. Tryharder and asked, "What are all the red zones on this map?" Ms. Tryharder replied, "Oh, those? Well they are the high-crime areas." The next question came from the clients, "Isn't that spot where all the red zones comes together where we were this morning at Mr. Hospitality's?" "Well, ah . . . yes, I guess so," said Ms. Tryharder. "But don't worry, Mr. Hospitality's hotel has excellent guards and even patrol dogs — they've thought of everything." The next morning at 9:00 a.m. sharp, Ms. Tryharder's phone rang and it was the same clients wanting to book the meeting at Ms. Tryharder's hotel. The group thought Ms. Tryharder's hotel might be a little better, in view of the fact that women were coming along to the meeting.

Think about this story as you go out to sell, and remember the three keys:

Knowledge of your product or service.

Knowledge of your client's needs.

Knowledge of your self-image.

## OVER-THE-PHONE SALES

Many times a hospitality industry product or service is sold without the opportunity for a direct face-to-face sales call. Booking business by telephone is an art in itself. There are a few golden rules to help achieve success. The first three are identical to the three keys we discussed in the previous section of this chapter, that is, knowledge of your product or service, knowledge of your client's needs, and knowledge of your self-image. We will comment on these as they apply to phone sales.

*First,* just as in face-to-face sales, know your product or service thoroughly. Do not hesitate or say, "I'll get back to you with those dimensions." *Second,* know about your prospect by doing your research before you call, not while you're talking to him or her. *Third,* your self-image can be detected or transmitted by your vocal expressions and telephone mannerisms. In addition, there are other keys to telephone sales beyond these three. The *fourth* key is perhaps the most important of all — *Listen!* Think for a minute of Mr. Hospitality on the phone telling his prospects a few jokes, reminding them of his famous third drink trick, and forgetting to ask if their spouses are coming to the meeting. Then there is Ms. Tryharder with her check-list of required information, listening intently and making sure each item mentioned or requested has been checked off, so that a clear, accurate, and prompt response is given right over the phone. Ms. Tryharder's phone call is going to end like this: "Well, Mr. Prospect, let me recap your needs, item for item," and then, "Now that we have all the details, should we book you on a tentative basis for the 3d through the 5th of next month?" The *fifth* key or step has just been completed — asking for the business. The *sixth* key is to say "thank you." Ms. Tryharder now goes on to steps 7 through to the end, making sure the booking becomes definite, the clients needs are met, and the meeting is a success.

## SALES THROUGH DIRECT MAIL

If you were to look closely at your mail for a week, you would be examining the results of great creative energies. Do you realize all the things you "may" have won, lost, or missed? From cashier's checks, to cars, to lifetime memberships, to your own vacation home — it all comes by direct mail. You open your charge card bill or your gasoline credit card bill and seven to ten pieces of fantastic offers "too good to refuse" fall before your eyes.

Selling the products and services of the hospitality industry via direct mail re-quires special knowledge and special challenges. In direct mail sales you do not have the chance to personally see or talk to your clients, as you do in direct face-to-face sales or telephone sales. Since it is impersonal, direct mail must be based on good mailing lists of *prospects* whose needs your product or service can fulfill. Then you must develop a direct mail "piece" that is not just a great picture, but a *com-munications vehicle that relates the client's needs to your product or service offering*. It is also necessary to know when to mail and when to *stop* mailing. Next, you must *fulfill* the positive response to your direct mail pitch promptly and accurately. Let's briefly discuss each of these key points to the success of direct mail sales.

**KEY 1:** GOOD LISTS
Knowing to whom your sales letter or promotion piece is going is of primary impor-tance. A simple thing like the correct spelling of a manager's name means a lot if you want your letter read. Lists should constantly be "cleansed" or "purged" of invalid or out-of-date information. Lists should be updated each time a new piece of information becomes available. Scan the media to identify those who are leaving and those who are coming so that your list is always as current as possible. Verify names, titles, and addresses from your most recent contact with the sales prospect. Constantly strive to be accurate.

**KEY 2:** THE COMMUNICATIONS "PIECE"
You can develop checklist upon checklist of do's and don't's for sales letters. There is no single "best" approach to sales letters. In some circumstances a personal ap-

proach may be appropriate. In other circumstances the second-person approach should be used. Some general rules for sales letters are always helpful, but if rules are strictly adhered to they may inhibit an engaging personal touch. One good guideline is to be sure to send an individualized letter or at least have it appear to be an original. No one wants to read a "personal" letter that has been copied or reproduced. Also be sure to include the key to any direct mail sales message — *relate the prospective customer's needs directly to your product or service*. Can all this be done on one page? The answer is an emphatic yes! Time is important to everyone, and your personal one-page letter has a lot better chance of being read by Ms. Decision-maker than a file containing lengthy, flashy, or even trashy promotion pieces.

### KEY 3: KNOWING WHEN TO MAIL

Consider the example of a large publishing company that just came out with a terrific consumer-oriented book on saving money on your federal income tax. The publisher is excited because this is a super book — new ideas, right price, and so on. So why doesn't the publisher promote it in June and July when the press runs are complete? The answer is timing. People buy books on federal income tax in October through March, not in June, July, and August. Furthermore, if possible time your letter to arrive on a Tuesday, Wednesday, or Thursday. You know what Mondays are like in a busy office. You also know if your letter arrives on Friday afternoon it may not even make the reading file. So, think it out — when do you need the business and when is the best time to send that letter?

Another example is that of Mr. Agressivo, a real go-getter sales manager for a large New York hotel. Mr. Agressivo compiled a list of prospective customers and prepared a personal, individually typed letter that concluded with, "I'll call you later this week to set up the inspection tour and complimentary luncheon." All 150 letters went out in the 4:00 p.m. mail on Monday afternoon so to ensure delivery on Tuesday. He then promptly caught the 5:30 p.m. flight to Los Angeles for a four-day sales blitz. The moral is simple. *Think!* Be there when your letter says you will and call when it says you will. Otherwise, you will have to start all over again, trying to land that prospective customer.

### KEY 4: KNOWING WHEN TO STOP MAILING

Promotion materials and sales letters are expensive; estimates are up to $8 a letter today. Thus, knowing when to stop mailing makes a lot of "cents." Many mailings may be sequential, with up to four or five pitches to the same list. Be sure you have a system that will eliminate the portion of the list that has already responded "yes" or "no" to your earlier mailing. Think of the example of the magazine renewal game. This past Christmas my spouse wanted to renew one of my favorite pictorial magazines as a Christmas gift. Having placed all the junk mail in a large stack, I began to wade through, looking for this magazine's renewal card and promotion. I found four offers! (I was on a "good" list.) Offer number one was for the "early bird" special offer. The $36.00 newsstand rate was reduced to only $24.00 if I renewed by November 1st. Offer number two was identical except for the date, which was November 15th. Offer number three was postmarked December 1st and offered this year's subscription on a "last chance for renewal" basis at $21. Finally, there was offer number four, postmarked December 20th — the absolute last chance and at only $19.95. By this time I was really angry — just think, the gold old loyal subscriber who took advantage of the "early bird" special was out $4.05. In mid-January I received another proposition letter saying they were sorry no one renewed by gift subscription, but "don't feel bad — we have a special discount for you at only $18.95." That's when I renewed and I never missed an issue! This publisher didn't know when to stop mailing, or did he? I renewed it, didn't I?

**KEY 5:** FULFILLMENT

Once you get that positive response, be sure you are in a position to fulfill what you promised on a timely basis. If you offered Mr. and Mrs. Jones a weekend vacation any weekend in May with the proviso that advance reservations be made, be sure you have their room ready when they arrive. If you fail to fulfill your offer you may as well eliminate the Jones's name from your "good" list along with the names of their friends and neighbors — they won't be responding either.

## RESERVATIONS

This is perhaps the most-often ignored point of contact in the overall sales process. Never forget that reservations is a key point of contact sales — not a computerized mechanical system. If you are in direct sales, be sure you spend a portion of each week talking with the reservations office. Tell the reservations office who is coming, what to do, and, if necessary, how to do it. Make sure you know the reservations personnel well enough to get a favor every so often. Just remember that they are like career service employees — once in a while a little extra attention can really help. Stories about reservations are more abundant than those told about hotels or rooms. You, the sales professional, have an obligation to see that your customers' reservations are handled without a flaw.

## CHECKLIST TO INCREASE SALES

\_\_\_\_ **1.** Shop Your Competition. Look for rate comparisons; make adjustments.

\_\_\_\_ **2.** Focus on Maximizing Revenue — versus just rate or occupancy.

\_\_\_\_ **3.** Communicate with Reservations. These personnel are the front line to the customer.

\_\_\_\_ **4.** Give Every Group Something. To close a sale, have some items to "give" — coffee break, suite, etc.

\_\_\_\_ **5.** Sell Up — to a higher-rated room or better menu item.

_____ **6.** Sell Down. If rate resistance is encountered, move it to a "valley" period and sell it.

_____ **7.** Regularly Review Your Sales Files. Look to convert tentatives to definites or check why a piece of business was lost.

_____ **8.** Review All Key Accounts. Are they being called upon regularly and by the correct person?

_____ **9.** Track Multi-Room Night Transient Accounts. Establish an account and track all transient accounts producing 50-plus room nights; treat as you would your best group customer.

_____ **10.** Review the Function Book on a Regular Basis. Sell into valley periods and push weak or questionable tentatives out of prime periods.

_____ **11.** Review All Lost-Business Reports. Ask how you can get this business back next time — and do it.

_____ **12.** Keep in Touch with and Entertain Key Contacts. These contacts include local car rental, airline, and motor coach managers.

_____ **13.** Develop a Support Letter. Use your general manager or owner to give you a support letter. It may make the difference to a group you're going after.

_____ **14.** Free Yourself and All Others in Sales — from all nonselling activities. The more time spent selling, the more sales that are realized.

_____ **15.** Regularly Meet with Key Meeting Planners. Show your personal interest.

_____ **16.** Post-meeting Follow-up Letter and Questionnaire — send both. One should be a thank you, the other a "May we help you again."

_____ **17.** Regularly (daily) View Your Competitors' Reader Board(s). (A "Reader Board" is the board on which meetings are listed in a hotel.) Make notes and prepare a game plan to land these firms and organizations for next year or next quarter.

_____ **18.** Get to Know Those Who Are in the Know. These are your local newspaper, city magazine, radio and television personalities. They are often the first to know who is coming to town — or what big event is about to occur.

_____ **19.** Know Your Transient Guests. They can lead you to your next group booking. Get to know them and their local contacts.

_____ **20.** Monitor and Befriend the Top Producing Travel Agents.

_____ **21.** Check Your Mailing Lists. Are they up to date?

_____ **22.** Test Your Reservations Department. Are your VIPs noted? Is the registration list accurate? Etc.

_____ **23.** Carefully and Regularly Review Your Group Rates. Nothing is worse than empty rooms. So what if the average rate is down. The revenue is what counts. Get it in the door!

_____ **24.** Go after Multi-Year Business — then service it well!

_____ **25.** Be Sure Your Rates Are Published and available to all local travel directories/corporations.

_____ **26.** Participate in City/Area Civic Functions — contacts result in business.

_____ **27.** Research — by phone and through publications (directories, etc.). Make a list and start calling.

_____ **28.** Upgrade Your Groups/Customers. If you want repeat business, use those empty club floor rooms or suites to upgrade your good customers or new customers. They will come back for more.

_____ **29.** Book It at Half Price. If there is a notorious rate shopper that your competitor routinely books instead of you, book him into one of your valley periods at 50 percent off — or below your competitor. You can use the revenue versus empty rooms.

_____ **30.** Appreciation Is Personal. Be sure you show you care by personally taking care of your accounts. Don't pass them on to an underling. Cultivate them!

Now that you have the tools described in this chapter and this checklist to increase sales, let's turn to another marketing weapon to bring in customers as we next look at advertising.

## KEY WORDS AND CONCEPTS

**Check-in** The time a person registers for a room. A hotel day usually starts at 6 a.m.; however, occupancy of rooms can occur any time they are made available, usually after 1 p.m.

**Banquet Business** Group of guests or people served in a room separate from the regular dining room with food service pre-selected at a flat price per person.

**Direct Mail** Promotional letters, pieces, or any sales-oriented correspondence sent to prospective guests.

**Hotel Representative** Companies that serve as an out-of-town representative for hotels and resorts that offer lodging operations at more cost-efficient methods to cover markets away from the home-base city of the hotel or resort. Hotel representatives promote individual reservations through travel agents, airlines, and corporations, and they develop group business for distant properties.

**Direct Face-to-Face Sales** Direct in-person selling or person-to-person selling.

**Sales Blitz** A concentrated short-term series of sales calls by a number of sales representatives to obtain a larger number of bookings or reservations.

**Telephone Selling** Contact by telephone whose primary purpose is to obtain a reservation for a room or a group commitment.

## ASSIGNMENTS

1. Design a confirmation letter for a selected hotel or resort that can be filled in while you are on the phone finalizing arrangements for a group meeting.

2. How would you organize a sales office to make maximum use of the time of all sales personnel? What would the receptionist or secretary be doing in his or her spare time that could help your sales effort?

3. Develop a script for a telephone sales effort that results in a definite booking.

4. Visit a local hotel or resort sales office. Review the sales and marketing audit checklists presented earlier in the chapter and determine if this property is organized to efficiently execute the task of selling.

5. Create a direct mail brochure or letter that sells!

# Applying Key Marketing Methodologies: Advertising

8

## PURPOSE

If used properly, advertising is another powerful marketing tool. However, if it is used unwisely, advertising can be very costly without being effective. This chapter will discuss when advertising should be used and which advertising techniques make the most sense for particular marketing opportunities. We will also examine how to create the proposition your advertising should convey and the platform, or promise, upon which it should be built. We will explore advertising at the national, major city, and local market levels. We will also discuss the relation of specific types of media and their applications to the hospitality industry and present useful techniques.

## OBJECTIVES

1. Relate your product or service to your advertising for maximum effectiveness with the consumer.

2. Develop a *platform* on which your advertising can be based and a *proposition* that will be the strongest "sell" for your product or service.

3. Identify when and how to advertise your product or service.

4. Select the best markets and media in which to advertise for maximum returns on your advertising dollar investments.

5. Understand how to trade the use of your product or service in order to double or even triple your advertising clout.

6. Explore themes, reasons, and actual case studies of a variety of ads.

Lists upon lists of do's and don't's for advertising proliferate. The interesting point about these biblical lists is that each contains a variety of golden rules: "tell the truth," "stretch the truth," or "be creative." Very few lists acknowledge two basic things: the product or service itself, and the role the advertising is to play in the overall marketing of that product or service.

## ADVERTISING GUIDELINES

Before any advertising can be created, a number of steps must be taken.

**STEP 1: Know Your Product or Service.**  What is the current level of your knowledge of the product or service you are offering or are about to offer through advertising? Do you really understand the current consumer perception (not your own) of your product's or service's acceptability and image in terms of price, quality, relationship to competition, consistency, and inconsistency? Knowing the consumer's current attitude, perspective, and image of your product or service is essential.

**STEP 2: Advertise as Part of the Total Marketing Strategy.**  What role do you anticipate advertising will play as part of your total marketing strategy? Do you know if you even need to use this marketing weapon? If so, should you use the narrow range but direct aim of a rifle or do you want to sweep a large region with a fleet of bombers? Later in this chapter a number of case studies will be presented; some will show how the rifle didn't work and others will demonstrate how the bombers missed.

**STEP 3: Develop a Proposition.**  Have you developed a general *proposition* to be conveyed in your advertising message? Is that proposition the strongest truthful statement you can make to the consumer on behalf of your product or service? Is that proposition in agreement with and support of your overall marketing strategy and in concert with the purpose of your advertising? For example, if you are trying to persuade people to use your product or service, does your advertising include a toll-free telephone number that consumers can call to order your product or service or get further information? A discussion of the purposes of advertising will be included within the case studies.

**STEP 4: Create a Platform.**  Once you have knowledge of your product or service, awareness of the consumer's perspective, knowledge of the role your advertising is to play as part of the total marketing strategy, and have developed your proposition, it is time to focus on the *platform*. The platform is an item-by-item listing of support for your proposition. These platform statements represent or demonstrate the foundation upon which your proposition is based. For example, when Hyatt Hotels says, "We offer you a touch of class," the company supports that claim with some pretty spectacular photos that demonstrate some "touches of class." We will return to other examples of propositions and platforms in the case studies later on in this chapter.

**STEP 5: Be Realistic About the Level of Expectation.** Regardless of the purpose of your advertising and regardless of its strategic role in your overall marketing plan, there is one key premise that you should always adhere to in the advertising of the products and services of the hospitality industry. This is the *level of expectation* premise: *Never promise more than your product or service can fulfill or deliver.* The level of expectation premise can be graphically presented as follows:

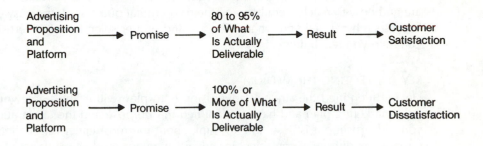

Think carefully about this basic premise and always remember it. How would you feel if you were led to believe "all of our Florida Rent-A-Car customers have a new Lincoln* assigned to them upon arrival" and you arrived to find a two-year-old Pinto? Upon reading the fine print on the contract you find that it says "*subject to availability, etc., etc." There are many, many other examples where hospitality industry firms have promised more than they could deliver and created customer dissatisfaction.

**STEP 6: Review for Customer Needs.** Does your advertising strategy relate to your customers' needs? Have you kept the needs of your customers or audience in the forefront of your advertising strategy? This is a simple step if steps 1 to 5 have been thoroughly addressed.

The preceding six basic steps are essential before one even begins the key considerations associated with actual advertising. Briefly, a list of key considerations follows:

**KEY 1:** PURPOSE
Clearly identify *one* purpose you expect your advertising to serve. Ensure this one purpose is dominant and *consistent* with your marketing strategy. If you need to use advertising weaponry to *persuade,* be sure it does just that — persuades people to buy your product or service. If you need advertising to *remind* people to use your product or service, be sure your advertising reminds the audience your product or service is still there for their consumption. If you need advertising to *inform* people about your product or service, be sure it tells them the product or service is available and informs them how to get it. Be it to persuade, inform, or remind, advertising

does not, in itself, make a sale; however, it can facilitate a sale if executed properly and if it is based on the six basic steps.

### KEY 2: TARGETING YOUR AUDIENCE

Assuming you know what you want to say and why you want it said, the next key is to precisely *identify to whom you want it said.* The obvious answer is, "I want to say it to people who will buy my product or use my service." Where these people are and how to reach them become the next critical questions to be answered. Market research can tell you where they are and proper selection of advertising media can help you reach them.

### KEY 3: SELECTING THE MEDIUM

Having identified the strategy advertising is to play within the framework of your total marketing plan and having identified the *purpose* and the target audience for your advertising, it is now time to think about the most effective, efficient, and affordable medium you can select for advertising your product or service. For some it may be television, radio, or magazine advertising; for others it may be direct mail, directories, outdoor advertising, or the yellow pages. This becomes a function of whom you are targeting and how much you have to spend. It also becomes a function of what strategy or role advertising is to play as part of your total marketing plan.

### KEY 4: CREATING THE AD

This is largely dependent upon all other steps and keys previously cited. Despite wide interest in great creative advertising, your product or service, purpose, and budget become the practical parameters of what you can and cannot do in your creative strategy. It is very difficult to show your customers your expansive beach when all you can afford is a 30-second radio spot or a three-line ad in a directory.

### KEY 5: PLACEMENT AND/OR TIMING

Your (or your agency's) creativity has hit upon a stroke of genius. Now, don't blow it! As critical as all the other steps and keys is the proper selection of *where* your advertising goes and *when* it is carried. The where and when encompass many details which should be in writing and based on the best available research. *Where* includes such things as the markets; the selection of media, be it *Sports Illustrated* or *Ladies Home Journal;* the issues; the page; the section of the page; and so on. *When* includes such things as the time of year; the month; the week; the day of the week; the hour of the day; the minutes during the hour of the day, such as after the sports on FM radio at 4:20 p.m.; and so on. And don't forget *who* actually does your ad — is the image, voice, appearance, or photo best for your product or service and message?

**KEY 6:** FULFILLMENT

Well, you ran the great creative ad with all strokes of genius, at the strike of the clock, and the results begin to come in. The phone is ringing off the hook! Is there *anyone* there to answer it? Being able to fulfill after you have motivated the consumer to purchase is now critical and should always be viewed within the total context of your advertising strategy.

## *DO IT YOURSELF OR SELECT AN AGENCY*

Depending on the skills you have and the size of your budget, executing an advertising campaign can be self-administered or contracted to an agency. The scope and breadth of the hospitality industry's advertising is immense, ranging from local entertainment ads in the local newspapers to national TV campaigns on major networks. This section makes a few suggestions for those of you who cannot afford the luxury of hiring a major agency.

*First,* regardless of your product or service, start your own *master book*. This master book should contain examples of clean ads that you or one of your employees can readily use. The book's content and organization are up to you. It will prove an effective way to review how, where, and what made your ad come together. In this same notebook set up a section labeled "Monitor." This monitor section should be both a log of the history of your advertising and a statement of results. For example, it could read as follows:

Tues., Feb. 20.   Print Ad "A-1" — *Telegraph* — Entertainment Page

Wed., Feb. 21.   Print Ad "A-1" — *News* — Sports Page

Thurs., Feb. 22. Print Ad "A-1" — *Telegraph* — Women's Page

*Results:* Covers for Wed. through Fri. up by 25% over same period last year and/or week.

     *or*

Beverage revenue up 16% Thurs. and 28% Fri. compared to same period last year and/or last week.

This simple procedure will give you or your replacement a history of which ads were run, where they were run, and the results.

Also consider keeping a clippings file of what appears to be the best of your competition's advertising. Analyze the file carefully to determine what strategy your chief competitors are executing through their advertising and what you can do to combat the moves of your competitor. For example, let's say your competitor has run "2-for-1" sales and has pushed these through advertisements. You should analyze this offer to determine if you can do the same or better and if there is a pattern as to when these sales are run. You might discover that the ad runs the fourth week of every month. One strategy you might employ would be to run your own "2-for-1" sale through advertising the third week of the month.

Selecting an agency is not an easy task. It is important that the agency you select knows something about your market and the customers of your product or service. This knowledge can be augmented by a good agency research function, either within the agency itself or contracted out to the better research suppliers. If an agency immediately wants to talk creative strategy, or media, or contract, take another look. A good agency will want to listen and learn as much as possible about your product or service, about your markets or consumers, and about you and your overall marketing strategies. Another helpful technique is to place your business "out to bid" or "out for proposal."

It is always amazing to see the amount of good work that comes from the "bid presentations" absolutely free of charge. By all means consider more than one agency in the proposal stage so that you will have some bases for comparison. There are all kinds of theories on how long to stay with an agency or how often to switch. Only you can be the judge of this, and you should make changes only when your objective measurements indicate that it is time for a change.

## MARKET COVERAGE

Assuming your product or service requires use of advertising marketing weaponry, it is now time to think about where your product or service should be exposed to the consumer. Since each case should be viewed individually and there are no real golden rules, the checklist of definitions that follows should help you understand the ways in which you can reach the market through advertising.

____ Nationwide. Simply stated, this is coast-to-coast coverage or exposure of your product or service. If your market is nationwide or if you are trying to develop the nation as your total market, it might make sense to look at this total market exposure. Nationwide campaigns are particularly useful for large chains seeking to increase their brands awareness levels or seeking to provide an "image" for their brand. Also, when a national product introduction or service offering is desired simultaneously in all markets, a nationwide campaign is utilized.

____ Select Major Markets. Advertising can be placed on a very tailored or "pick the markets" concept. This means that, based on research or for reasons of dollar expenditure constraints, you select only those major markets you want to penetrate with your campaign. There are many examples of applications of this cost-effective major market selection technique. One might be a restaurant chain with facilities in 20 major markets east of the Rockies — to this chain, major market selection makes sense.

____ Regional Markets. There are numerous methods of identifying marketing regions for your product or service. Advertising can be purchased or selected on a regional basis also. For example, a large chain of cafeterias selects only the southwest region for advertising exposure since this is the primary market for their locations and customers.

____ Population Markets/SMSAs. These are defined as major concentrations of population. There are various breakdowns available, such as standard metropolitan areas of over 1,000,000 population (or viewers, exposures, etc.), over 750,000 population, over 500,000 population, and so on.

____ Viewer/Reader or Subscriber Market Areas. TV stations, radio stations, and magazines provide detailed descriptions of the number of people within their range or on the circulation lists. In addition, various *buyer characteristics* are provided that will help correlate the best match of media to your product or service consumer. Selection by this methodology allows for a more pinpointed or defined market area for your advertising message.

____ City Pairs in Feeder Markets. Previously determined markets wherein the demand for your product or service is generated may also be selected for your advertising message.

____ Cities. Advertising can be placed on an individual city basis or even by area within cities. Utilization of local market research can be a valuable aid to selecting the proper media.

Note that today's sophisticated market analysis and customer research should help you select the best of the preceding methods or combination of methods to maximize the effectiveness of your advertising dollar.

## *MEDIA SELECTION*

Media selection is another concern which you should evaluate carefully before creating your advertising. *Broadcast media,* which includes television and radio, provides one type of exposure for your product or service. Only you can determine if broadcast media is the best to use. *Print media,* which includes magazines, newspapers, supplements, catalogs, directories, yellow pages, brochures, flyers, etc., provides other types of exposure for your product or service.

Prior to selection, you should carefully analyze the various media to determine a number of factors, such as the number of potential customers to be reached, expected return on investment, best method to convey advertising strategy, and the most cost-efficient method. Again, you will be best served by careful analysis of your needs and budget.

## TRADE-OUTS, BARTER, AND OTHER TECHNIQUES

Frequently it is possible to exchange your product or service for advertising space or broadcast exposure. There is an infinite variety of "trade-outs" or barter agreements you can negotiate, ranging from a "1-for-1" to a "5-for-1" or even greater trade. These terms simply mean that, for example, you will provide $1,000 in products or services for equal dollar value of space or air time. This would be a "1-for-1" trade. If it were $1,000 of your product or service for $2,000 worth of air time or space, you would have a "2-for-1" trade-out. If negotiated properly, trade-outs can be a very effective way to stretch your advertising dollar and to increase your business.

## CO-OPING

Another method of stretching your advertising dollar is to join with others to jointly advertise, thereby sharing the costs and the results. Resort areas frequently run cooperative advertising campaigns promoting the region or area and also list or mention your product or service. A more popular use of co-oping is also exemplified by two or more firms jointly advertising each other's services or products either individually or collectively in the same advertising campaign. For example, Marriott Hotels and Hertz Rent-A-Cars, or American Airlines and Avis feature each other in cooperative ad campaigns (see Figure 8.1).

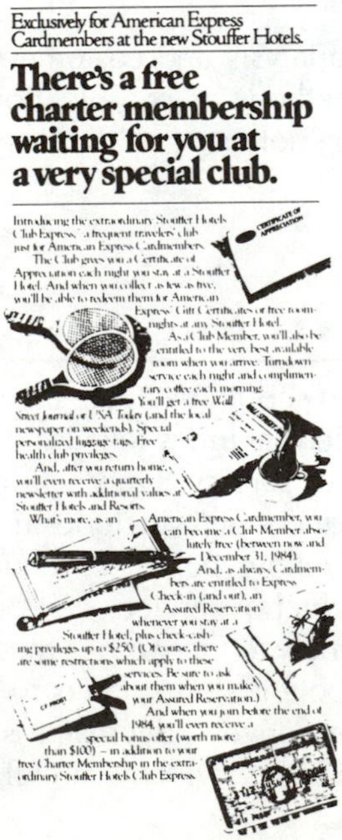

**Figure 8.1** Sample of a Cooperative Advertisement Campaign (*courtesy: Stouffer Hotel Co.*)

## *RHYMES, REASONS, AND THEMES*

An ad is not just the product of an idea. Planned and effective advertising begins long before the "great idea" stage. Some key questions need to be asked regarding the purpose of the advertising, the platform, and the proposition as previously discussed. Even the great idea must have a purpose, or it is an idea in a vacuum. In this section we will present and give examples of types and themes of ads as they relate to the purpose of the ad. We will examine some examples of great ideas in the case studies later in the chapter. As you will see, in some cases the great ideas backfire since the consumer may view the ad from his or her own perspective rather than that intended by the advertising. Reasons for, and themes of, a specific ad or ad campaign are many. Here are some examples.

**TYPE A: Reputation Builders.**  These are ads which seek to enhance the reputation of the product or service being represented by featuring *testimonials,* self-claims, or other-party claims, or by acknowledging leadership or professionalism. One such example is the testimonial or celebrity ad, in which a recognized celebrity speaks on behalf of the product or service or merely lends his or her photo or signature in association with or as an implied endorsement of the product or service.

Another version of this celebrity testimonial is the self-testimonial ad. In this case the CEO, president, or chairman of the firm speaks on behalf of the product or service. This is also referred to as the "ego trip" ad later in the case studies section of this chapter.

Another form of reputation builder is the *professional/trust ad* wherein the platform itself is self-implied professionalism. The ad features the entire staff in uniform standing at attention, just waiting to professionally serve. Finally, we have the ad that may be referred to as the "image" ad form of reputation builder: the rich-looking flower arrangements, the monogrammed towels, the Rolls-Royce at the portico (see Figure 8.2).

**TYPE B: Product/Service Touters.**  A product or service *touter* ad can take on a number of looks. The most obvious is the *direct* look featuring the facility (product or service) and stating boldly the reasons for its greatness. This touting of the actual elements of the platform gives results similar to those of the reputation-builder ads — they both enhance the product or service. Another more direct form of touter ad is the *comparative* approach. Here, the ad compares the product or service side by side with the competitor to plainly demonstrate that its platform of benefits outstrips the competition.

Sometimes a touter features an element or select aspect to achieve its goal. An amenity of unusually high quality may be the ad focal point. Sometimes a "touter ad" will feature a scene, such as an elegant-looking couple or a rich setting, as the "positioning" statement for the product or service. In this case the scene speaks for the product or service type. Product/service "touter" ads can have multiple elements (see Figure 8.3).

**Figure 8.2** Sample of a "Reputation Builder" Advertisement *(courtesy: Hyatt Hotels Corporation)*

**Figure 8.3** Sample of a Product or Service Touter Advertisement *(courtesy: The Breakers)*

**TYPE C: Brand Identifiers.**   In today's crowded marketplace, getting your brand known — achieving *brand awareness* — is not an easy job. What may be even more difficult is to effectively convey what that brand stands for — *brand identity*. Some approaches to achieving brand awareness and brand identity may include statements that boldly feature the brand. Another approach is to develop a *brand identifier,* something — a character, a voice — that becomes synonymous with the brand (see Figure 8.4). A simple approach is to make an introduction or announcement type statement about the brand. "US Air now serves Cleveland." In this case, US Air, the "brand" is the lead-in word in bold type. In essence, "we are now here to serve you." And finally, a more subtle or perhaps sophisticated approach is to seek to develop a niche or to break the clutter of other brands by providing a unique service as the associated identifier (see Figure 8.5).

**TYPE D: Offers.**   An offer ad is one in which the platform becomes part of the proposition. The variety and type are limitless. One prevalent ad is the straight *price offer.* "Newark $49 Round Trip." In the price offer, the actual price is featured and highlighted as the key motivator, not necessarily the product or service. Another variation of the straight price offer is what may be termed the *price offer plus.* In this instance, something additional is included with the implication or direct statement that there is no additional cost. Examples are inclusion of a meal such as breakfast, upgrade

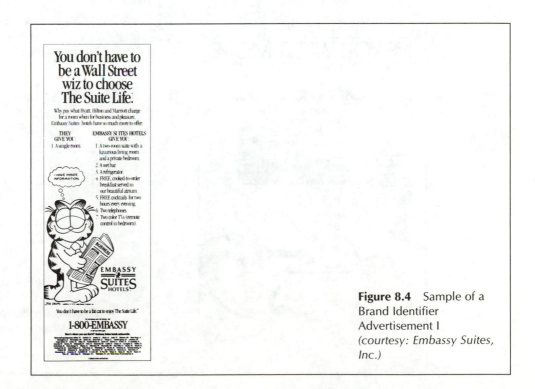

**Figure 8.4**   Sample of a Brand Identifier Advertisement I *(courtesy: Embassy Suites, Inc.)*

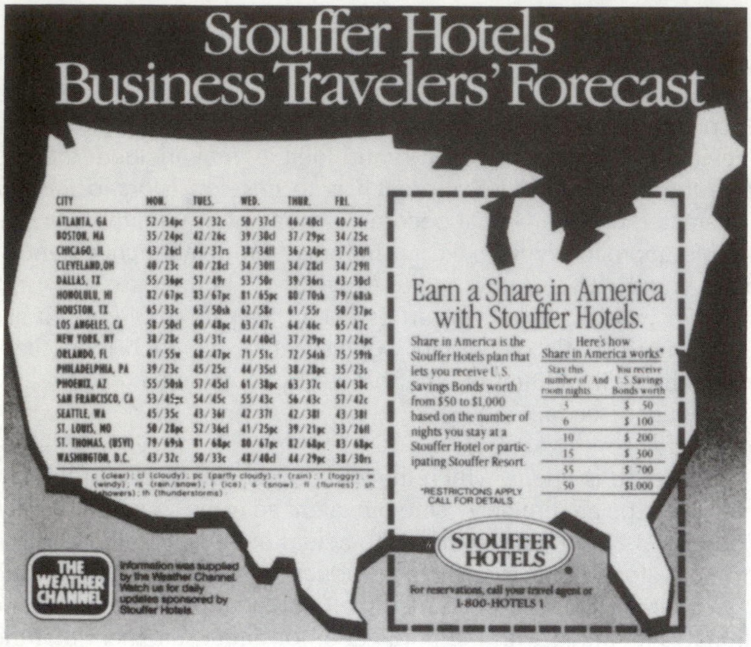

**Figure 8.5**
Sample of a Brand
Identifier Adver-
tisement II
(*courtesy: Stouffer
Hotel Co.*)

**Figure 8.6**   Sample of an
Offer Advertisement
(*courtesy: The Sheraton
Corporation*)

of a room or seat, or getting a luxury car at economy rate. Today, one of the strongest hitting offer type ads is associated with repeat or "build" promotions such as frequent traveler or frequent guest promotions. These ads feature offers or benefits for customers who repeatedly use one product or service (see Figure 8.6). Such sophisticated hard-sell ads for promotional offers recently have engulfed the hospitality business.

**TYPE E: Human Scenarios.** A long-standing type of advertising is designed around what may be referred to as the *human scenario;* the human is the focal point of the ad, either directly — by example or by inference — or by identifiable event or circumstance. One approach is the human element ad in simple form. The employee or group of employees is featured accompanied by a gratuitous statement or slogan (see Figure 8.7). Another version is the portrayal of the "exceptional employee" as representing the norm. On a more sophisticated level, and also more risky if it doesn't work well, is the "situation identification" scenario (see Figure 8.8). Here, the wrong-way scene is displayed and the statement made that this won't occur at our place or with us. Often humorous, these ads have been known to backfire. And, last but certainly not least, is the age-old "suggestive identifier" approach often featuring the promise of romance or sex to the weary reader or viewer. Here, the iden-

**Figure 8.7** Sample of a Human Scenario Advertisement *(courtesy: AVIS RENT A CAR SYSTEM, INC.)*

**Figure 8.8** Sample of a Situation Identification Advertisement *(courtesy: The Westin Galleria and Westin Oaks)*

**Figure 8.9** Sample of a Suggestive Identifier Advertisement *(courtesy: Broward County Tourist Development Council)*

tifier is an attractive person and the "hook" is a man's or woman's imagination (see Figure 8.9).

**TYPE F: Benefit.**  The *benefit* ad is akin to the platform in that it can state item-for-item why the consumer should purchase. Sometimes the ad will focus only on the primary benefit such as a straight locational pitch: "Located at Dallas-Ft. Worth Airport." In other cases the benefit becomes engulfed in an overall umbrella such as the case with most destination ads (see Figure 8.10). Benefit ads may become even more complex by seeking to present a "win-win" situation. Here, the game may vary; i.e., use our services: and "We pay you and we keep your client happy." For example, a resort states in its ad to travel agencies: "Send your clients to our resort and you will be paid a 15% commission promptly (win one), and our service will keep your clients happy so they'll thank you for selecting us (win two). (See Figure 8.11.) Often, meeting-related ads are benefit-oriented; they seek to convey the benefits sought by the meeting planner.

**TYPE G: Series.**  Perhaps one of the most famous series ads run in print was for Porsche. In bold ads actually numbered 1, 2, etc., Porsche stated the "numerous" reasons why Porsche was a superior automobile. The series ad campaign, while used

**Figure 8.10**  Sample of a Benefit Advertisement I *(courtesy: St. Louis Convention & Visitors Commission)*

**Figure 8.11** Sample of a Benefit Advertisement II *(courtesy: AVIS RENT A CAR SYSTEM, INC.)*

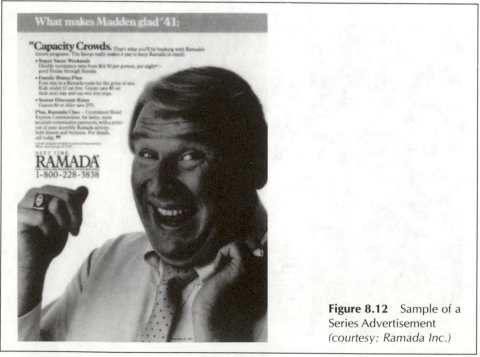

**Figure 8.12** Sample of a Series Advertisement *(courtesy: Ramada Inc.)*

in the automotive industry and outside the U.S. market, has only been used on occasion in the domestic hospitality industry (see Figure 8.12).

**TYPE H: Line Art and Silhouettes.**   More of a technique or production treatment than ad reason or approach, line art and silhouettes have become more and more popular. Their popularity stems largely from their ability to be effective in a newspaper or other black and white setting (see Figure 8.13).

**TYPE I: Trade.**   With the increasingly complex purchasing decisions caused by airline deregulation and the resultant pricing, overcapacity in the lodging sector, and market share wars in the rent-a-car sector, the trade ad takes on a meaning all its own. Today, firms in the hospitality business understand the growing importance of the travel intermediaries and are seeking to gain their attention. Naturally, many elements of the previously described ad types have been employed to reach the travel intermediary. The theme of the trade ad depends to some extent on the travel intermediary per se. For example, an ad aimed at a travel agent might very well strike home with "benefit numero uno" — the commission check — highlighted (see Figure 8.14). The message directed to the meeting planner may be very different: "Meet with us — we know your job is on the line."

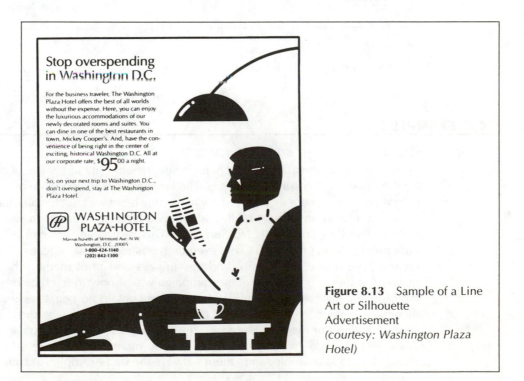

**Figure 8.13**   Sample of a Line Art or Silhouette Advertisement *(courtesy: Washington Plaza Hotel)*

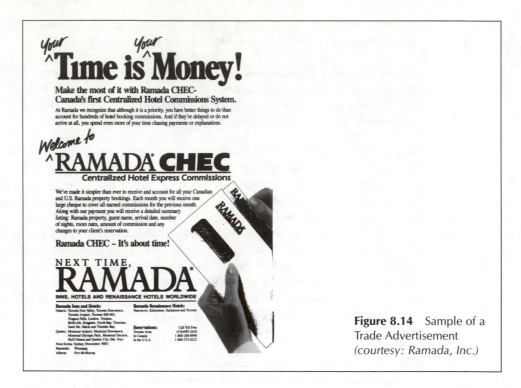

**Figure 8.14**   Sample of a Trade Advertisement (*courtesy: Ramada, Inc.*)

Let's now examine a few of the ad types and approaches in more depth as we look at a few select case examples.

## CASE EXAMPLES

### CASE EXAMPLE A: *THE B-52 THAT BOMBED*

In the late 1970s the major hotel chains made increasingly larger use of national TV for their major advertising campaigns. The largest dollar expenditure of all belonged to Holiday Inns, whose aggressive new marketing team was out to gain market share. Creativity was at an all-time high, and a new advertising campaign was launched, called "The Best Surprise Is No Surprise." This campaign was carried by normal nationwide TV, in print media, and even on the napkins and matches. The ads were creative, the music was catchy, and the airways and print media schedules were heavy. The theme or concept of the campaign was simply to tell the consumers that their lodging experience at Holiday Inns would contain no negative surprises. Sub-themes, like your reservation won't be lost, your room won't be dirty, and so on, were contained in the ads. Moreover, this was a hard-hitting campaign in that the "us" versus "them" was treated in a sarcastic manner within the ads. "Us" was always the good example, and "them" always the bad example. To sum it up, Holiday Inns had a fully loaded fleet of B-52s and saturated the airways with "The Best Surprise Is No Surprise at Holiday Inns."

What was the response to this massive campaign? What was good and what was not so good? The good list is very long and includes: quality creative work; excellent selection of broadcast and print advertising; part of the overall marketing strategy to gain market share; excellent execution, placement, and timing; complete coordination throughout the marketing areas and within the in-house promotional materials; and a pre- and post-measurement mechanism in place to determine the very positive results expected. Technically, there were many plus marks; after all, Holiday Inns was the biggest advertiser in the industry. The bad list is brief, with only a few, but very important, items. *First,* the key premise of advertising was violated in that the level of expectation expressed in the ads was at the 100 percent level and the actual fulfillment at the property level was less. The result was not only customer dissatisfaction, but an increase in the volume of complaint mail. *Second,* the platform, which is the item-by-item list that supports the proposition, was not 100 percent fulfilled at the operational level. There were still surprises, especially in a chain with 1,700 properties where quality control and consistency are major challenges. *Third,* the campaign inferred that the rest of the industry, other chains and independents, would give the consumer all kinds of bad surprises. In essence, the advertising "knocked" or degradated the competition. It is unwise to offend everyone else in your industry! Needless to say, this ad campaign was widely recognized and talked about. Was it a B-52? Yes, in terms of volume, placement, and air time. No, in terms of the results — a negative consumer and industry reaction.

### CASE EXAMPLE B: *THE EGO TRIP*

It is not surprising that advertising agencies often have success with their clients when they employ none other than the Chief Executive Officer of their client-company as the main star in the firm's ad campaign. Naturally, the CEO believes in his or her product or service and really doesn't mind gaining personal exposure. Let's examine a few of the CEO ads and dissect the good and the bad from each.

Perhaps the most famous example of an ego trip or testimonial ad came from Chrysler with Lee Iaccoco as its chief spokesperson and CEO. This was more than a chairman's ego trip — it was a credible, very good ad campaign. The man, the product, and the ad all gelled into a believable story, aimed straight at the emotional desires of the consumer for the underdog to win and then boldly displayed the red, white, and blue. In all likelihood it will go down in history books as one of the all-time winners.

In the hospitality industry, the CEO testimonial ranges from the straightforward to the strictly absurd. I don't know where Chrysler's agency dreamed up that campaign, but somewhat earlier Marriott launched a self-testimonial campaign with like credibility. The theme was centered around Bill Marriott, Jr. and his personal involvement in ensuring that things were right in the hotels. As he said, "That's my name on the door." The campaign's theme was really product consistency and the tie-in was the boss making sure it was right. As self-testimonial ads go, this campaign was pretty good.

One risk inherent in self-starring testimonial campaigns is that not everyone loves the star. Think about human nature and the average person's response to Mr. or Mrs. Millionaire. In some cases it can still be fairly positive. Those who know Bill Marriott know he works hard, inspects, and is "in place" doing the ad. Even given all this and even given the success of an ad campaign, other self-testimonials have backfired. For example, Leona Helmsley's many appearances as the "queen" have done much to publicize the Helmsley Hotel chain. There are many whose reaction to self-proclamation to the level of queen is to be turned off to the product. Hence, a well-meaning ad campaign, achieving its product positioning and image objectives, loses customers because some customers experience negative reactions. There are even worse cases. Take the over-the-hill chairman talking about his over-the-hill product. Things can always get worse. The fundamental problem with such ads is human nature and credibility. Is the proposition there? If so, is it believable? Where is the platform? And, where are the real people — the consumers? What measurable results are derived from such ads.

There is a big difference between testimonials to a product or service and the CEO ego trip advertisement. Yes, it is important for the consumer to know someone cares about his or her firm's product or service, but does this expression or advertising relate to the benefits the consumer seeks from the product or service being offered?

### CASE EXAMPLE C: *LEVEL OF EXPECTATION AND WHAT WAS THAT NUMBER?*

Occasionally an advertising campaign can be so well done that the fulfillment by the product or service cannot live up to the level of expectation created by the campaign. For a number of years, Sheraton has run a very skillful campaign or series of campaigns featuring an attractive female vocalist singing the praises of Sheraton. The ad content has always featured quality photography of superior rooms, food, beverage, and an overall feeling of class. The advertising leaves the viewer with the distinct impression that Sheraton Hotels and Inns categorically offer a "class"-quality experience. The ads also build an unrealistically high level of expectation which is difficult for any hotel or inn to fulfill.

Sheraton's advertising over the past few years has included perhaps the single greatest number of exposures for any toll-free 800 number. The number has been in print advertising, on matchbooks, in TV commercials, and even vocalized for listening enjoyment. (Do you remember the number?) Think about it. There are approximately 5 million heavy travelers in the United States. For the same cost how many times could a gold embossed card with the 800 number have been mailed to each person. (Finally, do you remember the number?)

### CASE EXAMPLE D: *HUMANIZING THE ALL-BEEF PATTIE*

On the food side of the hospitality industry one firm has won practically all the advertising awards created. McDonald's advertising campaigns have humanized the all-beef pattie and fast-food experience. Be it the birthday party or the promise to a little child, McDonald's has gone right to the heart of the consumer. More important, the product, service, and level of expectation are all positively known commodities. Further, the creative character of the advertising, the tie-in to promotions, the responsiveness to overall marketing strategies, and every technical element are almost works of precision. In addition, McDonald's has successfully improved their customers' eating experience by upgrading facilities, logically expanding the menu offerings, and never sacrificing quality or confusing their image. The proposition is there, as is the platform to support it. Most important of all is the fulfillment in terms of value. The value is an inexpensive quality product easy to obtain and enjoy, and McDonald's is a master of market segmentation relationships — ranging from small children to their grandparents.

### CASE EXAMPLE E: *BUILDING AN IMAGE OUT OF BRICK, GLASS, AND MORTAR*

For years, Hyatt Hotels spent very little money on advertising, yet their image as a class hotel operation continued to build in the consumer's mind. Hyatt's advertising centered around its unique designs for its spectacular properties (see Figure 8.15). In this case, the physical product itself was so out of the ordinary that it advertised itself. Hyatt's advertising fully capitalized on these spectacular physical properties and succeeded in its effort to place Hyatt in a class by itself. While this may not be

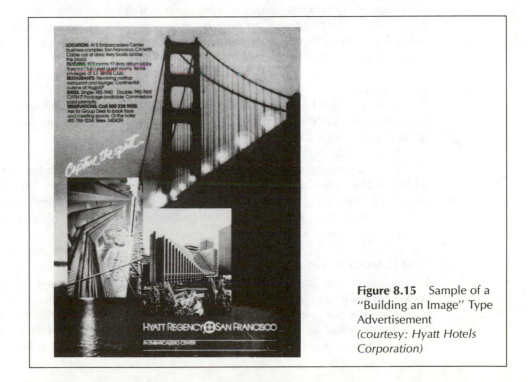

**Figure 8.15** Sample of a "Building an Image" Type Advertisement *(courtesy: Hyatt Hotels Corporation)*

always true from an operational or financial perspective, to the consumer of a first-class lodging experience, Hyatt does stand out. Design of a product or service can be an advertisement in itself if it is so unique as to trigger a psychological response mechanism in the consumer's mind. Pizza Huts, Golden Arches, Taco Bells, and even L'eggs Panty Hose receive the benefits of advertising from their physical packaging. How many consumers recognize McDonald's or a Holiday Inn by its neon sign alone?

### CASE EXAMPLE F: "FRIENDLY," "NICE," "PEOPLE PLEASIN' PEOPLE"

Recognition that consumers of the hospitality industry's services are people away from home can be exemplified by three distinct advertising campaigns. Each of these campaigns has recognized a person's needs of warmth and help when away from the security and comfort of his or her own home and environment. These campaigns were big 15 to 20 years ago — and still play today. United Airlines' "Friendly Skies" advertising campaign was one of the earliest in the industry to recognize the human and psychological needs of consumers away from home. United Airlines ads were a direct response to the consumers' fear of cold or impartial treatment or the strange feeling associated with a new travel experience. Eastern's "Wings of Man" campaign and American Airline's "Doing What We Do Best" ads picked up on the same response mechanism.

Second, Ramada's "Nice People Doing Nice Things for People" advertising campaign really brought home the message that there is a "hospitality" service industry. The advertising was sincere and, again, directly related to the consumers' needs for a warm, friendly environment of helping people away from home. Unlike advertising that preached about "standards," "policies," and other items of little interest to the consumer, this "nice people" advertising reached the consumers' needs directly.

Third, Holiday Inns' "People Pleasin' People" advertising campaign also related to the real needs and concerns of the traveling consumer. The theme was simple — make the travel and lodging experience human and warm. The consumers' response had to be acceptance.

There are many other examples that demonstrate everything from effectively advertising to reach a market segment to building a new image. The key to the successful advertising examples lies in the fact that the six steps and six keys have all been followed or, as one of Marriott's advertising campaigns phrased it, "When we do things — we do them right."

### CASE EXAMPLE G: THE CAT THAT MADE THE BRAND ROAR

Earlier in this chapter we displayed a character ad showing Garfield the Cat as the spokesperson for Embassy Suites (Figure 8.4). This ad campaign presents a dilemma similar to that discussed in the Helmsley campaign. Like the "queen," Garfield the Cat gets the brand awareness aspect of the job done very well. In fact, I can't recall an ad campaign that created such high brand awareness so quickly. From this perspective, the campaign was a stroke of genius. Using an endearing character, easy to love, to look at, to believe, and, most important of all, easy to remember. Yes, he was the "fat cat" leading the "suite" — Embassy Suite — life.

So what's the dilemma? Well, does Garfield the Cat convey the brand or product identity from a positioning perspective? Yes and No. Yes, he is synonymous with an all-suite hotel concept? No, he is not the image of $100-plus per night that Embassy Suites could have capitalized upon. As a brand name, Embassy Suites conveys the top-of-the-line. However, identified with the "cat" and "fat cat" campaign, it appeals to the middle-tier wanting to step up — but pay less. If you have the great name, a superior product concept (all suites), then why not design a campaign that merits or conveys a higher rate and image awareness. Insiders will answer, "Go for market share — get identity." They well may be right. In any event, this campaign will go in the books as one of the classics.

*CASE EXAMPLE H: BREAKING THROUGH THE CLUTTER BY BUILDING A NICHE*
For years the "Camel Scoreboard" (providing baseball scores in local newspapers under the "Camel" banner) gave Camel cigarettes strong brand awareness and at the same time imparted to the consumer a good feeling by providing a service. Camel broke the clutter by carving a niche with a service. The cigarette market was flooded with brands and more brands, some with substantially more ad dollars than Camel. By carving its niche and appearing regularly, Camel retained a high level of brand awareness in a fragmented and overcrowded market. Camel survived.

Today, sporting event sponsorships are common and expensive. Think about the $600,000-plus 30-second hotel ad appearing on the Super Bowl just when everyone (but the hotel company executives and members of their agency) got up to take a break. However, one hotel was able to carve a niche in this overcrowded marketplace in a unique way: Stouffer Hotels became the sponsor of the "Business Travelers' Weather." Because the name Stouffer was associated with one of the daily concerns of the traveler, the hotel achieved dramatic increases in brand awareness (despite a tough name with which to work). The "Business Travelers' Weather" appeared in two major papers, the *Wall Street Journal* (see Figure 8.5) and *USA Today*. Stouffer sponsored the "Business Travelers' Forecast" on CNN, The Weather Channel, and on news TV programs. Stouffer's weather forecasts accomplished exactly what "Camel's Scoreboard" and Garfield the Cat had done so well — they achieved brand awareness by breaking the clutter, carving a niche, and being unique.

## THE ADVERTISING AUDIT

Just as a checklist style audit of your sales methods is helpful, a similar audit of your advertising can determine if it is organized and working. The following checklist of questions can be adapted to your own product or service advertising efforts and may prove to be a useful tool for your organization.

### Advertising Audit and Checklist

____ Do your advertising plans support the objectives and strategies of the current marketing plan?

____ Does your chief marketing officer understand the responsibilities of persons and parties involved in executing the advertising strategy for your product or service?

____ Is the sales manager or director involved in the planning and execution of the advertising strategy and program? To what extent?

____ Do your key marketing and advertising people have good rapport with the media? Are they capable of executing trade-outs or barter agreements?

____ Do you have a "master book" containing up-to-date examples of your advertising?

____ Do you have a monitoring and results measurement system in place to determine the outcome or effectiveness of your advertising expenditures?

____ Is there a "Clippings" file, and is someone specifically assigned to analyze what the competition is doing?

____ Does the director of marketing have the request forms, exceptions reports, insertion orders, sample copy, and sample ads readily accessible?

____ Is there a master file for all media and trade-out contracts?

____ Are there advance advertising schedules prepared?

____ Are advertising work request forms being used? Are they sent in with sufficient lead time? Are copies on file?

____ How is the advertising production budget being managed? Have all ads and expenditures received proper approvals?

____ Are insertion orders submitted to the media on time? Are copies of completed orders properly distributed?

____ Do all key marketing personnel understand the conditions of all media contracts — print, broadcast, outdoor, airport display, and trade-outs?

____ What is the condition of outdoor boards? When were they last checked? When are they scheduled for reprint?

____ Is a verification process in place? Are all invoices supported by tearsheets of affidavits? Are copies of invoices and tearsheets on file? Are they checked for accuracy against insertion orders?

____ Are rates and discounts verified? Are rate changes supported by new rate cards?

_____ Have there been any major changes in the approved advertising schedules? Has everyone been posted on these changes?

_____ Have all deficiencies from the previous audit been corrected?

While not every audit checklist question may apply to your advertising area, the concept of an audit checklist can do more than save you money. If religiously followed, such an audit checklist provides a cross-check to ensure that advertising, sales, public relations, and so on, are all working together to execute the marketing plan and strategies.

This chapter has concentrated on helping you relate your product or service and advertising to the total marketing plan for your product or service. We began at step 1, understanding your own product or service and the consumer's perspective. We discussed the necessity of knowing your audience and of tying your advertising into your total marketing plan before you create your ad. We have touched upon identifying the strong statement you make on behalf of your product or service — the proposition — and supporting that statement with an item-by-item list, called the platform, upon which your advertising is premised.

Further, we defined the level of expectation concept to ensure that your advertising resulted in satisfied purchasers of your product or service. We have reviewed when, how, and where to advertise and the various media selections available. We've touched upon the concepts of trade-outs and cooperative programs, and we've also presented and commented upon a number of case examples. You may have agreed or disagreed with the critiques; however, your own self-analysis and cross-check against the six steps and six keys should provide you with some insights as well as stimulate your ideas regarding advertising of your own product or service.

## *KEY WORDS AND CONCEPTS*

**Proposition**  The strongest factual statement you can make on behalf of your product or service.

**Platform**  The item-by-item list of things that directly support your platform.

**Level of Expectation**  The extent or quality of your service or product that your customers expect. The basic premise of advertising is that you never promise more than your product or service can actually fulfill.

**Media**  The vehicles by which you can advertise. Broadcast media includes television and radio. Print media includes magazines, newspapers, direct mail, brochures, yellow pages, outdoor advertising boards, etc.

**Placement**  Where your advertising actually appears, be it a time slot on radio or the January issue, page 6, upper right-hand quarter-page.

**Exposures** The number of consumers actually hearing or seeing your advertising. One ad may reach 100 million people if it is on national TV at prime time or provide you 100 million exposures.

**Trade-outs/Barter** Exchange of your product or service for advertising coverage in either the broadcast or print media.

**Co-oping** Joining with others to advertise where dollar constraints would normally prohibit you from advertising alone, or joining together to promote a common bene-factor to all, such as the region or market.

## ASSIGNMENTS

1. Select a current advertisement, and analyze it against the grid of the six steps and six keys to determine how many of each has been adhered to by the ad.

2. Create an ad and list the six steps and six keys you followed by describing each and the rationale you employed.

3. Work with a local hospitality firm to develop a trade-out or barter agreement.

4. Develop a cooperative ad campaign for a group of hospitality industry firms in your market area.

5. Develop your own advertising audit checklist or guide, and apply it to a local firm's advertising efforts.

# Applying Key Marketing Methodologies: Public Relations

9

**PURPOSE**

The purpose of this chapter is to help you understand how public relations can help improve sales and employee morale. We will focus on internal or "within-the-house" public relations applications and the full gamit of external public relations techniques and methods. We will discuss programs that have proven their worth in the hospitality industry. Finally, we will examine productive public relations in a discussion of how to tie your public relations effort to your needs and how to measure the results.

**OBJECTIVES**

1. Relate public relations to your overall operations, problems, and marketing plan.

2. Focus on how to implement effective internal public relations programs to motivate employees and increase revenues and productivity.

3. Apply public relations as a powerful marketing tool to help solve your sales and image problems.

4. Show how to measure your public relations effort and improve your program systematically.

Public relations is a marketing weapon. It is the communications vehicle between the hospitality industry's products or services and the current customers, potential customers, and the variety of audiences in the marketplace. Early in this book we discussed how marketing's perspective must include the *total audience,* which could include the investment community, shareholders, franchisees, and, of course, all the intermediaries and individual consumers. As a marketing weapon, public relations can effectively reach and affect everyone in this broad external audience. Furthermore, public relations can prove to be a very effective internal marketing device with which to communicate and motivate employees.

You may frequently hear the expression that "so and so really got publicity from that event." *Publicity* is only one facet of public relations. Publicity can be free, but it can also be of a negative or positive variety. Think of all the publicity surrounding hotel or casino fires. The publicity is enormous — it is free, and, unfortunately, negative. We'll discuss publicity later in this chapter.

## COMMON FALLACIES ABOUT PUBLIC RELATIONS

There are many fallacies about public relations: "PR is B.S." "Public relations is undefinable; it doesn't do anything and can't be measured." "It's a waste of time and money." "Anyone can do PR work." These comments are made as a result either of not understanding public relations or of having been exposed to a disorganized public relations effort. Yes, public relations does not directly make a sale; however, it can be very influential in seeing that a purchase is made. Let's look at some ground rules for various aspects of public relations, as well as explore what public relations is, how it can be applied, and how it can be measured.

## WHAT PUBLIC RELATIONS IS

As a powerful marketing weapon that is capable of reaching all marketing audiences, public relations can go on the offensive or be defensive. In positive applications, public relations is on the offensive; in negative situations, public relations can provide a strong defensive strategy.

Public relations involves dealing with all publics, including individual potential consumers, the financial community, the local community, the media (all broadcast and print sources, and the trade publications), and even your own employees. Effective public relations can mean a good, competitive advantage within your own business area — be it hotels, airlines, restaurants, or travel services. The competitive advantage is frequently overlooked, even by public relations personnel. In essence, a well-executed public relations program can provide a good image within your industry segment. That image is reflected in consumer preference for your product or service, and it may also result in attracting and retaining good employees.

Public relations creates a favorable attitude for your company, product, or service. It creates this favorable environment most effectively if it is part of the overall marketing plan. Objectives, strategies, target markets, expected results, timetables, and measurement can and should be established for all public relations programs. Of equal importance in a formal plan for public relations is selection of the trained professionals to create and execute the plan. It is an absolute fallacy to believe "anyone can do public relations."

The resources that can be utilized in public relations are unlimited. Here is a brief listing of vehicles public relations uses to reach its targets or audiences:

| | |
|---|---|
| Announcements | Civic, social, and community involvement |
| Broadcast media (TV and radio) | |
| Print media (newspapers, magazines, etc.) | Employee relations |
| | Speeches |
| News conferences | Interviews |
| News releases | Photographs |

In addition to these outlets for public relations, there is an infinite number of techniques that can be employed to obtain exposure. Numerous articles and texts provide list after list, but many authors forget one basic thing — the planned purpose or strategy for achieving such exposure. Even if one's relationship with the media is superb, the use and placement of publicity must support an overall marketing objective. The caution is simply stated, "Make your PR count." Some ideas are contained in the following list of suggestions. Each of these should be viewed within the context of a marketing strategy.

### Suggestions for Public Relations Opportunities

Accomplishments of employees or firm

Activities involving your company employees

Anniversary dates

Appointments of key people

Awards received by firms or employees

Celebrities who visit you (obtain individuals' approval)

Community awards

Contributions to charities and local community by firm or employees

Displays of all types

Entertainment appearing in your facility

Events occurring on your property

Events of special interest — humorous or creative

Grand openings of all types

Groups of interest meeting or eating with you

Guests of interest (upon approval)

Industry-related events

Interviews with visitors, guests, etc.

New management, ownership, employees, etc.

Openings of all kinds

Operating changes of major significance to the public

Organizational changes

Public service events/activities

Receipt of certificates, awards, etc.

Recognition of people, places, things, etc.

Special displays, features introduced, etc.

Special events of all types

Speeches of employees, groups meeting at your facility, etc.

## HOW PUBLIC RELATIONS CAN BE APPLIED

Once the objectives for your public relations plan have been established and tied into the overall marketing plan, it is time to consider how to apply or execute those ideas. You must first answer some questions:

1. What medium can best execute this strategy?

2. Who are the key contacts for this task?

3. Is it necessary to establish or resolidify any personal relationships before executing the strategy?

4. Is our approach carefully thought out? What are the potential downside risks?

5. Do we have a delivery package ready for the media?

The *delivery package* is essential and should contain any required copy, plots, key contacts, phone numbers, and so on. Although there is no guarantee your copy or materials will be used, it is much more likely that your public relations message will correspond to your intentions if you make a delivery package available. The following list will aid you in compiling a package that will be useful to the media.

### Delivery Package Requirements

Addresses and phone numbers of key media contacts

Addresses and phone numbers of key corporation personnel

Approval procedures and required forms

Biographies of key personnel

Briefing sheets on individuals, company, product, etc.

Brochures, if applicable

Cancellation procedures and policy

"Canned" formats, releases, letterheads, logos, symbols, etc.

Confidentiality statements/procedures

Contacts list and phone numbers/procedures

Copy samples and actual copy

Displays, podiums with logos, etc.

News conference procedures list

One person to call and his or her phone number (usually public relations contact)

Photo inventory of product, people, etc.

Photo library and selection ready for press

Previous problems files and checklist

Previous questions files and checklist

Price/rate information

Procedures for distribution

Promotion package on firm or product

Request forms — data, photo, product information, etc.

Scrapbook or clipping files

Speech copies for distribution

Other forms for utilizing public relations involve personal appearances and statements. Speeches, press conferences, meetings, and interviews all involve a direct relationship and reliance on the human element. If you are going to employ one of these direct contact methods, you need to prepare the individual(s) who will be making the direct contact with the media. *Thorough preparation is essential for successful direct contact public relations.* Ground rules and suggestions abound as to how to prepare a speech (the content, delivery, and do's and don't's). Assuming one is smart enough to follow the rules, there is still one critical mistake that can be made — using the wrong person. Simply stated, be sure you use the right speaker. If the talk is technical, be certain that the speaker has total command of the technical terms. If the talk is on corporate strategy, be sure the individual has the authority to make it believable. If the talk is on your own product or service, make sure the speaker can relate it to the audience's perspective. The following is a brief list of do's and don't's.

## DO'S AND DON'T'S OF PUBLIC SPEAKING

### Do's

Carefully organize and allow yourself enough time to prepare.

Be prepared — write out the talk, memorize it, and keep notes.

Rewrite, review, and rewrite again.

Create an outline or plan for your speech and follow it.

Change postures, positions, intonations, emphasis, etc.

Use pauses for emphasis, to make thoughts last.

Check and double-check the visuals, equipment, room, visibility, etc.

Speak out and deliver smoothly.

### Don't's

Speak on subjects about which you are not qualified.

Speak ad lib.

Guestimate numbers.

Read in a monotone.

Use excessive pauses either in number or length of time.

Prepare unreadable visuals.

Mumble, slur, laugh to yourself, etc.

Wait to read what you are going to say until the plane ride or cab ride.

## THE PRESS

Dealing with the press is one of the most difficult tasks marketing and public relations personnel have to undertake. It is difficult for many reasons, but most of all because the press is *powerful*. It reaches many consumers with a message in writing, so you must be absolutely certain that the press has your facts correct.

Again, many good articles have been written on public relations and the press, many golden rules layed down, and many do's and don't's have been listed. The recognition factors that follow represent a composite of a number of such lists. These are not all-inclusive, nor are they intended to be golden rules. They are factors that may keep your public relations efforts on a positive note — on the offensive rather than in a defensive position.

## PUBLIC RELATIONS AND THE PRESS

### Recognition Factors

1. *Identify your purpose.* What is your purpose or reason for seeking the public relations exposure? If your purpose is to make others aware of your new restaurant theme, be sure that is exactly what you convey — don't let it be lost in a story about your chef's auto collection. Be precise and be sure your intent is communicated.

2. *Identify your target.* Who is your target? Is it prospective consumers of your product? Is it the local financial community? Is it recognition of one of your employees, thus employees' morale? Is it food sales, beverage sales, room sales, brand awareness? Think it out and identify how and where in the media you will best achieve your objectives.

3. *Understand the other perspective.* You know your purpose and you now know your target. That is your perspective. What is the press's interest? Identify and understand their interests. *Determine how you can place your purpose and target within a package that directly meets the interest of the press or other media.* To be successful here, think about what will help their circulation, listening audience, etc.

4. *Tailor your preparation.* Having identified your purpose, your target, and the media's perspective, tailor your preparation to include all three. Be sure to *include everything* that the press will need to convey the story — photos, names, releases. Be sure it's typed, double-spaced, and in the style the medium is currently utilizing. *Follow the editorial style of your selected medium at all times.*

5. *Know the transmission channels.* Knowing where to send your material means knowing the difference between a news and a feature story. News should be directed to the city desk; feature stories should go to the appropriate editor, such as the entertainment editor or the restaurant editor. Better yet, get to know the editors who can be of most help to you and cultivate the relationship, but don't wear it out.

6. *The human elements.* People do not like extra work or being pressured, and most cannot afford the time to tell you the ground rules. People are basically lazy. This sounds cruel, but it should help you understand how to deal with the human element. Find out the deadlines in advance. Do not waste your time or the valuable time of media contacts. Do as much of their work as you can. Remember, if it is well prepared and you do most of the work for them, your material may be used. If you do not do the work, you can expect nothing to appear. Also remember to be available for immediate response to any questions or clarifications the media may have on your story. If you are unavailable, your material may be scrapped or come out wrong.

These six recognition factors will only bring you to the door. Now you will need some guidelines for answering questions, which will eventually allow you to turn the lock of the door and enter. The keys that follow are not all-inclusive, nor are they original, but they are very practical.

### KEY 1: TELL THE TRUTH

The message you want to convey should be pure fact. The media want credible, straightforward, and truthful material and relationships. This simply means your materials should be thorough and honest. It does not mean you need to reveal every detail, confidential data, or private source, nor does it mean you should violate confidentialities.

### KEY 2: BE RESPONSIVE

You may not provide nor have all the answers at your fingertips for every question or inquiry. Do not lie; say, "It's not available," or "I can't comment on that," or "I do not have that information with me; however, I will call you and provide it today." Then get the information fast and provide it accurately.

### KEY 3: PROVIDE THE FACTS AND FOLLOW UP

Supply the key facts and provide them in print or a handout to lessen the chance of being misquoted on key data. If at all possible, follow up and seek to go over the facts or key numbers for accuracy. If you do not have a requested statistic, get it and follow up with a phone call and/or note to be sure the accurate numbers reach the media.

### KEY 4: BE CONCISE

People usually get into trouble with the media for what they say, not what they do not say. Provide the facts in a concise, uneditorialized, and unexaggerated manner. By all means, be precise and accurate. Ranges may be okay, but pulling the numbers out of the blue sky is a disaster.

### KEY 5: BUILD THE RELATIONSHIP

If you follow steps 1 through 4 by being truthful, responsive, factual, and concise, you are on your way to achieving the fifth practical key — building a good relationship. Hostile attitudes, reactionary statements to sensitive questions, aloofness, or a combative position destroys relations and may result in very negative reactions. Work hard at being in control of yourself and your responses, no matter what you think of the media, interviewer, or individuals with whom you deal in these relationships. After all, an enemy or someone who dislikes you is not going to give you space or air time.

## INTERNAL PUBLIC RELATIONS

The jobs of many people in the hospitality industry are challenging and often not very rewarding. The hours are frequently long, and keeping employees motivated and building pride in the job is a difficult task. One of the most effective devices for combating these problems is a well-organized internal public relations effort. This does *not* mean promoting the goods or benefits of the company to the employees. It can take many shapes and forms: (1) An especially effective technique is to promote or provide special recognition of employees, their efforts, or even their interests. "Employee of the Month" awards, posters, photos, and so forth, all work well. (2) Special incentive awards and related public relations also are a valuable tool. Cash, prizes, or even novelty awards or plaques to deserving employees will help morale and spirits. (3) Grouping activities and events jointly with management — a bowling club or a joggers' group — will help build a team spirit. (4) Common goals, such as total support of a selected charity, is another type of internal PR device for building unity. (5) Perhaps most important of all is the continual recognition of human dignity, pride, and respect. Make internal public relations your key incentive for productive and happy employees.

## HOW CAN PUBLIC RELATIONS BE MEASURED?

You frequently hear this comment: "You can't measure public relations; therefore, it is useless." This is absolutely false! If a public relations program is well organized, it can be measured in many ways. One way is to measure the number and type of exposures received: keep a current log or scrapbook of clippings and categorize each type of exposure. Set goals for the number and type of exposures, then measure actual performance versus targets. A second method is geared to evaluating the effectiveness of internal PR efforts. Look at questionnaires that assess employee morale, as well as employee turnover rates, breakage, pilferage, etc. If your internal PR is working, certain quantifiable trends should emerge. Do not, however, ignore a more subjective yardstick of your efforts: have you improved the "esprit de corps" in your organization? Are employees busy and enthusiastic? Specific public relations activities may be measured by increases in sales. For example, if a major event is promoted through PR, and bar or food volume directly increases as a result of additional customers coming in to view the event or display, you know public relations is working for you.

### Sample Public Relations Audit Checklist

_____ Does a PR plan exist and does it support the current priority areas of marketing?

_____ Do the director of marketing and all personnel understand their responsibilities with respect to the press, PR firm, and other outsiders?

_____ Do key management personnel have good relations with the local media?

——— Are press release mail lists up to date, accurate, and readily available?

——— Are *fact sheets* readily accessible to all and near the phones?

——— Are *photo files* up to date and fully stocked? Is there an up-to-date black-and-white photo file?

——— Are brochures and other collateral material accessible?

——— Are there definite plans, budgets, reviews, and measurement procedures in place for PR?

——— Is there a property or product press kit? Is it up to date?

——— What is the quality of photos and stories, and how are they to be used?

——— Are all key employees briefed and knowledgeable about the value of public relations and related procedures to follow for press inquiries?

——— Are PR network memos kept on file? Where? How often are they looked at or discussed?

——— When was the last PR audit? What were the results, and were all follow-up steps completed?

## EXAMPLES FOR YOU TO THINK ABOUT

Public relations can be an offensive weapon or a very effective defense for your firm. The two examples that follow depict one example of each.

### THE OFFENSIVE WEAPON

A large hotel located near a major airport and within a substantial minority population area of the city conceived this public relations offensive weapon. The goals were multifold and included: (1) improving the morale of its minority employees, (2) increasing food and beverage sales, (3) increasing room sales, (4) improving community relations, and (5) overcoming a location problem. Briefly, the hotel offered its 24-hour coffee shop as a nightly broadcast facility to the largest Spanish-speaking radio station in the city from midnight to 6 a.m. Over 50 percent of the hotel's employees were Spanish-speaking, as well as a larger percentage of the cab drivers in the airport area. Cab drivers were offered free coffee and given a "chip" redeemable for coffee or food each time they brought a "late arrival" guest from the nearby airport to the hotel. This scheme was devised to address the hotel's problem of being too close for the cab drivers to get a good fare, thereby losing "walk-ins" (in this case, "fly-ins") to more distant hotels. In short, the coffee shop became the focal point of community activity as a result of the radio broadcast. Food and beverage sales set records from midnight to 6 a.m., employee morale and attitudes toward the hotel were at all-time highs, local community relations were superior, walk-in/

fly-in room sales increased, and the locational problem was overcome. The hotel succeeded in becoming part of the community and a place of pride for the employees.

## THE DEFENSIVE WEAPON

Another large urban hotel was the site of a tragic event which could have seriously damaged the hotel's reputation had it not been for a well thought-out press release. The hotel, also located in an airport area, was targeted for a police raid on a suspected abortion ring. Undesirable elements had been operating out of a number of hotels in the area and a number of deaths had occurred. The hotel volunteered its security personnel (off-duty city police) to help. The raid was staged, a woman was found dead, and the ring was captured. Instead of the front page reading "Raid Reveals Murder and Bloody Abortion Ring at Hotel," the story appeared on page 3 under the headline "Hotel Security Force Helps Chicago Police Resolve Airport Area Crime Problem." A well thought-out public relations and press approach can take a tragic and damaging event and turn it into a more acceptable defense for you. Think about it!

## PUBLICATIONS

The hospitality industry is fortunate to have excellent trade or industry-related publications. These publications are widely read by not only those within the industry, but frequently by consumers of the product. Some of the major publications are listed here.

### *Major Hospitality Industry and Trade Publications*

Association Management
1011 16th Street, N.W.
Washington, DC   20036

Association & Society Manager
825 South Barrington Avenue
Los Angeles, CA   90039

Association Trends
7204 Clarendon Road
Washington, DC   20014

ASTA Travel News
Travel Communications, Inc.
488 Madison Avenue
New York, NY   10022

Aviation Daily
1156 15th Street, N.W.
Washington, DC   20005

Business Travel News
CMP Publications, Inc.
600 Community Drive
Manhasset, NY   11030

Canadian Hotel and Restaurant
Maclean-Hunter Publishing Company, Ltd.
481 University Avenue
Toronto, Ontario
Canada   M5W 1A7

The Cornell Hotel and Restaurant Administration Quarterly
School of Hotel Administration
327 Statler Hall
Cornell University
Ithaca, NY   14853

FIU Hospitality Review
Florida International University
Tamiami Campus
Miami, FL   33139

Corporate Meetings & Incentives
747 Third Avenue - 7th Floor
New York, NY   10017

Corporate Travel
A Gralla Publication
1515 Broadway
New York, NY   10036

Food Executive
International Food Services Executives Association
508 IBM Building
Fort Wayne, IN   46815

Hotel & Resort Industry
488 Madison Avenue
New York, NY   10022

Hospitality Lodging
Penton/IPC, Inc.
614 Superior Avenue, West
Cleveland, OH   44113

Hospitality Restaurant
Penton/IPC, Inc.
614 Superior Avenue, West
Cleveland, OH   44113

Hotel and Motel Management
Robert Freeman Publishing Company
845 Chicago Avenue
Evanston, IL   60606

Incentive Marketing
633 Third Avenue
New York, NY   10017

Incentive Travel Manager
825 South Barrington Avenue
Los Angeles, CA   90049

Insurance Conference Planner
695 Summer Street
Stamford, CT   06901

Lodging
American Hotel & Motel Association
888 Seventh Avenue
New York, NY   10019

Lodging and Food-Service News
Hotel Service, Inc.
131 Clarendon Street
Boston, MA   02116

Lodging Hospitality — see Hospitality
   Lodging

Meetings and Conventions
Ziff-Davis Publishing Company
1 Park Avenue
New York, NY   10016

Meeting News
1515 Broadway
New York, NY   10026

Meetings & Expositions Magazine
22 Pine Street
Morristown, NJ   07960

Motel/Motor Inn Journal
Tourist Court Journal, Inc.
306 East Adams
Temple, TX   76501

Nation's Restaurant News
Lebhar-Friedman, Inc.
425 Park Avenue
New York, NY   10022

Resort Management
Box 4169
1509 Madison Avenue
Memphis, TN   38104

Restaurant Hospitality — see Hospitality
   Restaurant

Restaurants & Institutions
Cahners Publishing Company
1350 East Touhy Avenue
Des Plaines, IL   60018

Restaurants, USA
National Restaurant Association
One IBM Plaza
Suite 2600
Chicago, IL   60611

Sales and Marketing Management
Sales Management, Inc.
633 Third Avenue
New York, NY   10017

Successful Meetings
633 Third Avenue
New York, NY   10017

Tableservice Restaurant Operations Report
National Restaurant Association
One IBM Plaza
Suite 2600
Chicago, IL   60611

Texas and Southwest Hotel Motel Review
Texas Hotel & Motel Association
8602 Crownhill Boulevard
San Antonio, TX   78209

TravelAge East
TravelAge Mid-America
TravelAge Southeast
TravelAge West
Travel Magazines Division
Official Airlines Guides, Inc.
100 Grant Avenue
San Francisco, CA   94108

Travel Agent
American Traveler, Inc.
2 West 46th Street
New York, NY   10036

Travel Management Daily
An Official Airlines Guide Publication,
   Inc.

888 Seventh Avenue
New York, NY   10106

Travel Master
645 Stewart Avenue
Garden City, NY   11530

Travel Trade
Travel Trade Publishing Company
605 Fifth Avenue
New York, NY   10017

Travel Weekly
Ziff-Davis Publishing Company
1 Park Avenue
New York, NY   10016

Trends in the Hotel-Motel Business
Harris, Kerr, Forster & Company
420 Lexington Avenue
New York, NY   10017

U.S. Lodging Industry
Laventhol & Horwath
1845 Walnut Street
Philadelphia, PA   19103

World Convention Dates
Hendrickson Publishing Company
79 Washington Street
Hempstead, NY   11550

Worldwide Lodging Industry
Horwath & Horwath International
   & Laventhol & Horwath
919 Third Avenue
New York, NY   10022

### News Bureaus

News Bureaus In The U.S.
Richard Weiner
1984
Public Relations Publishing Company
New York, NY   10106
(References major newspapers and maga-
   zines)

Society of American Travel Writers
Membership Directory
1986
Society of American Travel Writers
Washington, DC   20036
(Membership list of all writers)

## KEY WORDS AND CONCEPTS

**Public Relations** A marketing weapon that is the communications vehicle between your firm and current customers, potential customers, and the variety of audiences in the marketplace.

**Publicity** One facet of public relations, it is the mentions or exposures received from announcements, events, and releases.

**Delivery Package** The essential tools, including required forms, copy, photos, fact sheets, and biographies, to ensure that you are ready to effectively execute public relations programs.

**Trade Media** The group of publications and/or broadcast media that follow your specific industry and product or service.

## ASSIGNMENTS

1. Are you organized for a public relations effort? Create a public relations plan for a firm or a product or service.

2. Conceptualize an "event" and develop a public relations plan to promote that event.

3. Develop an internal public relations program for a local hotel, restaurant, or other hospitality industry firm.

4. Select a negative public relations problem and develop a defensive public relations effort to resolve the problem.

5. Conduct a public relations audit of a selected hospitality industry business or firm.

6. Develop a public relations scrapbook for a selected hotel, restaurant, or other services industry firm, including a measurement system.

# Applying Key Marketing Methodologies: Promotions

# 10

## *PURPOSE*

In the last three chapters we have just begun to load your marketing arsenal of weapons to improve revenues and profits. We have discussed sales, advertising, and public relations, both internal and external. This chapter focuses on another very powerful and effective marketing weapon for the hospitality industry — promotions. Special attention is given to helping you determine *what* to promote and how to use this technique. We further examine how to execute specific promotions by applying market segmentation and critical timing factors. Finally, we look at how to measure the end result.

## *OBJECTIVES*

1. Tie promotions into your total marketing plan by providing an understanding of their role within the total plan context.

2. Identify all you have to promote and when and how it should be promoted.

3. Apply market analysis of segmentations, needs, or problems to your promotional efforts.

4. Develop your own methods to measure the real value of your promotional campaigns.

Promotions have been used widely in many industries for a long time. Perhaps the earliest promotion ever used in the hospitality industry goes back to the offer of the first free cup of coffee. As we move through the 1980s, promotions are becoming an increasingly sophisticated marketing weapon. There is an infinite number of promotions with their diversity limited only by the limits of people's imaginations. Promotions may be classified in many ways. However their one common denominator is that they must be designed to fulfill a marketing need. This need may be to: build trial (new) business, get a greater share of existing business, keep business, or get repeat business. Regardless of the type of promotion, the objective is to help the overall marketing effort.

Just as there are many reasons for promotions, there are many ways in which to execute a good promotion. The keys to a well-defined promotion are discussed next.

## KEYS TO SUCCESSFUL PROMOTIONS

**KEY 1:** PURPOSE

Why is the promotion needed? Answering this key question will give you the lead-in to executing a good promotion. Is it to create new business? Is it to stimulate demand in a down period? Is it to take business from a competitor? Key number 1 is to clearly state *why* the promotion is needed.

**KEY 2:** TARGET IDENTIFICATION

Who is the promotion going after? Be specific in identifying your target. Is the promotion going after potential first-time users of your product or service? Is it going after previous users? Are they young, old, male, female, upscale income, etc.?

**KEY 3:** TYPE MATCH-UP

What is the best type of promotion for the purpose and target identified? Granted, there are many types of promotions; not everyone will be compatible with your creative idea or, more important, marketing objective. Some key questions to ask here are: What is it I want to promote and to whom? What is the demographic and psychographic profile of my target?

**KEY 4:** EXECUTION DETERMINATION

Assuming you know what your purpose is, who and where your target is, and the type of promotion you require, it is time to take the critical series of execution steps. You must carefully consider these questions: What is the best method to reach the target? When is the best time to promote the target? Where is the best place to promote?

### KEY 5: FULFILLMENT

This key is a preventive one that should keep you from hurting, rather than helping, yourself. Anticipate your expected results and be sure you can fulfill them. Ask yourself this critical question: If this promotion works as planned, will I have enough available products or services to meet the demand? If you are promoting a food item, drink, weekend, seat, or space, be sure it is there when your turned-on customer arrives to accept your promotional promise. Otherwise, you may well lose that customer or sale for good.

### KEY 6: FALLBACK

No one is ever 100 percent correct in terms of predicting behavioral response to every promotion. In order to avoid the problem of customer dissatisfaction by not being able to fulfill because of an unexpected overly successful promotion, plan a *fallback*. It can be a menu item substitution, an upgraded room, a first-class seat, whatever, *but provide it*. An important key to your fallback is to ensure it is of like or better value. Even if you use the "raincheck" fallback, consider giving that raincheck some extra value to offset the inconvenience caused the customer.

### KEY 7: REAL EXPECTATION

Another important factor is to remember to promote only what you legitimately intend to deliver. Don't even chance your creative copy stretching the truth: never lie, exaggerate, or make any false promises. Always remember the *level of expectation* your promotion creates *must* be fulfilled in order to have a satisfied customer.

### KEY 8: COMMUNICATIONS

Don't forget to tell everyone exactly what you promoted and how it is to be fulfilled. Be sure you clearly communicate, in writing, such key items as price, quantity, acceptance procedures for the promotion, dates, times, and every other detail. Nothing is more irritating to a consumer than responding in good faith to the product of your creative genius only to find that no one knows about the promotion when he or she arrives to take advantage of it.

### KEY 9: MEASUREMENT

Why did you go through the entire effort? Establish a goal(s) and measure the results of your effort. Did the promotion do what you wanted it to do? More or less? If more, will it work again? If less, what was wrong?

### KEY 10: RECORD IT

Write down what you did and how it worked. Don't find yourself reinventing the wheel. How often have you heard, "What was that promotion we ran so successfully a few years ago?"

## TYPES OF PROMOTIONS

The variety of promotions is numerous; however, there are a number of types or classifications into which many can be categorized. These are:

1. *Price.* A promotion in which the incentive to purchase is based on price. The price is the main attraction and featured prominently in the message (see Figure 10.1).

2. *Trial.* A promotion with the objective of getting your target to try your product or service. Price is one frequently used method to motivate customers to try something.

3. *Share.* A promotion in which the primary purpose is to take market share away from competition through some form of incentive. Price, an upgraded product, or another advantage is clearly established over your competition and is the focus of your promotion.

4. *Introduction.* A promotion designed to introduce a new product or service to the market. Like a trial promotion, the premise is to get people to try your product or service. The purpose may be to familiarize the market with your new product or service and to then build repeat purchases (see Figure 10.2).

**Figure 10.1** Sample of a Price Promotion
*(courtesy: US Air)*

**Figure 10.2** Sample of an "Introduction" Promotion *(courtesy: Stouffer Hotel Co.)*

5. *Build.* A promotion designed to build repeat business through an increase in the reward or payoff for multiple purchases. Today's frequent flyer and frequent guest promotions are forms of build promotions (see Figure 10.3).

6. *Give-away/Sweepstakes.* A promotion designed to bring people to your product or service using the "chance" of a win or an actual "give-away" item (see Figure 10.4).

7. *Ego/Recognition.* A promotion designed to appeal to the individual's desire to be recognized. Such promotions may offer such things as first-class upgrades, club-floor upgrades, and complimentary suites.

8. *Tie-ins.* A promotion of your product or service that ties into another product or service. Usually the tie-ins are undertaken where there is a clear benefit to both parties.

9. *Co-ops.* A promotion similar to a tie-in where two firms cooperatively promote a product or service for a mutual benefit. It may be for maximizing exposures in view of limited budgets, or it may be because the products or services are of more value promoted together. An example would be a fly and drive promotion involving an airline and rent-a-car company (see Figure 10.5).

# Northwest WORLDPERKS Awards

| | AUTOMATICALLY ISSUED AWARDS | | | OPTIONAL PICK-A-PERK™ INTERNATIONAL TRAVEL AWARDS | | | |
|---|---|---|---|---|---|---|---|
| MILEAGE LEVEL | NORTHWEST DOMESTIC TRAVEL AWARD | CAR RENTAL AWARD | HOTEL AWARD | NUMBER OF DOMESTIC TRAVEL DOCUMENTS** | NORTHWEST TO HAWAII/ MEXICO/CARIBBEAN (Between the Domestic U.S. (including Canada and Alaska) and Hawaii, Mexico, or the Caribbean) | NORTHWEST TO EUROPE (Between the Domestic U.S. (including Canada and Alaska) and Europe) | NORTHWEST TO THE PACIFIC (Between the Domestic U.S. (including Canada and Alaska) and the Pacific) |
| 20,000 MILES | 1ST FREE Roundtrip Coach Class Certificate | 2 Car Class Upgrade | Purchase 1 Weekend Night Get the 2nd Weekend Night FREE (any rate) | 1 | 1 FREE Roundtrip Companion Ticket | OR 1 One Class Roundtrip Upgrade on any Full Fare | — |
| 40,000 MILES | 2ND FREE Roundtrip Coach Class Certificate | 2 FREE Weekend Days (premium car) | 1 FREE Weekend Night | 2 | 1 FREE Roundtrip Economy Class Ticket | OR 1 FREE Roundtrip Economy Class Ticket | OR 50% Off Companion Ticket – Executive or First Class |
| 60,000 MILES | 3RD FREE Roundtrip Coach Class Certificate plus First Class Upgrade* | 3 FREE Weekend Days (premium car) | 2 FREE Weekend Nights | 3 | 2 FREE Roundtrip Economy Class Tickets | OR 2 FREE Roundtrip Economy Class Tickets or 1 FREE Roundtrip Executive Class Ticket | OR 1 FREE Roundtrip Economy Class Ticket |
| 80,000 MILES | 4TH FREE Roundtrip Coach Class Certificate plus First Class Upgrade* | 1 FREE Week (mid-size car) | 3 FREE Weekend Nights | 4 | 2 FREE Roundtrip First Class Tickets | OR 2 FREE Roundtrip Executive Class Tickets or 1 FREE Roundtrip First Class Ticket | OR 2 FREE Roundtrip Economy Class Tickets or 1 FREE Roundtrip Executive Class Ticket |
| 100,000 MILES | 5TH FREE Roundtrip Coach Class Certificate plus First Class Upgrade* | 1 FREE Week (premium car) | 4 FREE Nights | 5 | — | 2 FREE Roundtrip First Class Tickets | OR 2 FREE Roundtrip Executive Class Tickets or 1 FREE Roundtrip First Class Ticket |
| 120,000 MILES | 6TH FREE Roundtrip Coach Class Certificate plus First Class Upgrade* | 1 FREE Week (luxury car) | 5 FREE Nights | 6 | — | — | 2 FREE Roundtrip First Class Tickets |

\* Domestic First Class Upgrades valid on any published fare
NOTE: 1) FREE Northwest Domestic Travel Certificates are valid for travel between points in North America (including Alaska and Canada; excluding Hawaii), or between points in the Pacific (excluding Hawaii), or between points in Europe.
2) Car Rental award is valid for National Car Rental OR Thrifty. Hotel award is valid at Mandarin Oriental Hotels OR Marriott Hotels OR Radisson Hotels.

\*\* Travel Documents include any **unexpired** Free Flight Plan Travel Certificates, Republic "Timesaver" tickets or Northwest WORLDPERKS Domestic Travel Certificates

WORLDPERKS PARTNERS  // National   Thrifty   MANDARIN ORIENTAL   Marriott   Radisson

**Figure 10.3**  Sample of a "Build" Promotion *(courtesy: Northwest Airlines, Inc.)*

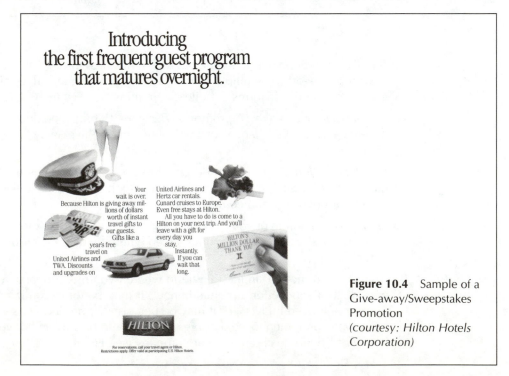

# Introducing the first frequent guest program that matures overnight.

Your wait is over. Because Hilton is giving away millions of dollars worth of instant travel gifts to our guests. Gifts like a year's free travel on United Airlines and TWA. Discounts and upgrades on United Airlines and Hertz car rentals. Cunard cruises to Europe. Even free stays at Hilton.

All you have to do is come to a Hilton on your next trip. And you'll leave with a gift for every day you stay. Instantly. If you can wait that long.

HILTON

For reservations, call your travel agent or Hilton.
Restrictions apply. Offer valid at participating U.S. Hilton Hotels.

**Figure 10.4**  Sample of a Give-away/Sweepstakes Promotion *(courtesy: Hilton Hotels Corporation)*

**Figure 10.5** Sample of a "Cooperative" Promotion *(courtesy: AVIS RENT A CAR SYSTEM, INC.)*

There are many other types of promotions or variations of those previously listed. Some promotions may be intended to build good will, others as paybacks for utilizing your product or service, and still others to expand awareness of your product or service into new market areas or to expose new market segments to your product. Always keep in mind your *purpose* for entering into a promotion and the *benefit* you will receive from the promotion.

A word of caution is appropriate at this point. Do not enter into a joint promotion without ascertaining the impact on your base business, image, or overall market. While it is enticing to be offered a low-cost tie-in into someone else's package or promotion, it may not always be beneficial. In fact, it could be detrimental. Look closely at your own image and reputation and make it your rule of thumb not to enter into a promotional agreement unless the other parties have an equal or better overall reputation.

## METHODS FOR EXECUTING PROMOTIONS

It is no secret that one of the key reasons promotions fail is because the wrong method of execution is used. Take extreme care in determining the best promotion method to achieve your purpose *and* reach your target. The full gamut of weaponry is at your command. If you need a shotgun, don't select a pistol! The weapons include advertising (outdoor, displays, TV, radio, print); direct mail; tent cards; publicity; personal, direct selling; handouts; telephone sales; a special benefit to loyal customers or club members in monthly billings, and so forth.

You may promote your purpose and reach your target by yourself by directly appealing to the end-users of your product or service, or you may reach your target through the appropriate intermediaries such as travel agents, retailers, wholesalers, traffic departments, suppliers, secretaries, tourist organizations, associations, convention bureaus, franchise affiliates, and distributorships. You may use credit card mailing stuffers, mailing lists, someone else's outlets, and posters and flyers of all types. Most important is to select the methods that most efficiently and effectively reach your target and accomplish your purpose.

## INTERNAL PROMOTIONS

Up to this point we have been discussing some general aspects of promotions. Frequently a major way to increase the revenue and profit yield from your existing customers is to promote to the customers once they are inside your door. This can be achieved in many ways but should be done selectively and with a specific purpose or goal in mind. Internal promotions should be created and executed with the same care as external promotions. In fact, there are some additional considerations to take into account when promoting internally. Assuming all the keys to successful promotions have been followed, consider these additional items:

### COMPATIBILITY
Is my internal promotion compatible with what my customer perceives of my product or service? Never cheapen your image with your loyal customers by a slapped-together, poorly thought-out and executed promotion.

### BENEFIT
Will my internal promotion not only meet my purpose, but, moreover, will it offer a perceivable benefit to the customer? Will it keep the customer as a friend, or will he or she be offended?

### VALUE
Does the internal promotion provide my customers with a perceived value for their money? Value means quality at a fair price — not cheapness.

### CLUTTER AVOIDANCE
Will my internal promotion piece clutter or detract from the table, desk top, wall, or wherever it is presented? Be sure your overall product quality is not cheapened as a result of the physical promotion piece or content of the promotion.

These four additional considerations should be viewed as essential steps prior to doing any internal promotions of your own or allowing anyone else's promotions to be viewed by your customers.

## CASE EXAMPLES

There are many examples of both good and bad promotions in the hospitality industry. A promotion that works to produce positive results need not be likable to all. It is more important that your target market responds favorably to it. Here are a few case examples of promotions that display both success and failure. Look closely at *why* the promotion succeeded or failed; you will see that the keys to successful promotions were either fully and correctly employed or violated.

### CASE EXAMPLE A: THE GREAT IDEA

In a medium-sized New England city an independent motel owner/operator was trying to compete with a nearby national chain franchised motel. Overall this was a good occupancy sector of the market, averaging 80 percent. The chain motel had a slightly better location, but the independent motel had a better physical property. The chain motel was running an 83 percent occupancy and the independent motel a 73 percent occupancy. Mr. Owner/Operator watched that occupancy percent weekly and was getting frustrated. He came up with an unresearched but logical (to him) "great idea."

He called a friend who painted signs and said, "I want a large sign with red letters reading 'Low Discount Rates — Stay Here' with a large red arrow pointing to my entry." This great idea resulted in Mr. Owner/Operator's occupancy gradually declining to 63 percent and his bottom line sinking even further. In desperation he called in a marketing consultant.

The consultant examined the market and determined "rate" was of less significance than "quality of the facility." Mr. Owner/Operator had a high-quality facility; however, his great idea had given his property the image of a cut-rate lower-quality (than the chain motel) independent motel. The consultant recommended that Mr. Owner/Operator do some upgrading in the landscaping, lighting, and painting of the entry facade. The consultant further recommended that the homemade price-war sign come down and be replaced with a permanent high-quality brick and brass sign with a new name, incorporating the name of the city, such as "The Burlington Inn" or "The Lexington Inn." The consultant also recommended a new awning canopy (cost $850) and a new rate structure $2.00 above the chain franchised motel. The final touch was a promotional slogan on the marquis: "The new _____ Inn — the finest in town."

The results were dramatic. Occupancy recovered and went to 83 percent with a rate averaging $2.00 higher than the franchise motel and $7.50 higher than a year earlier for the same independent motel. The chain franchised motel's occupancy dropped to 74 percent.

*CASE EXAMPLE B: THE SIMPLE IDEA*

Many times the simpler the promotion and the less complicated its execution, the more successful it is. Two national chains have succeeded in getting a large share of the summer family market with very simple promotional concepts. Holiday Inns' "Kids Stay Free" and Ramada Inns "Four for One" programs have both succeeded. "Kids Stay Free" simply meant that children under age 18 accompanying their parents stay free in the same room as their parents at Holiday Inns. Ramada's "Four for One" permits four persons to stay in the same room for the price of one person in Ramada Inns.

These promotions are successful for two basic reasons. First, each meets the needs of the market segments; each offers a tangible, perceived value. Second, each is straightforward and easy for the consumer and operations to understand. Other hotels/motels have tried similar promotions, but have confused the market/consumer with such restrictions as "only children under 12 years," "no extra beds allowed," or "only at the following Inns. . . ." In essence, both Holiday and Ramada have kept it simple for both the consumer and the front desk. They offered a value and succeeded.

*CASE EXAMPLE C: ANOTHER SIMPLE PROMOTION*

Omni Hotels ran a very simple promotion in the mid-1980s which simply stated: "Stay four nights and the weekend is free."

*CASE EXAMPLE D: THE ADDICTING IDEA*

The fast-food business is tremendously competitive. Market share and repeat business factors are constantly measured and monitored. Advertising and promotions demand the best of creativity. A major challenge is to get market share without having price promotions putting major dents in franchisees' financial statements. Recognizing this factor, a major chain recently executed an extremely effective promotion. The concept was also simple — give people a reason to come in and come back. Let's take McDonald's "Build a Big Mac" promotion and label it one big success. Why? Because it had a clear purpose, a well-defined target, and was simply executed. The purpose was to build volume in a recessionary period. The method was "hope" — the chance to win up to $100,000 instantly. The repeat factor was the intrigue that only one more piece of the puzzle was needed to win. The idea appealed to both kids and adults. It as a winning promotion because every key to a successful promotion was used and tuned to perfection.

*CASE EXAMPLE E: THE PAY-OFF*

There are many case examples that could be featured here: airline frequent traveler programs such as UAL's Mileage Plus, American's AAdvantage Program, Continental's TravelBank, and hotel frequent guest programs such as Marriott's Honored Guest Program, Hyatt's Gold Passport Program, and Stouffer's Club Express program. These are all examples of "pay-off" programs, a type of promotion which blossomed

**Figure 10.6** Sample of a "Payoff" Promotion I *(courtesy: Inter-Continental Hotels)*

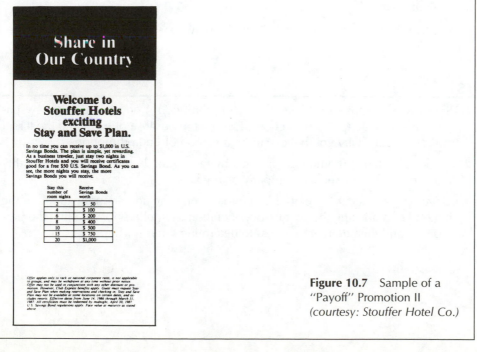

**Figure 10.7** Sample of a "Payoff" Promotion II *(courtesy: Stouffer Hotel Co.)*

in the 1980s. We'll look at these generically because the elements are basically the same, as are the premises. The pay-off works along these lines. A discount or "cost" is figured — say 5 percent. This is then equated to points, credits, miles, or other measurements applied on a scale. Achievement of points, etc., on the scale corresponds to pay-off levels. The pay-off increases with the volume of consumption. For example, fly 30,000 miles and get a free first-class round-trip ticket; fly 50,000 miles and get two free first-class tickets (see Figure 10.6). Another example: stay 10 nights and receive a $100 U.S. Savings Bond; stay 15 nights and receive $200 in U.S. Savings Bonds (see Figure 10.7).

## KEY WORDS AND CONCEPTS

**Promotion** A creative idea that is aimed at providing business and which supports the overall marketing efforts. It may be used to stimulate new, trial, repeat, or incremental sales.

**Test Card** An internal promotion tool that rests on the top of a table, desk, bureau, or other flat surface. It may be more than a single fold or contain more than one promotion.

**Price Promotion** A promotion in which the incentive to purchase is based on "price."

**Introductory Promotion** A promotion designed to introduce a new product or service to the market.

**Cooperative Promotion** A promotion involving two or more suppliers of services and/or products joined together in a common promotion for their mutual benefit.

## ASSIGNMENTS

1. Select two examples of different types of promotions from the Sunday newspaper travel or entertainment sections. Identify the purpose of each and the target audience. State why you believe these are good or bad promotions.

2. Create an internal promotion for a nearby restaurant, hotel, or other hospitality industry product or service company near you.

3. Develop an execution plan for a promotion; include identification of the method of marketing the promotion, operations guidelines for fulfilling the promotion, and measurement process to determine the results.

# Applying Key Marketing Methodologies: From Collateral Materials to VIP Clubs

# 11

## PURPOSE

In order to effectively market your products and services, you must clearly communicate what you are offering, where the consumer can obtain your products and services and why the consumer should buy from you. This chapter focuses on these points and demonstrates how to make your collateral materials sell for you. We will discuss a variety of instruments such as directories that sell and in-house collateral materials to which your customers will respond. We will also introduce club concepts that result in profit and employee programs that enhance morale and help capture your own in-house market.

## OBJECTIVES

1. Determine additional and inexpensive ways to market your products and services.

2. Learn an effective way in which to use traditional communication vehicles like directories, brochures, tent cards, and many more.

3. Apply methods to capture your own employees as customers.

4. Apply techniques that give you the competitive edge in capturing your customers' dollars.

Collateral materials are the print support materials that assist in the marketing of your product or service. As used by the hospitality industry, they include brochures, maps, guides, menu inserts, tent cards, photo displays, and posters. The cost of the preparation, printing, and distribution of these materials is an easily measured expense.

It is important to understand that you should approach the preparation of each piece of collateral with the same care you would give your best advertisement or most important sales call. Your collateral materials are always in view of your potential market and customers. In essence, the same "do's and don't's" that apply to promotion pieces in general apply to all collateral materials. There are some key points to note with respect to these materials.

**KEY 1:** RATIONALE IDENTIFICATION

Before you determine whether you need color, what quality of paper stock to use, and what shape, size, and so forth you should make any item, ask yourself what is the primary purpose of the piece and who is the audience.

**KEY 2:** FALLACY ABOUT QUALITY

Don't fall for the fallacy about quality that states: "If it's four colors and on high-quality stock, it's got to be good." Too often the real quality of a collateral piece of material is confused with its physical appearance versus its marketing purpose.

**KEY 3:** COMPATIBILITY

Whatever "image" your product or service has should be reinforced, not contradicted, by your collateral materials. If you are running an upscale gourmet restaurant, be sure your materials are compatible with the image you are trying to establish. There are times when one tries to improve on image through improving the collateral materials. An example is the new brochure. One word of caution, however: Does the new brochure violate the number one premise of advertising, that is, does it build a level of expectation beyond what the product can deliver? If so, you could be doing yourself more harm than good.

**KEY 4:** CONSISTENCY

The single greatest fault with collateral material in general usually rests with its lack of consistency. Does your collateral material have any consistency with your other marketing and image-related visual aides? Simple things such as use of a logo, certain colors, print styles, and so on, will help build consistency. You may want your piece of collateral material to stand out, and it should, but not at the cost of detracting from your image.

**KEY 5:** PRACTICAL DETAIL

Does the piece of collateral material convey the marketing purpose it was designed to convey? Too often things like picture selection take precedence over clear directions and a useful map. The result may be great photos, but no one can find you! Remember to review the materials and be sure of every detail.

### KEY 6: VISIBLE AVAILABILITY

If you want customers to pick up and respond to your collateral materials, don't hide them! How often do you check to see that these materials are where they belong (where the customer or potential customer can clearly see and pick up the material)?

### KEY 7: CLUTTER AVOIDANCE

Be sure you are not a victim of "the more-the-better" syndrome. Yes, it's great to have good information for your hospitality industry customers, but too much results in clutter. Or you may even find that the customer has left you to pursue and spend time and money at an attraction you promoted over zealously.

### KEY 8: KEEP IT CLEAR

Regardless of the collateral piece of material, do not overload it with photos, copy, or detail to the point that it loses its purpose as a marketing vehicle. Be sure its purpose is clear and visible. A customer or potential customer picks up the material to get a message — don't bury that message in fine print or, worse, too much print.

## TYPES OF COLLATERAL MATERIAL

Given these general keys, let's look at some specific types of collateral materials employed in the hospitality industry.

### BROCHURES

A brochure is a highly specialized piece of collateral material. It's preparation requires careful thought. It is not a collection of sexy photos and some copy. A successful, well-prepared promotional brochure for a property should contain the following 10 elements:

1. Identification of the facility, including logo
2. Descriptive facts on the facility
3. Directions on how to get to the facility
4. A map with commutation times
5. Telephone number
6. Address
7. Person or individual to contact for more information (sales director, catering department, etc.)
8. Amenities within the facility (recreational, food and beverage, etc.)

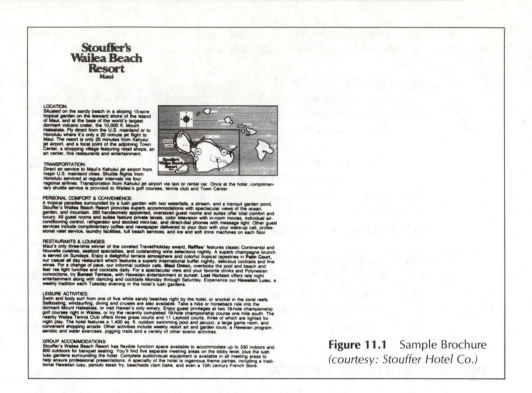

**Figure 11.1** Sample Brochure *(courtesy: Stouffer Hotel Co.)*

9. Nearby attractions and items of interest to the guests/customers (i.e., shopping, tourist attractions, etc.)

10. Transportation information (limo service, bus, airlines, rail, interstates, rent-a-car companies, etc.)

Inclusion of these 10 elements will not necessarily ensure that your brochure is successful. You must also consider the eight keys to successful collateral material mentioned earlier and, of course, use professional photos, art, design layout, and copy to produce a quality final product (see Figure 11.1).

## DIRECTORIES

If you list your firm, establishment, or operation in a directory, observe the following points:

1. Proof everything twice.

2. Be careful about being too specific with prices/rates; use ranges (especially if it is an annual directory).

3. Check and double-check your address and phone listing (and telex if applicable).

4. Ask to review the final copy.

5. Ask to review the actual placement.

6. If a photo of your product or service is used, be sure it is up-to-date, representative, and a sales tool; otherwise, do not use it.

There are both large volume reference directories and pocket-size or briefcase directories. If you produce a directory that you want to be used by the traveling consumer, be sure it fits in a briefcase or purse. No one wants to (or will) carry a book. Make it easy to use. Follow a format that is logical — to the customer, not you — and include an index and a key. Put your phone number wherever possible, preferably on every page, as well as the front and back covers.

## DIRECTORY LISTINGS

Today there are over 5,000 different reference directories, ranging from the local yellow pages to a relatively new publication, *A Directory of Directories*. Not every product or service establishment in the hospitality industry can benefit from directory listings. In order to determine which directory listings are helpful to you, you will need to analyze *where* your business is coming from, *how* it finds out about you, and *what* type of business you are getting. Answer the following questions designed to help you determine which directories you should list in for the most exposure for your product or service:

1. Do I currently receive business as a result of a directory listing?

2. Does my competition receive business I do not, as a result of a directory listing?

3. Will I receive enough business from a directory listing to offset the cost for the listing?

4. Are there any key directories in which other competitors are listed and I am not?

5. How should my product or service be featured in a directory (i.e., one line, block ad, photo ad, etc.)?

While these five practical questions should provide you with some rationale to list or not to list in a directory, often trial and measurement will be the best test. If you decide directory listings will be helpful in marketing your product or service, be sure that the content and the placement of that listing is well thought out to convey your marketing message. Directory listings often require similar information for all contributors. It is to your advantage to fill in every line in the listing questionnaire. If the directory you select allows leeway, be sure to include the following: address (directional locator if possible; for example, "next to the Metro Station in Crystal City"), phone number, and any special information that will give potential customers a reason to call you (this reason can be referred to as the "why statement"). Insist that you review the placement of your listing — the actual spot in the directory where your listing will appear — and, most important, that you have an opportunity for a final review of the copy that goes into the directory. Do not scan it — read it word for word, number for number. Once it is in print in a directory it is widely circulated — errors, wrong phone number, and all. And, again, if you must list rates/prices, use a range. Most directories are published annually, and rates of inflation are high. You do not want to commit to fixed published rates.

## GIFT CERTIFICATES

Another very useful application of a promotion piece using collateral materials is the gift certificate. The gift certificate provides the opportunity for an individual to purchase your product or service for someone else. Gift certificates can take on many different forms and be promoted in many different ways. One example is McDonald's seasonal promotion of the gift certificate book of coupons as a Christmas gift. Another, more creative example was executed well by a lodging facility that sold "gift boxes" containing "escape weekend tickets along with empty champagne glasses" — to be filled on a complimentary basis. Restaurants offer "dinner for two" gift certificates with all sorts of variations. These programs have become increasingly popular, fulfilling people's need to give an unusual gift. Merchandising in general, and especially through gift certificates, may well increase applications in the hospitality industry in the 1980s.

## ENTERTAINMENT PIECES

Collateral materials in support of entertainment come in many shapes, forms, and levels of quality. Most entertainers will supply photos, posters, or flyers. Most hospitality industry establishments use these as supplied. This is fine if the quality and, most important, *taste* in the collateral material is compatible with the establishment's image. There are no standard criteria by which to screen entertainment collateral materials; however, there are some steps that can be taken to ensure the materials are compatible to the establishment.

1. Consider developing a standard marquis-type poster display case.
2. Request entertainment groups to supply appropriate photos or posters to fit the display case.
3. Reject all "home-made" posters, signs, and other wall hangings.
4. Consider your print advertising as part of the total campaign for the entertainment — make it stand out from the rest (see Figure 11.2).
5. Be sure that the supplied photos, copy, and any related public relations or press releases are in good taste and compatible with the image your establishment is trying to convey.

**Figure 11.2** Sample of Advertisement for In-house Entertainment *(courtesy: Ramada Inc.)*

6. Be sure the entertainment itself is representative of how you want your customers to perceive your place. Think of your image at all times.

## FLYERS

Flyers are announcements usually printed for quick distribution to stimulate interest in a special event or promotion. Flyers may be used as reminders or even announce an event when time does not permit using another method. If you use flyers, take care that they have a professional appearance and are compatible with other materials used to promote the event. It is important that you control distribution to ensure that potential customers (and not your parking lot) get the message. Use flyers only when no other organized collateral material or promotional method is possible.

## GUEST SERVICES CARD

There are two approaches to guest services collateral materials: the clutter method, and the organized approach. The clutter method is best depicted by a hotel room dresser or desk top full of everything from credit card applications to room service menus, all set up alongside instructions on how to work the TV, save energy, and so forth; the net result is a guest room with a cluttered appearance.

There are many ways to organize guest services information. One method is to use a folder with inserts related to the various services (i.e., room service menu, amenities, etc.). The second method is to use a display made of laminated plastic with slots for inserts. Either is acceptable, and both are preferred to the clutter approach. The guest room materials should reflect some consistency in color and print style, and, most important of all, they should be readable. Often too much is squeezed on an instructions card with print too small to be of help to the guest, resulting in unnecessary calls to your telephone operator. One final note. Be sure a pen or pencil is included with the collateral materials in the room. The guest will not only appreciate it and use it, but he or she will probably take it, so be sure it is imprinted with the name of your establishment.

## LOUNGE MATERIALS

Collateral material promoting a lounge in the lodging facility should adhere to the same guidelines as materials used to promote the facility itself. The lounge materials need not only convey the environment, theme, and so on, but should include a marketing message that relates to the needs of the consumer. The message can be: "a place to relax," "a place to unwind," "a place to discuss business or pleasure," or whatever.

If there is something special about the lounge, say so in the collateral material. Collateral material promoting the lounge should tell the reader where it is in the facility, indicate any dress requirements, and be placed in visible locations throughout the property. Visible places include, but are not limited to, the restaurant, the elevator lobby, elevator display panels, the lobby, and the guest rooms. Collateral materials should convey, via photo contents, the reason to come to the lounge, be it relaxation or the promise of intimate discussion. A photo of four walls does not sell or motivate the consumer. People visit lounges to get away from the room, seek companionship, avoid loneliness, or relax. Be sure your collateral materials convey that your lounge meets these needs.

## MAPS

A good map will indicate a clear way to reach your establishment, and will identify landmarks, key roads, and distance or travel time. With respect to distance or travel time, use the indicator that is most advantageous to you. If you are three miles from the airport, but it takes 25 minutes to travel the distance, indicate three miles. If you are nine miles from the airport, but only 15 minutes via the expressway, indicate fifteen minutes. If you can get your establishment listed on other maps, do so — it is an additional exposure for you. Rent-a-car company maps, chamber of commerce materials, realtor maps, bank maps, and sightseeing maps are but a few opportunities to get your establishment noticed.

## MENU SPECIALS

A frequently used piece of collateral material is that which promotes a special food or beverage item promotion. These promotions take many forms, ranging from the mimeographed clip-on to multicolored menus or table-top displays. Regardless of the formality of the collateral piece, its objective is to increase sales and profits by getting guests to opt for the special. In today's market environment these promotions can be extremely effective "value" as perceived by the potential customer. The promotion can be on a regularly scheduled day of the week, week of the month, or month of the year. If you use the material as part of an on-going program, you can more easily implement and control the promotion and measure its effectiveness. The Denny's restaurant chain uses this type of collateral sales material. Their restaurants regularly promote two items as specials. The items frequently change; however, the clip-on collateral material is well prepared and its quality is compatible with the neat appearance of the menu.

Menu specials can be designed to achieve a variety of objectives. The purpose may be to increase volume by offering a relatively low-priced special, or it may be to build "trial" by offering a low-priced special to attract new clientele. Specials may be designed to increase profits by promoting low-cost items that provide a higher profit margin, such as pasta dishes. Others may be designed to build volume for a specific item, or to increase beverage sales, or to increase the average check amounts through dessert promotions, and so on.

Menu specials can work to meet your specific objectives if you clearly identify the purpose and result expected and you conscientiously and methodically measure your results, and if your collateral promotion piece is well planned.

Finally, remember to tell the waiters, waitresses, hosts, and hostesses about the "special" and *how* to promote it to the customer. A waitress who answers, "I don't know" when your customer asks about a special is not going to make a sale.

## MEETING FACILITIES BROCHURES

If you decide to prepare a brochure about the meeting facilities in your establishment, be sure to include the items of interest to meeting planners. This means every detail, not just photos. Details to include are as follows:

### Meeting Brochure Details

Room sizes/dimensions

Ceiling lights

Seating capacity, referencing different set-ups (theater style, classroom, U-shaped, etc.)

Audiovisual equipment

Display capacities (maximum width and height of entries)

Sketches or diagrams of the rooms

Break-out room and additional conference room information

Adjoining banquet facilities

Meeting and feeding set-ups

Special features (acoustics, tables, etc.)

Rates and discounts, if applicable or appropriate

Location of the facilities

Proximity to transportation (subways, airport, etc.)

Other property amenities that will help sell meetings

Service procedures and policies, focusing on the human aspect rather than the physical facility

Telephone number and name of person to contact

Group transportation services

Make the meeting facilities brochure easy to read and responsive to the meeting planner's needs. Include the banquet services menu and any other related collateral materials as support information for the meeting planner.

The meeting facilities brochure should answer every question a potential customer might ask about the physical facility and services available. Inclusion of a "things to do" section or as an attachment can also help sell your facility. This section or attachment should reference nearby or in-house shopping, entertainment, cultural attractions, recreational attractions, and so forth.

Again, and most important of all, be certain that there is a telephone number and person to call. If that person is not available, be sure that the person answering the telephone is completely versed on procedures to follow in answering questions or ensure that the appropriate salesperson can quickly contact the potential customer. Finally, be certain that there is an adequate stock of all materials on hand to supply the potential customer.

## RATE CARDS

Perhaps the single most debatable piece of collateral material today is the rate card. Rates change frequently and, moreover, are often discounted or tailored for special types of business (for instance, corporate clients, airline crews, family rate plan). If rate cards are used, they should be constructed with frequent replacement in mind, and designed to allow the flexibility to sell. This means using ranges, clearly defining special rate programs and qualifying rules, clearly stating dates for which the rates are in effect, and defining any special policies.

Printing your rates may not always legally obligate you, but it certainly builds an expectation among your potential customers on what your product or service will cost. Always have a disclaimer, "rates subject to change," but, more important, strive to have the correct current rate clearly defined for your customer. Likewise, be sure every employee who has contact with potential customers knows the current rate policy and procedures, and has the current rate card in front of him/her or accessible at all times.

## RECREATIONAL FACILITIES GUIDE

Amenities, be they within the hospitality facility or in nearby areas, are an asset to be promoted. Internal collateral materials can support this goal and help satisfy the guest and attract a repeat visitor. Select reference materials to nearby local attractions can also benefit a property that lacks the internal amenities or facilities. The caution here is avoid the "clutter" syndrome of having many different collateral pieces which vary in quality. Also, discard any out-of-date brochures. Cooperative programs can work very well between lodging facilities and nearby attractions by increasing the exposure and perceived value through jointly referencing each other. Again, be sure to give careful thought to consistency and image before you enter into such cooperative promotions.

## SHOPPING GUIDES

Shopping consistently ranks high on the list of needs expressed by leisure travelers. Collateral materials pointing out nearby or special shopping areas can thus add another perceived value to the hospitality lodging facility. If there is a "shopper's guide" for your area, getting your hotel (or restaurant or airline office, etc.) identified within the publication as a reference point or map point can also provide additional marketing exposure.

## TENT CARDS

Tent cards are another popular form of collateral material. They can be used to promote everything from a restaurant within a hotel to a drink or dessert special within the restaurant. Tent cards come in all shapes, sizes, and forms. Some practical considerations are:

1. Use all sides of the tent card.
2. Design it in a practical manner to rest on the table or desk top.
3. Make it attractive, including the item featured.
4. Avoid the temptation to have the "totally unique" tent card — it will usually be costly to produce, difficult to use, and constantly in need of replacement.
5. Be sure that size and locational placement of the tent card are in concert with the purpose or message on the card.
6. Monitor and measure the results of each tent card promotion to determine its real value to you.
7. Avoid clutter or promotions that cheapen your overall product or service offering.

## EMPLOYEE MOTIVATION

There are other in-house marketing methodologies that can be very useful in the hospitality industry. As a labor-intensive industry, *employee motivation* and attitude are very often the keys to a successful operation. Ensuring employee motivation is a very difficult task in the services business. In-house materials that help employee morale are important and have a direct impact on the "sale" of your product or service. Do not ignore these motivations; they are a key marketing tool. Some examples are included here.

## EMPLOYEE-OF-THE-MONTH PROGRAM

One of the more successful applications of motivational principles in the hospitality industry has been an "employee-of-the-month" program. The visual execution of these programs is important; often a photo poster is prominently displayed in a high-traffic employee area.

An even more meaningful and potentially more beneficial method is to establish a permanent display case for such a poster, thereby allowing your guests to also see this recognition award. This method of placement provides even further recognition for the employee and fosters additional feelings of good will among both employees and guests. Executing this internal employee program requires a well-planned program of support, frequently including external public relations and some form of reward for the deserving employee. Selection criteria, fairness in judgment, and the involvement of other employees are often keys to success in making such a program work. Management's involvement and respect for the employees and their achievements are also critical factors.

## EMPLOYEE INTEREST PROMOTION

Motivating employees can also directly help in marketing your product or service. "Employee interest promotions" help to achieve both the motivational goal as well as increase the marketing exposures for your establishment. An employee interest promotion begins by identifying a hobby or special interest of an employee. One example is that of a chef in a large hotel whose hobby is driving race cars. The hotel successfully placed a number of human interest stories in the media about the "fastest chef in town," featuring their employee and his hobby. The recognition aspect of the program included displaying the news clippings and photos of the chef and his autos in a number of high-traffic employee areas within the property. Employee interest promotions are limitless, but they should be used on a limited basis or their internal value may dissipate.

## EMPLOYEE COMMUNITY SERVICE RECOGNITION

Another very effective program is recognition of employees' efforts in their local community. Many employees do volunteer work, have made special efforts on behalf of a charity, or have made special contributions to their community. Identifying and providing public recognition for these employees and their service efforts benefits both your firm and the employee. These are "win-win" promotions. Examples include employees who walk, run, or rock for contributions to charity; employees who perform volunteer work for the sick, disabled, or elderly; and employees who help save lives as volunteer fire fighters or rescue-squad personnel.

## CLUBS

Clubs are another internal as well as external marketing device that can work for you. Regardless of the sector of the hospitality industry, you can create a "club" concept to promote business. Here are a few examples:

### VIP CLUBS

Just as employee recognition programs identify employees most important to you, VIP clubs recognize segments of customers who are very important people to you. Examples of such concepts are numerous in the hospitality industry and include: Hertz #1 Club; Hertz Platinum Service; the various airline frequent-traveler clubs such as United's Red Carpet Club, TWA's Ambassador Club, and American's Admiral's Club. The lodging sector also uses a variety of VIP concepts and promotions. Each has some common denominators: membership recognition symbols ranging from wall plaques to plastic wallet cards; special privileges in recognition of the customer loyalty or importance as a heavy user of the product or service; and the appeal factor, the attraction of belonging to a specially recognized group of individuals (see Figure 11.3).

Today's VIP club concepts are sophisticated and require skills in everything from building direct mail lists, to publishing special magazines, to complete merchandising programs. VIP clubs can also exist *within* a lodging or food and beverage facility. It can be a concept as simple as designating upgraded rooms or floors for VIPs or sectioning off an area of the dining room for VIPs. Recognition, appreciation, and appeal to the repeat user are the motivators behind such VIP club concepts. A synopsis of key factors for a VIP club concept is as follows:

1. Recognition of heavy users of the product or service
2. Perceivable benefits to membership
3. Special services
4. Exclusive items or services for members only
5. Membership symbols (membership cards, wall plaques, etc.)
6. Emphasis on taking problems out of the travel experience
7. Simplifying the product or service purchase

### SECRETARIES CLUB

A very important intermediary in the hospitality industry is the secretary. A secretary is often in direct contact with the customer and, more important, is often a decision maker. Hotels have been the leaders in the industry in recognizing this and devel-

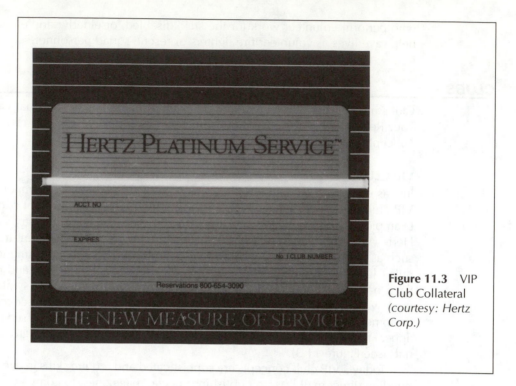

**Figure 11.3** VIP Club Collateral *(courtesy: Hertz Corp.)*

oping special appreciation club concepts. One such club concept offers various incentive awards in appreciation for various levels of business directed to their establishments. The concept is well thought out and exemplifies how to organize a productive secretaries program. Here's a sketch of how it works.

The establishment assigns an individual to identify secretaries who are providing reservations on a regular basis. A list is developed, and those secretaries are invited to join the "club." The club provides everything from a quarterly appreciation luncheon, to flowers on each secretary's birthday, to free weekends for certain volumes of room nights, to free trips for even larger volumes. While this is an oversimplified explanation, the concept is "business is appreciated and, more important, so are you." It's no wonder that the chains' highest percentage of repeat business comes from the secretaries club. The building of lists, enrolling of members, personal letters, gestures of appreciation, incentive gifts, and all other aspects of this club concept are highly sophisticated and geared to the premise of building repeat business through loyal intermediaries and friends.

## SALESPERSON'S APPRECIATION CLUBS
Special club or VIP concepts are particularly applicable to the commercial transient salesperson. These individuals form the loyal core or base for many hospitality in-

dustry establishments as a result of a heavy consistent travel pattern. Building loyalty to your product or service with this market segment can be very beneficial. The club or VIP concept assumes many different forms; however, they have as a common premise the recognition that it is desirable to keep this particular customer's brand loyalty. Special rates, rooms, first-drink-free promotions, every tenth room free, free coffee and breakfast, and even free car washes have been offered as part of the special treatment for salespersons.

### DINING/MEAL-OF-THE-MONTH CLUBS

Building a loyal or regular following in today's food and beverage market is increasingly difficult because of the many new concepts and plethora of competition. One method of ensuring a regular following is to develop a concept of a dining-out club. The club concept can have a number of different appeals, ranging from price and value, to a variety of themes, to entertainment tie-ins. Regardless of the method selected, the idea is to build a core of regulars through a club concept.

### OTHER IDEAS THAT CAN WORK FOR YOU

There is no limit to creative promotional ideas within the hospitality industry. Everything from 10-year pocket calendars, to desk top reminders, to engraved pen sets have been used and can be used to promote new and repeat business. The criterion is simple — getting a good return on your investment. That return may be difficult to calculate, since it may not occur for months or even years. However successful your creative idea, there will always be need for another. Build an inventory, time the introduction, and go after that customer.

This chapter has identified a variety of additional marketing weaponry you can employ. We discussed collateral materials, in house promotions, and "club" types of recognition programs. These weapons, viewed on an individual basis, are analogous to rifle shots at the consumer market. In the next chapter we will discuss putting a number of weapons together to take a larger shot at the market — it's called packaging!

## KEY WORDS AND CONCEPTS

**Collateral Materials** Print-based support materials that assist in the marketing of products and services. Included are brochures, tent cards, posters, directories, maps, guides, menu inserts, flyers, and entertainment promotion pieces.

**Flyer** An announcement of a special event or promotion usually created and printed for quick distribution by "drop" (leaving at a location), for "pick-up" (by consumers passing by that location), or "tag-a-long" (being included with other materials or stuffers).

**Stock** The type of paper or material used for printed materials; usually defined by weight, grain, or texture.

**Placement** Actual location of a print message within a publication (for instance, "sports section, page 2, upper right-hand corner").

## ASSIGNMENTS

1. Design a brochure for a local lodging facility; include all the key elements.

2. Develop a tent card promotion for a food item or beverage for a local restaurant.

3. Obtain a local resort's brochure and analyze it, pointing out its strengths and weaknesses based on a check against the key elements.

4. Scan your yellow pages directory, and identify three hospitality firms' listings. Analyze each to determine the clarity of the listing.

5. Design an "entertainment" promotion piece that can be used in a lobby area of a hotel or restaurant to attract patrons into the lounge.

6. Select a menu item, and design a "menu special" piece to promote the item.

# Applying Key Marketing Methodologies: Packaging

# 12

**PURPOSE**

Today, more than ever, people are buying a complete product or service. The travel experience, be it or a week or a weekend, can also be presented to the consumer in a complete "package." Packages may contain every ingredient or some of the components of the total travel experience. Packaging makes the purchase more attractive to the consumer: it simplifies a multiple purchase and may, in addition, offer price advantages. Packaging is an important marketing weapon and is becoming increasingly popular in the hospitality industry.

**OBJECTIVES**

1. Understand what packaging is and who benefits from this marketing weapon.

2. Determine how packaging works to the benefit of the consumer, as well as to the benefit of the individual hospitality product and services firms participating in the "packaging."

3. Apply packaging concepts as a marketing weapon by determining when, where, and for whom packaging will work most advantageously.

4. Understand the role of packaging vis-a-vis the arsenal of other marketing weaponry.

Earlier in this text we referred to the fact that travel as a product or service was just beginning to fully develop. One sign of this development is expressed by the marketing concept of packaging. Packaging in the hospitality industry can be defined as offering more than one product and/or service, together, to the consumer for one total price. The price may be less than, equal to, or more than the sum of each component's cost to the consumer. Examples range from an "escape weekend" that may include rooms, food, and beverage — a "weekend package" — to a more elaborate packaging scheme that might involve a "fly-drive-cruise" package. Let's examine packaging as a marketing weapon, then come back to some "package" examples.

## BENEFITS

As a marketing weapon, a package should offer certain benefits to the consumer as well as to the participating hospitality group product or service firms. The consumer should feel that he or she is benefitting from the package offer by (1) having had the many travel-related decisions simplified and (2) getting a value or cost savings.

While these perceived consumer benefits from packaging seem straightforward and reasonable, the challenge to meet these needs is substantial.

Assuming the consumer gets a benefit from the packaging concept, what is in it for the individual hospitality industry product or service supplier? Sometimes very little; other times substantial multiple sales. Included here are a few of the many reasons for being part of a package:

*Reasons to Participate in Packaging*

1. Increases sales
2. Fills fringe or down periods with sales
3. Makes own product easier to acquire by being part of another, better known product
4. Makes own product or service appear more attractive than if offered on a stand-alone basis
5. Achieves economies of scale by being offered through many sales channels
6. Gains recognition or builds reputation in a new market or for a new product or service

Assuming we agree that the consumer gets a benefit out of packaging, and that marketing packages also benefits the participating hospitality industry firms, who else profits? Usually the person or firm that puts more than one travel product or service together into a package also benefits. As we discussed in an earlier chapter, *packagers* may buy more than one travel product or service and then put them together in a package and sell them directly to the consumer — this is known as

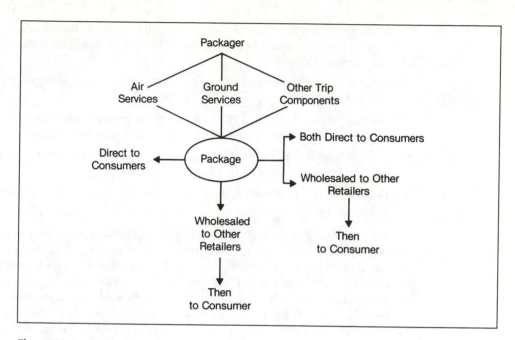

**Figure 12.1**   Packaging

*retailing a package.* The packagers may also perform another role — contracting for many components of the travel product or service, placing them together, and in turn selling these packages to others to sell directly to the public. This is known as *wholesaling a package* (see Figure 12.1).

Regardless of whether a package is offered directly to the consumer by the packagers or wholesaled through other retailers to the consumer, it must be attractive from a marketing base as well as a financial base. In order to be attractive from a marketing perspective, the package must meet the needs of the customer. These needs are often complex and defining them requires considerable thought.

## PARTICIPATION

Not every hospitality industry product or service lends itself to packaging. There are periods when participating in a package at a discounted rate can hurt you. There are packages that "sell" and "don't sell." Let's consider some questions to ask yourself prior to putting a package together or participating in someone else's package.

### Questions for Package Participation

1. What benefits will my product or service receive from participation? (More room nights? When? In season? Or when I need them in off-season?)

2. Will my participation and identity within the package be advantageous or detrimental to my product or service image? (Am I the Cadillac among Fords or the Ford among Cadillacs?)

3. What is the downside risk in committing my product or service to the package offering?

4. Are my "partners" in this package going to keep my customers happy or dissatisfied up to the point I relate to them and/or after they leave me?

5. Who is handling the details and/or do I have enough control over my portion of the package to keep my customers satisfied?

6. How is payment for my share of the product or service offered in the package to be handled.

Let's assume that your answers to all these questions point to your participating in a package, and you want to either be part of an existing deal or you want to put one together and reap the benefits of being the packager. Let's also assume you have the financial resources, the key contacts, and the willingness to accept the risks of being a packager. How do you now create the package? This question should lead you to think about some things we have already addressed in this book, such as: Which market segment is my package going to go after? What are the needs of that market segment? Where do I go to reach that market segment? To what kind of pricing structure will that segment respond? A package must be thought out with all the skill and depth of a marketing plan because it is just that — a plan to bring products or services to the market for purchase. Packaging is a complex and sophisticated marketing weapon that requires training before firing or misfiring.

## TYPES OF PACKAGING

Let's now examine packaging more in depth by looking at examples and types of packages that work in the hospitality industry. Because a package is a type of special promotion, there are virtually limitless applications of packaging. We have included some of the most popular applications.

### ALL-INCLUSIVE PACKAGES

All-inclusive packages are complete in that they include air services, lodging, ground services, rent-a-car, admissions to attractions, taxes and gratuities, and so forth. Examples include such packages as: "One week for two adults at Walt Disney World via Eastern Airlines" (hotel, rent-a-car, admissions included), or "Complete three-day Las Vegas Spree — $249" (air fare, deluxe rooms, meals, and shows). All-inclusive packaging lends itself to destinations since it simplifies the purchase of the complete trip.

Frequently, price promotions can be arranged as a result of averaging off-season and in-season rates, bulk purchases of rooms or seats, and so on. Such packages may be offered directly to the consumer in local newspaper ads, through clubs, churches, or civic organizations, or through retail travel agents. A packager or wholesaler may supply the same package to one or more retail outlets and in turn to the consumer.

### FLY-DRIVE PACKAGES

Fly-drive packages are popular and continue to grow. In this instance, air services and auto rental are combined into a package. For example, "American Airlines California Fly-Drive" included air fare to Los Angeles or San Francisco, a rental car for five days, and return air fare from San Francisco or Los Angeles. The concept was that you could fly to California, then drive up or down the coast, all for $499. For many years air carriers and rent-a-car firms on the east coast have successfully marketed Florida. Fly-drives prove particularly popular in markets or times when renting cars is difficult (for instance, in-season in Florida or when the destination is one with many attractions best seen by automobile). (See Figure 12.2.)

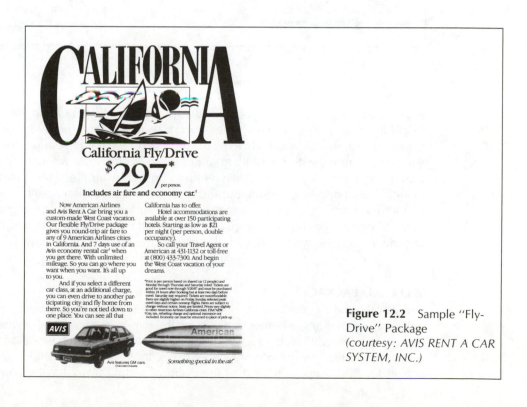

**Figure 12.2** Sample "Fly-Drive" Package
(courtesy: *AVIS RENT A CAR SYSTEM, INC.*)

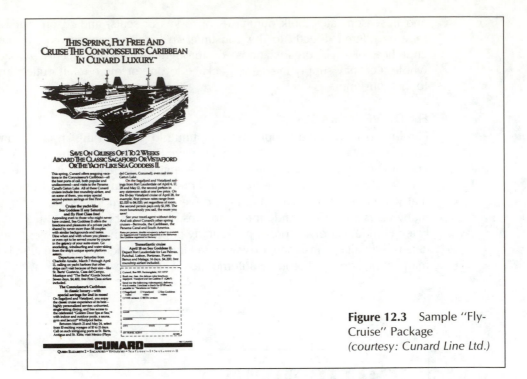

**Figure 12.3** Sample ''Fly-Cruise'' Package
*(courtesy: Cunard Line Ltd.)*

## FLY-CRUISE PACKAGES

A variation on the fly-drive package is the fly-cruise package. Originally conceived to eliminate lengthy cold days at sea for cruise passengers, the fly-cruise flew the customer to a warm seaport where he or she began a week-long cruise. For example, vacationers from the northeast fly from Boston to Miami, from where they sail to the Caribbean and back to Miami, then return to Boston by air. Recently, the struggle to maintain long-distance cruising (for instance, a transatlantic service) has resulted in a fly-cruise variation. The package is first-class air fare one way and a cruise in the other direction. Essentially, the packaged transatlantic fly-cruise, offers the cruise experience sought, while reducing the return time by offering air travel (see Figure 12.3).

## WEEKEND PACKAGES

Perhaps the most common and one of the simplest forms of packaging centers on weekend promotions, whether they are for the family or second honeymooners. In these instances, while convenience, price, or other logical purchase rationale would seem important, they are not preeminent. Yes, those factors are important, but the reason for the escape weekend or the event of getting away for the weekend has

**Figure 12.4** Sample "Week-end" Package *(courtesy: Marriott Corporation)*

become a strong need that "weekend packaging" fulfills. Examples include family escape packages geared to family fun and value (for example, the kids stay free Friday and Saturday nights, or four in the room for the price of one); second honeymoon escape packages (deluxe room, champagne, breakfast in bed, all geared toward getting away from it all — even the kids); and the hundreds of other escape weekend concepts, from ski packages to sporting event packages (see Figure 12.4).

## SPECIAL INTEREST PACKAGES

A package can be successfully created to appeal to people's special interests. The concept is to provide the basic service or product of the hospitality industry packaged with a special interest such as skiing, golf, tennis, swimming, boating, or horse riding. Special interest packages need not be limited to sport or recreational activity tie-ins. They may also relate to history, religious interests, or hobbies.

One of the most successful bus-tour packages has been a weekend "foliage" tour to see the changing landscape of New England as fall unfolds. Meals and rooms at quaint New England inns are usually packaged along with the scenic bus tour, complete with photo-taking sessions at scenic overviews along the highway. Other examples include "Friday Night at the Races" via motorcoach with dinner, cocktails

**Figure 12.5**  Sample "Special Interest" Package *(courtesy: Stouffer Hotel Co.)*

on board, and general admissions tickets all included in the one-cost package and an "Around the World Tour" to see the "seven wonders of the world." Packaging for special interests has no limits and can be applied to help many businesses while meeting customers' very special needs (see Figure 12.5).

## SPECIAL EVENT PACKAGES

Packaging around a special event is another form of package marketing. Each year tens of thousands of people purchase such packages to the Super Bowl, Mardi Gras, college bowl games, major boxing events, world series, and many more special events. The event is the reason to go — the package provides the easiest method to purchase everything in one step.

More creative individuals have developed not only the packages but even the special event to be promoted. These have included transcontinental balloon flights, nationwide bike races, and weekend dinners and festivals honoring people and places.

## SPECIAL DESTINATION/ATTRACTION PACKAGES

There are special places and times that lend themselves to being promoted via a package. These include such places as the Holy Land; the Vatican; Israel; Washing-

**Figure 12.6**    Sample ''Special Destination''/Attraction Package *(courtesy: Regency Cruises Inc.)*

ton, D.C., and capitals in general; theme parks (Disney World, Six Flags, Marriott's Great American); Atlantic City and Las Vegas; the mountains (Catskills); the beach (Myrtle Beach, Virginia Beach, Cape Cod); Alaskan cruises; and so on. Making it possible to purchase the experience offered by the special destination along with the method of travel, services upon arrival, and taking the problems and worries out of the consumers' minds — all make packaging work. Perhaps one of the best examples of a destination attraction that is packaged for the young (school-aged children) as well as for the old (retirees) is Virginia's Colonial Williamsburg Village (see Figure 12.6).

## THEME PACKAGES
Another common reason to develop a package can be the ''theme,'' or literally creating the reason for the package. An example of a successfully created theme package recently was promoted in the New York City area. A number of hotels looking for weekend business in New York City have successfully used variations on the theme of a ''weekend in New York including dinner in Central Park and an evening at the theater.'' The theme requires the packaging to include rooms, theater tickets,

meals, and most even offer the buggy ride in the park or limo to the theater as part of the attraction. Other theme packages have related to art shows, cultural displays at museums, gambling, and even "celebrity weekends," which center around the appearance of a celebrity.

### HOLIDAY PACKAGES

"Winter vacation week of 12/28 to 1/5 in sunny Florida via Delta only $469 air fare, room (double occupancy) included" is a frequent type of holiday package promoted on college campuses in the Northeast. Others include everything from "Easter in the Holy Land" to "St. Patrick's Day in Dublin" to a week in sunny Spain to witness Pamplona's running of the bulls. While the reason to travel is the holiday event itself, the packaging of that event with other hospitality industry products and service for one price is the key to making the promotion sell.

### "TWO FOR ONE" AND OTHER "PRICE" PACKAGES

There are many more types of packages. Another successful concept in packaging is the "give-away," frequently called the "two for one" concept. Here the marketing message focuses on value or price. Two dinners for the price of one is a frequently used food promotion. The "second drink free" is another promotion making use of price. These examples of food and beverage promotions seek to capitalize on the attraction of getting something "free." Travel can be similarly promoted or packaged, such as weekends at 50 % off, a free suite, the spouse goes free, the second week is free, or "two extra days on the Costa del Sol included at no cost," and so on (see Figure 12.7).

## PACKAGING IN PERSPECTIVE

In the 1980s packaging has become a very useful and widely applied marketing weapon. Packaging is more than a promotion concept; it involves every step of the marketing process from pricing to identifying customer needs. As travel and the products or services of the hospitality industry continue to grow, the acceptance and need for simplified purchasing will increase. Packaging directly meets that need. While packaging employs the weapon of advertising, promotion, sales, and other marketing tools, it is a weapon or tool unto itself. As we look further into the 1980s, packaging will in all likelihood occupy its own line or industry segmentation on organization charts. That line, "packaging," will interrelate with all other lines, as well as directly with the consumer.

## KEY WORDS AND CONCEPTS

**Packaging** The combining of more than one hospitality product or service into a single purchase item for a single price.

**Figure 12.7** Sample "Two for One" or "Price" Package (*courtesy: Sugarbush*)

**Wholesaling** The selling of a package to travel agents, airlines, and other travel companies who, in turn, sell it directly to the consumer.

**Retailing** The selling of a travel product or service directly to the consumer.

**Ground Services** Broadly defined as all the services received at a destination (excluding method of travel to the destination), such as rooms, food, beverage, and local tours.

## ASSIGNMENTS

1. Identify two types of packages advertised in the Sunday travel section of your newspaper. For each ad, determine the type of package, if it is being marketed on the basis of price, if a wholesaler is offering it directly to the consumer or if it is being offered through a retail outlet, and who the target market is.

2. Develop a package that includes air and ground services, pricing rationale, identification of the target market, your media approach, and a list of benefits to the participants or suppliers of the package.

3. Analyze a local lodging facility and identify its occupancy pattern. Then develop a packaging concept that fills the voids in the pattern.

4. Create a package based on a theme or event, including the pricing, promotion plan, and identification of the market for your package.

# Applying Key Marketing Methodologies: Understanding Rates

# 13

## PURPOSE

The hospitality industry applies a different rate virtually for every day of the week, every market segment, and every event one can think of — or create. In fact, one of today's most powerful marketing weapons is rate, and terms such as "discount," "special offer," "trial," "preferred" proliferate in marketing and promotions. The purpose of this chapter is to set forth a rate guideline which shows the relationship of various rate types. This will form a base for understanding the role of pricing strategies which are covered in Chapter 14.

## OBJECTIVES

1. Provide a definition of the various rate categories used in the hospitality business today.

2. Show the relationship between rate types.

3. By suggesting prioritizations of rate types, develop a base for maximizing revenue.

4. Demonstrate appropriate rate steps through provision of a competitive rate analysis procedures.

5. Provide a general discussion of rates and rate management.

6. Demonstrate how and why rate management is a key tool of marketing today.

A key to any discussion of rate is a clear and consistent use of terminology. This is especially important as it relates to the consumer whose patience with fine print, restrictions, and the way the game is played is just about exhausted. Many in the industry use rate terminology very loosely, causing confusion and undermining their credibility. Rate definitions should be specific and consistent. We are going to define the key rate terminology used by the hospitality industry first. Later, we will discuss air fares and rental car rates. A caution here is that rate categories and associated terms or conditions are in constant flux even within the framework of the same carriers or rental agency.

# HOTEL RATES

## STANDARD RATES

**Corporate Rate.** As used in today's marketplace, the corporate rate is a "competitive" sell rate to attract frequent travelers. Depending upon the quality of the hotel and location in relationship to its top competition in the marketplace, a hotel's corporate rate should be the same as, or within five dollars of, that of its four major competitors. Obviously, if you have the clearly superior location and product, you can be the rate leader if your hotel is established in the market. If your hotel is new, or not yet established, your corporate rate should be used to bring in trial business — thus, be lower than the competition.

As it plans its rate strategy, a hotel should establish its corporate rate first. A hotel should strive to ensure that the corporate rate that it advertises on airline terminals and in directory listings should be the lowest — but in a competitive range — corporate rate offered. A hotel may, and in all likelihood should, use a range (as with rack rates discussed next) based on room type, location, or other selected criteria.

**Rack Rate.** A hotel's rack rate should be used as a "positioning" rate. Rack rates provide the consumer and intermediary a perception of the quality level of the hotel in relationship to its competition and all other hotels in a given market. Rack rates provide the optimum opportunity to maximize rate *or* to obtain revenue. In general, the broadest range is desirable for rack rates, beginning with your lowest-rated room category and topping out above your nearest competitors to *create the perception of the best hotel in the marketplace as well as allow for revenue maximization* through controlled sale and inventory of the *lowest*-rated rooms. These lowest-rated rooms should be entered in the airline terminals, directories, and in a central reservations system.

**Preferred Rate.** Also known as a preferred corporate rate, this rate is a specific amount charged to a *volume consumer* of rooms. There may be — and should be — many different preferred rates. Preferred rates are *lower than* corporate rates. Usually, the higher the room volume consumption, the lower the preferred rate.

Preferred rates should not be called such. Rather, they should be referred to by the name of the company or organization to which such rates have been provided, such as the IBM rate, the 3-M rate, or the Nestle rate.

**Super Saver.**  The super saver is a rate established which should be lower than corporate and used for *rate resistors* or as a *loss leader* when conditions merit. The super saver can and should be used to fill empty rooms in valley periods or days. Just as do rack rates, super savers help maximize revenue by filling what would otherwise be empty — "zero-revenue" — rooms. This rate also should be used to steal business from competition. The super saver rate can be changed as needed. It can be offered to any market segment and is usually *capacity controlled,* that is, *applied to a limited number of rooms* in the inventory. *It is ultimately the responsibility of the general manager to close off this category daily — or hourly — if necessary.*

**Weekend Rate.**  Weekend rates are those in effect for weekends, meaning Friday/ Saturday/Sunday. These are flat *room rates,* not person rates. Depending upon market and local events, this room category can be closed off for any day or period. For instance, you may wish to close this category on Sundays in a high Sunday-arrival market, which may be the case for football weekends or other events. Weekend rates should be promotionally oriented; that is, they should be set at fixed amounts of $49, $59, $69, $79, or $89 and should lend themselves to being advertised nationally.

**Summer Rate.**  Usually in effect from Memorial Day to Labor Day, summer rates are promoted to attract summer vacationers. These are usually a specific market: families. Summer rates can be either flat room rate or person rates. The rates are flexible and capacity controlled based upon local market conditions. The category can be open or closed at discretion of the hotel. Because it is a promotional rate, the summer rate should be of the $49, $59, $69, $79, $89 type of rate offer.

**Club-level Rate.**  This rate is assigned to rooms located on the club floor(s) or concierge-attended areas. This is a *premium* type rate which should be above regular room rates, that is, $15 to $20 above rack or corporate rates for the same room type. When competing with hotels which also have club or tower floors, your hotel rate should be competitively priced as with — and in line with — the hotel's total positioning strategy.

## OTHER RATES
The following rates, while not uncommon, apply to very specific markets.

*Package Plans* provide rates for a room plus other items, such as food, amenity, or car.

*Contracted* rates apply to rooms contracted for a period of over 30 days; these may be crew rooms, relocation rooms, training rooms (if not preferred or another category).

*Seasonal* rates are premiums added or subtracted based on locational desirability due to climate. These rates are usually in season or peak, shoulder, and off-peak.

*Group* rates are given for volume or length of stay.

*Suite* rates vary as to pricing strategy. At the lower end, be competitive; at the upper end, go for top dollar and positioning as the best hotel.

*Government* rates are based on the market and competition and need for business.

*Military Personnel or retirees* are often given a lower rate. This rate is applied to a limited capacity or number of rooms allocated for these market segments.

## RANGES

Ranges of rates should be used in the following rate categories: corporate, rack, club level, and any other category for which there is not a flat room rate. *Ranges should be broad* to allow for selling-up or selling down within the range. As mentioned earlier with respect to corporate rate, and may be applied in general, a hotel should publish or list the *low end of the range* in directories, airline terminals, or other listings in case capacity does not allow for a full range; i.e., "$99 and up." Ranges may relate to various criteria, such as room types, room locations, and views (see Table 13.1).

**Table 13.1** Hospitality Hotel (Four-Diamond–Rated)

|  | *Standard Room* | *Superior Room* | *Delux Room* |
| --- | --- | --- | --- |
| Rack | $155* | $125 | $145 |
| Club Level | 135 | 145 | 164 |
| Corporate | 95* | 105 | 115 |
| Corporate Club | 115 | 125 | 135 |
| Super Saver | 89† | | |

*Rate published in airline terminals and directories.

†Rate which is managed and controlled by hotel and is used to sell empty rooms in "valley" or down periods.

## *MAXIMIZATION OF REVENUE*

A hotel must control *and* manage its rate categories. It must know when to open or close these categories and must effectively manage or limit the number of rooms in each rate category. The hotel must know how to take full advantage of rate ranges *by selling up or down* in the range.

### OBJECTIVES

The hotel's goal is to maximize revenue through:

Sale of all empty rooms

Sale of all rooms at maximum rates possible

Control and management of type or nature of group business *and* transient business

Management of sales and catering function to ensure maximum revenue

Hourly, daily, weekly, monthly, quarterly, etc., management of the room rates, room reservations, room sales, and catering functions

### STRATEGIES

Now that you have identified your objectives, here are some suggested strategies to achieve your goal.

Adjust your corporate rates plus or minus five dollars to be competitive with top four competitors.

Tell someone — everyone!

Establish rack rates to allow for optimizing revenue — both top-end and low-end rates. Publish the low-end rate.

Shop your competition *daily* via direct calls to the hotel. Call the competitions' "800" numbers or call through the airline terminals.

*Publish* your corporate rate and list it wherever you can especially at airline terminals, in directories, etc.

Establish a super saver rate and appropriate room allocations, timing, etc.

Establish a task force to implement this rate strategy and provide (1) ongoing training, (2) daily management responsibility, (3) checks and balances, and (4) measurement.

Price your product appropriately. This is your single most important management responsibility.

## EXAMPLES OF REVENUE-MAXIMIZATION STRATEGIES

The following examples are based on the grid-positioning concept which was presented in Chapter 6. Your position on the grid, which is a function of both the strength of your market and the position of your product within that market, helps determine what steps you should take to maximize your revenue (see Figure 13.1).

### Strategy 1: Strong Market/Strong Product

Maximize your rate in periods of strong demand (sell up and/or raise rates).

Stay ahead of your competition in servicing accounts.

Use your quality to steal business in valley periods at competitive rates.

Move business to days or periods of lower demand.

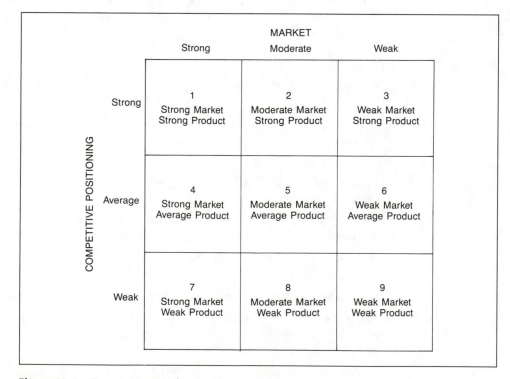

**Figure 13.1**  Competitive/Market Positioning Grid

### Strategy 2: Moderate Market / Strong Product

Go for market share via competitive pricing.

Tie up better (rate) market segments for the future.

Use your product strength to sell up.

Don't price yourself out of the market.

### Strategy 3: Weak Market / Strong Product

Go for repeat business by building loyalty. (Also, "Love thy intermediary.)

Build the base — shrink the empties. Go for *all* the business!

Put a competitor out of business.

Use several different pricing strategies that relate specifically to different market segments.

### Strategy 4: Strong Market / Average Product

Price slightly below competitor to take market share.

Go after the value-oriented market, that is, the segment that wants quality at a fair price.

Be sure your product is sold and perceived as an acceptable alternative: not as the most expensive, but as the best.

Tie up a corporate or preferred "base" — then sell up.

### Strategy 5: Moderate Market / Average Product

Go after market share with lead promotions and rates.

Distinguish your product with a specific market segment, and *own* that segment.

Price your product to the public as number 2, but concentrate heavily on selling corporate and super saver rates (as a better value by stressing price).

Give a reason to come back (have a $50 concept).

### Strategy 6: Weak Market / Average Product

Go after competitors — hit on their weaknesses. Steal the business via pricing.

Go after all market segments with short-term promotions.

Create new market segments or reasons to stay (such as your town day, etc.).

Shrink the product by building the base.

| RATES | Competitor I | Competitor II | Competitor III | Competitor IV | Your Hospitality Hotel |
|---|---|---|---|---|---|
| **800 Tel. No.** | | | | | |
| Rack | $  –$ | $  –$ | $  –$ | $  –$ | $  –$ |
| Corporate | $ | $ | $ | $ | $  –$ –$ |
| Corporate Club | $ | $ | $ | $ | $  –$ –$ |
| Super Saver | $ | $ | $ | $ | $ |
| **Hotel Direct Tel. No.** | | | | | |
| Rack | $  –$ | $  –$ | $  –$ | $  –$ | $  –$ |
| Corporate | $ | $ | $ | $ | $  –$ –$ |
| Corporate Club | $ | $ | $ | $ | $  –$ –$ |
| Super Saver | $ | $ | $ | $ | $ |
| Weekend | $ | $ | $ | $ | $ |

**Questions**
1. Are we competitively priced?
2. What are the publicized rates in airline terminals?
3. Are we positioning our hotel correctly?
4. What actions should be taken immediately?

**Figure 13.2**  Weekly Intelligence Sheet

## RATE ANALYSIS

One of the benefits of knowing more about your competitors' rates is that it enables you to assess your rate strategy and implement new strategies if required. Figure 13.2 is an example of a weekly intelligence sheet. Many hotels chart information about their competitors' rates on a regular basis so that they can effectively develop rate strategies.

## AIR FARES

The principles of rate strategy for air carriers are not terribly different from those for hotels. Whereas hotels deal with occupied rooms, average rates, and rooms revenue, airlines deal with load factors (occupied seats), average revenue per passenger mile, and passenger revenues. Instead of the term "rate," airlines use the words "fare" or "tariff." There is general consistency among airlines in their use of symbols

**Table 13.2**  Competitive Rate Profile

|  | Competitor I | Competitor II | Competitor III | Competitor IV | Hospitality Hotel |
|---|---|---|---|---|---|
| **General** | | | | | |
| Rack | $100–$125 | $105–$135 | $110–$140 | $115–$155 | $100–$165 |
| Corporate | $ 95 | $ 95 | $101 | $103 | *$ 98–$103–$108 |
| Corporate Club | $105 | $115 | $120 | $122 | $118–$123–$128 |
| Super Saver | $ 85 | $ 89 | $ 95 | $ 99 | $ 88 |
| **Corporate*** | | | | | |
| City I | $ 79 | $100 | $120 | $135 | *$ 98–$108–$128 |
| City II | $115 | $118 | $119 | $130 | *$115–$125–$135 |
| City III | $ 86 | $ 95 | $105 | $105 | *$ 95–$105–$115 |
| City IV | $ 89 | $ 98 | $ 99 | N/A | $ 99–$104–$109 |
| **Corporate*** | | | | | |
| City V | $ 92 | $ 91 | $ 81 | N/A | *$ 79–$ 89–$ 99† |
| City VI | $ 79 | $ 86 | N/A | N/A | *$ 85–$ 95–$105† |

*Publicized rate in airline terminals.*

*†Not best product—Here we have better hotels with which to compete.*

and definitions, although frequently the fine-print disclaimers and restrictions vary by carrier. Following is a list of the various fares and related symbols used for classes of airline service.

**A**   First class discounted

**B**   Coach/Economy discounted

**Bn**  Controlled inventory or limited number of seats available — night coach rate (usually after 9, 10, or 11 p.m., depending on carrier)

**C**   Business class: a class of service and related fare between first class and coach aimed at the international business traveler

**Cn**  Night or off-peak (peak travel hours/days) business class

**D**   Business class discounted

**F**   First class service, usually the highest fare

**Fn**  Night/off-peak coach in first class compartment (a lower than usual first class fare which allows seating in first class)

**H**   Coach economy discounted

**J**   Business class premium

| | |
|---|---|
| **K** | Thrift: usually capacity-controlled or offered in off-peak hours; a fare lower than coach |
| **L** | Thrift discounted |
| **M** | Coach economy discounted |
| **P** | First class premium |
| **Q** | Coach economy discounted |
| **Qn** | Night coach economy discounted |
| **R** | Supersonic |
| **S** | Standard class |
| **T** | Coach economy discounted |
| **U** | No reservation services/baggage check limitations |
| **V** | Thrift discounted |
| **Vn** | Night thrift discounted |
| **Y** | Coach economy |
| **Yn** | Night/off-peak coach in other than first class compartment |

## CARRIER STRATEGIES

The plethora of fares just defined suggests the broad range of rate strategies that air carriers use to achieve market share of profitability: from offering all first class to offering all deep-discount services, with virtually every variation in between. Some carriers select a strategy for competitive reasons, others because of their market position or even based on the hour of departure per flight. In essence, the revenue management game for the airlines is not unlike that of hotels or any other business. The bottom line on the revenue side is to maximize revenue per flight, in other words, to get the highest yield (of revenue) out of each seat or each flight. How this yield is achieved — be it by low price/high load factor, or by maximizing first class and coach fares and sacrificing some load factor — is fairly well defined as the selected marketing strategy of the carrier. Also, like hotels, a lot of your strategy is dictated by your labor costs, fleet (size of aircraft or hotel), and route structure (locations). Then, there is the consumer: the consumer who is loyal to a brand or carrier responds to the price and service-level levers based on his or her changing needs. So, when airfare wars break out, the consumer benefits. The winner is usually the carrier with deeper pockets (to absorb more losses). And, the loser is the less financially stable carrier.

## RENTAL CAR RATES

How rental car rates are presented often depends on who is presenting the rates as well as the month of the year. Here is a general overview.

**Weekdays:** Usually applied to Monday through Thursday, this rate generally is a premium rate (except in the case of a weekend destination location for which a weekend rate may be the premium rate).

**Weekends:** This rate is usually in effect for Friday, Saturday, and Sunday. (Many define it 12:00 noon on Thursday through 12:00 noon on Monday.) In most locations a substantially discounted rate is offered.

**Daily:** Usually one of the highest rate categories, this rate is applied if the car is rented for a 12-hour or 24-hour period only. Hourly rates, if offered, are usually at a premium over daily.

**2-Day, 3-Day, 4-Day, 5-Day:** Car rental firms often offer some form of discounted rate based on the number of days (12-hour or 24-hour period) for which a car is rented.

**Weekly:** This rate is even further discounted based on a 5-, 6-, or 7-day weekday rental.

**Monthly:** This discounted rate is applied to long-term rentals.

**Corporate:** This rate is usually a 10 percent, 20 percent or even deeper discount based on a company's levels of use.

**Preferred Corporate:** Car-rental firms may offer even deeper discounts to corporations that are very heavy or frequent users. Discounts of 20 percent, 25 percent, 30 percent, even 38 percent are not uncommon.

**Class of Car:** Another variable in the car rental formula, day of the week, period of time for the rental, etc., is the class of car. The actual rental rate will vary based on the type of auto, generally luxury, standard, compact, or subcompact. A problem with using this criterion is that not all firms' definitions of each car type — "standard," for example — are the same.

**Other Rates:** Holiday specials, seasonal rates (in Florida, for example), and event-related rates (such as for the Super Bowl) can also be developed and offered.

## RENTAL CAR STRATEGIES

Using the variables of rental periods, classes of cars, special rates, and car upgrades the strategies are plentiful. Some firms rent luxury class vehicles at standard class rates or at fixed rates, for example, "Lincolns at $39.95." Others opt for straight price sells — only $19.95/day. Still others may use service as their marketing pitch: "No lines. We'll meet you at baggage claim with your rental car."

Of course, there are the charge-per-mile and free-unlimited-mileage marketing options as well. These strategies depend on competition and other variables such as fuel costs, location history, days used, distance traveled, and other variables. And, again, the location(s) and number of rental points is a strong factor in brand selection. Just as with its hospitality industry partners, airlines and hotels, brand loyalty in the car rental industry is a function of price and service in meeting the challenging and changing consumer needs. Just as occupied seats or occupied rooms are critical to revenue production, rented units per day for car rental firms are likewise critical. Whether the break-even point is achieved through volume, price, or a combination of both factors, the game is the same — rate, rate management, and maximization of revenue.

## CRUISE SHIP RATES

Rate options and strategies are largely dependent upon the actual itineraries and the actual configuration of the specific ship. In general, cruises are priced according to the number of days/nights, for example, "5 days/4 nights." The rate is usually *inclusive*, that is, it includes three meals per day. In addition, the rate will vary based upon a particular ship's room or cabin layout. Generally, the higher level cabins or rooms with outside windows will command maximum rates, whereas rates for the inside cabins on the lower deck will be the least expensive.

## CONCLUSION

A rate is simply the price which is established for the service offered. It is not, in itself, an active item. How rates are managed and mixed moves the term "rate" into the active mode — this management is called *pricing strategy*. We have commented on some of the pricing strategies of carriers, car rental firms and, of course, hotels. In the next chapter we will look even more closely at pricing strategies.

## KEY WORDS AND CONCEPTS

**Corporate Rate** A discounted rate given a company because of its volume usage.

**Disclaimer** Usually a statement in fine print defining conditions of an offer.

**Preferred Rate** A specially discounted rate for a frequent customer — usually based on volume and set lower than corporate rate.

**Restrictions** Limitations and requirements which must be adhered to in order to qualify for the offer; for example, "Tickets must be purchased three days in advance."

**Super Saver** A popular rate terminology for a deeply discounted rate or fare.

## ASSIGNMENTS

1. Using a Weekly Intelligence Sheet, as presented in this chapter, conduct a rate survey of three competitive hotels by filling in the chart and answering the questions.

2. Analyze each hotel (of the three above) through a positioning grid, and determine if their rate strategies are appropriate.

3. Develop a rate strategy for a theoretical hotel which is positioned as the second best in a strong market.

4. Set up defined criteria for how you would price car rentals in your market, including time periods (length of rental), day-of-the-week variables, and classes of cars.

5. Conduct a complete rate survey of a major rental car company in your area.

6. Price an airline ticket between two cities, and identify all fares available and all applicable restrictions.

# Applying Key Marketing Methodologies: Pricing Strategies

# 14

## PURPOSE

The gamut of marketing weaponry extends beyond generating revenue through sales, advertising, public relations, promotions, and packaging. The ultimate generator of revenue and profit is *pricing*. Pricing should maximize your revenue and profit by applying a variety of techniques that capitalize on strong demand periods or periods where discounting may prove advantageous. Pricing is the application of rates in a selective manner to generate sales.

## OBJECTIVE

1. Apply methods and techniques to maximize revenue and profit through pricing.

2. Understand the concept of selling up.

3. Know when discounting price works to maximize revenue.

4. Go beyond the standard traditional concepts of "average rate," "average checks," and "average fares" for evaluating the success of your marketing efforts.

Having deployed your arsenal of marketing weaponry and implementing your marketing plan you now have a base of business for your hospitality industry product or service. The challenge then becomes *how* to maximize revenues and profits, build beyond the base, and squeeze every ounce out of marketing. The keys to achieving this success are a creative mind, a practical perspective, and a willingness to work hard at implementing ideas. Furthermore, inherent in these three keys are a willingness to listen and to discard sacred beliefs or measurements of success traditional to the hospitality industry. Let's now focus on *how*.

## MAXIMIZING PROFITS THROUGH MARKETING

### KEY 1: OFFER A PRICE RANGE

For years Marriott and Hilton have been outstanding performers at offering a price range. They give the consumer a choice of rates from which to select when rooms are discussed. This multirate structure permits the consumer to selectively choose, and the operator to *sell up*. Other chains (for instance, Holiday Inn) have believed that stating a fixed rate for singles and doubles is the strongest promise they could make to the consumer. Let's look at Holiday Inns and determine the impact of selling up by using a price range versus stating the fixed rates. We have made broad assumptions for the purposes of this example which are *not* intended to represent actual financial results. They are used solely to point out the potential advantages in using ranges of rates and selling up.

### CASE EXAMPLE I: HOLIDAY INNS

With over 300,000 rooms, Holiday Inns is the world's largest chain. Assuming the chain's occupancy averaged 70 percent, there would be 210,000 occupied rooms on a nightly basis. Further, assume that in order to achieve a 70 percent annual occupancy, there are a number of days during the year in which occupancy is 100 percent. Let's conservatively assume that selling up can occur in half of the locations and only 50 times (days) during the year. The 210,000 occupied rooms per night thus is reduced to 105,000 occupied rooms per night multiplied by 50 nights that can be sold up due to sell-out situations. Therefore:

$$
\begin{array}{rl}
105,000 & \text{eligible rooms} \\
\times\ 50 & \text{potential sell-up days} \\
\hline
7,750,000 & \text{room nights}
\end{array}
$$

Let's now assume that, rather than stating a fixed single and double rate, Holiday Inns chose to go to price ranges and trained its front-office personnel to sell up in locations or days of high demand. Let's conservatively assume this selling up process resulted in only a $1.50 more in rate on the average room per night. The result: $1.50 x 7,750,000 room nights = $11,625,000 in incremental room revenues from selling up. Holiday Inn must have felt very strongly about making a promise to the consumer.

Offering a price range is a simple technique that maximizes profits through marketing. The technique offers the consumer a choice, while taking advantage of up-cycle demand. There are many methods of offering price ranges; for example, hotels may vary rates based on room amenities, location, view, floor, furnishing, and so forth. The key is to offer the choice and benefit for the customer's selection. Even if your range is narrow ($62–$68), you can still realize the benefits by ensuring the low end of your range ($62 would be equivalent to the fixed rate you normally would request). After all, is there really a downside risk in using ranges when the low end of the range is identical to the fixed published rates and both are equally available and accessible to the consumer?

How to achieve both a firm promise to the consumer and still have the ability to offer a price range can also be shown using Holiday Inns in an example. The next case example provides Holiday Inns' answer to doing both.

*CASE EXAMPLE II: HOLIDAY INNS*

Perhaps because it believed in the value of the promise of charging its stated rate but recognized the need to maximize room revenues, Holiday Inns changed its approach to room rates in the 1980s. The approach was not unlike Hilton's, which offered a selection of rooms and related rates to the customer. Holiday's approach was to do away with the traditional single- and double-room classifications and stated rate. Holiday Inns decided to offer the customer three choices: "special," "standard," and "king leisure." The Inns now have some ability to go after maximizing room revenue through the consumer's selection of desired accommodation. This approach to categorizing the room structure also relates to the different needs and desires of the market segments. The "special" category appeals to the older clientele, retirees, or those on restricted expense allowances; the "standard" appeals to the broader spectrum of the market; and the "king leisure" to the executive travelers, weekenders, escape weekend couples, and those whose physical height requires a larger bed. While most of Holiday Inns' rooms are in the "standard" category, this approach offers the consumer a choice of rooms and the operator the ability to offer a price range.

**KEY 2:** SELLING UP

Making money is seldom easy. It frequently requires hard work, research, and timing. Given these facts, let's examine a second technique called *selling up*. The hard work involved means keeping records, analyzing data, plotting trends, identifying the right times, and doing your homework. Selling up has many applications; it can mean promoting a higher-priced item on the menu or offering higher-priced vacation. The case examples that follow may help you make money by selling up.

*CASE EXAMPLE I: THE WELL-TRAINED WAITER/WAITRESS*

Dimitri owned an upscale restaurant and always managed to show better profit margins and higher check averages than his competitors. His technique for achieving this exceptional performance was called "recognition, recommendation, and results," or the 3 Rs technique. Dimitri trained his service help to *recognize* regular customers, those trying to impress others, and the "nothing's too good for my little gal" man attempting to make an impression. He instructed his personnel to first ask what entrees interested the customer the most. Depending on the response, the waiter or waitress was then to take one of three courses of action.

If the choice of entree was a high-priced and profit item, the course of action was to agree with the customer's selection by saying, "An excellent choice this evening — we have had many compliments on that." If the choice was a mid-priced item, the response was simply, "Usually that is a superb dish; however, tonight I would highly recommend (same as above item)." If resistance or indecision was noted, due to the price of the recommendation, an interjection was then appropriate: "May I also recommend (alternate mid-priced item which had a high profit margin) — it is really outstanding this evening." The third approach was reserved for the really indecisive high flyer who just could not decide. It was called the Dimitri *recommendation*. In this situation the waiter or waitress was instructed to say, "Please take your time to make your selection. I'll be right back." Then Dimitri would appear, introduce himself, welcome his guests, and, of course, provide his personal recommendation for the highest-priced item with the highest profit margin on the menu. Who could resist the owner's recommendation? The *recognition* of the opportunity to sell-up and the *recommendation* technique resulted in the third "R" — *results*.

*CASE EXAMPLE II: THE HOURLY FORECAST*

There are a number of hotels that have mastered the art of selling up by using forecasting. This method requires keeping a detailed history by day of the week, by week of the year, and, on certain key days, by hours of the day. Computers facilitate the process considerably. The history provides a record of the days in which 100 percent occupancy has been attained by the hotels. Based on pre-sold rooms, actual check-ins, and a no-show factor, an hourly forecast is developed. The correlation analysis might read:

MONDAYS, 4 p.m. — If 80 percent occupancy reached from check-ins, guarantees, and reservations, 90 percent to sell-out is likely. No more rooms available at $62 (assume range being used is $62–$72) and only $65 rooms for walk-ins or on preconfirmed check-ins for which no rate stated.

MONDAYS, 5 p.m. — 90 percent occupancy reached. No more $62 or $65 rooms available — only $68 and $72 rooms available.

MONDAYS, 6 p.m. — 95 percent occupancy reached. Only $72 rooms available.

The technique requires knowledge of one's historic performance, knowledge of the market (likelihood of competition being sold out also), communications and clear instructions at the front desk, and, most of all, management judgment.

Methods of selling up are virtually limitless. The technique requires judgment and discretion, for if it is abused or poorly applied, the result can be considerable customer dissatisfaction and loss of business. This brings us to:

### CASE EXAMPLE III: HOW NOT TO SELL UP

Recently a government employee was checking into a large hotel in downtown Chicago. She was given a government employee rate of $56 and assigned to room 733. Her associate unexpectedly had to make the same trip to Chicago and did not have time to make a reservation. He arrived at the same hotel after 6 p.m. (after the 6 p.m. forecast) and requested a room, preferably near his co-worker. He also requested a government rate. The poorly trained front-desk clerk, proud of having the opportunity to sell up, said, "We are virtually sold out. I do not have any government rate rooms left; however, we do have a room on the seventh floor for $68 — room 753." Tired and already late, the man accepted the room. About an hour later he went to meet his associate for dinner and knocked on the door of room 733. He walked in and observed the identical room and asked, "How much did they get for this room?" His associate replied, "The government rate of $56." That's called getting caught at selling up.

### KEY 3: SELLING DOWN

Demand is a variable. When it is at a high point, the opportunity to sell up exists; when it is at a low point, the opportunity to *sell* is even stronger. Understanding that revenue in excess of cost is desirable, even if average rate or profit margins may decline, is the key premise to *selling down*. Knowing periods of weak demand for your product or service and knowing your fixed costs are essential to successfully applying this technique. The *cost-plus theory* simply states that revenue in excess of the cost of the unused product or service (be it an airline seat, hotel room, bus seat, or whatever) is desirable. Let's examine the following case example of how the cost-plus theory can work.

### CASE EXAMPLE IV: COST PLUS THEORY

A 200-room motel owner charted his occupancy pattern and analyzed his costs per room. He discovered that for four months per year his property never exceeded 50 percent occupancy. He further learned his average costs per room were $6 (whether the room was occupied or not). He then calculated the incremental costs as a result of occupancy (maid service, laundry, utilities, etc.) at $4 per room. His total costs were then $10 per room. The motel's single rate was $32 to $38 per night. The owner, using the cost-plus theory, recognized that four months of the year half his rooms were empty and costing him $6 per night. Applying the "cost plus theory," he solicited business for the four-month period with a special program. He offered "new" customers who stayed in his motel three to six nights during the slack period single rooms for $20, six nights to ten nights for $18 and ten nights or more for $15. The results were dramatic — occupancy went up to 68 percent (an 18 percent increase for the four-month period). Furthermore, when the program ended he was able to retain more than 40 percent of the newcomers as regular repeat guests at the standard rates. His competitors' perceptions were, "He must have a very low average rate" or "He's in trouble." In reality, he was not only covering his costs and earning excess revenues, he was also converting trial business into repeat business.

## KEY 4: REVENUE AND PROFIT PER UNIT

Over-emphasis on average checks, rate, or percentages can become counterproductive. Unless your product or service is in constant strong demand and in a strong market area, focusing on revenue and profit per unit is a technique that can be of help to you. Reflecting on the previous case example, think about the motel owner's competitors who turned away the low-rate rooms business because it diluted the average rate. What actually occurred was that they lost an opportunity to generate revenue. The revenue and profit per unit technique seeks to maximize total revenues and total profits per unit. In the case of a lodging facility, the unit may be available or occupied rooms. In the case of a food facility, the unit may be seats. Focusing on revenue and profit per unit is critical where the unused unit (room, airline seat, bus seat, and so on) is a perishable item. This means that once the night is gone, the plane has left, or the bus has pulled out, the fixed costs per unit remain, but the opportunity to generate per-unit revenue is gone. Zero revenue and less overall profit are the end results.

## KEY 5: INFLATION RATE PLUS FACTOR

For many years a large national chain that relied on royalty revenue from room sales was concerned about its franchisees' aggressiveness in raising rates. Many of the franchisees were absentee owners, some were looking for tax write-offs, and others lacked business sense. The chain published a directory twice a year and solicited new rates prior to printing the new directory. An analysis of the return cards from the franchisees revealed that a large group consistently raised their rates 5 percent every six months. Another smaller group only raised their rates for the January directory and indicated "no change" for the June directory. When the inflation rate was very low, the concern was not very intense; however, in one 12-month period the inflation rate jumped over 12 percent and the ramifications started to become apparent. The buying power of the royalty revenue and fees based on rooms revenue began to shrink dramatically. The costs for media, personnel, supplies, and so on, was increasing at double the rate of the inflow of incremental royalty fees. The company realized it needed to take action.

Using the *inflation-plus factor,* it began an intense program to educate its franchisees that rates should increase in proportion to the inflation factor for costs associated with their facilities. The *plus* concept suggested that increasing rates beyond the inflation cost factor (where demand allowed) would enhance the profit margin. This step worked well, but timing was another factor. Rate changes were required 90 days in advance of publication, and these rates were in effect for six months. Even if the franchisee were conscientious and raised his or her rates, by the time the directory was published (based on the 12 percent inflation factor), 3 percent was lost to inflation. Also, by the time the directory rates were replaced, an additional 6 percent would have been lost to inflation. To help alleviate this problem the chain's management invested in an alternate printing approach and directory format which cut the 90-day lead time to 30 days. In addition, the chain went from publishing two directories per year to four. Yes, publications costs were up, but were more than justified by the increase in the incremental royalty revenues being received.

**KEY 6:** INTUITIVE JUDGMENT AND FLEXIBLE BREAK-EVEN ANALYSIS
Establishing the most effective price to charge for your product or service is based on many factors. The local market and competition will, in all likelihood, prove to be dominant factors in influencing a pricing decision. However, the local market conditions and your need to break even need not overly restrict your judgment or creativity in establishing a pricing strategy. Frequently, the most important factors in selecting the optimum rate or pricing strategy will come from your own intuitive judgment about what will work best for the product or service in view of the local market and competition.

Once the market has been analyzed and the competition profiled, a break-even analysis is another tool to assist in selecting the optimum pricing strategy. A break-even analysis is simply a look at the relationship between total sales and total expenses for an establishment, be it a lodging facility, airplane, or restaurant. Often depicted on a simple graphic display, the analysis demonstrates the effects of changing the levels of total sales in terms of dollars or volumes. The vertical scale shows the quantitative measurement, which can be expressed as rate or price, in dollars. The horizontal axis represents volume in units, which can be expressed as occupancy, occupied seats, and so on. Total costs at the various levels of volume (or sales) are plotted with a straight line. Total revenue expected as total sales is also entered as a straight line. The point at which these lines cross represents the *break-even point,* the point at which sales are adequate to cover costs. To the left of this break-even point are losses; to the right, profits. In the sample shown in Figure 14.1 the break-even point can be stated either in dollar volume ($24,000) or in unit volume (2,400 units).

Break-even charts are useful tools, although they are not always precise. There are also two mathematical equations that can be used to reach the break-even points for sales or units.

The break-even point in units is determined by first subtracting the variable cost per unit from the selling price per unit. The result is then divided into the total fixed costs.

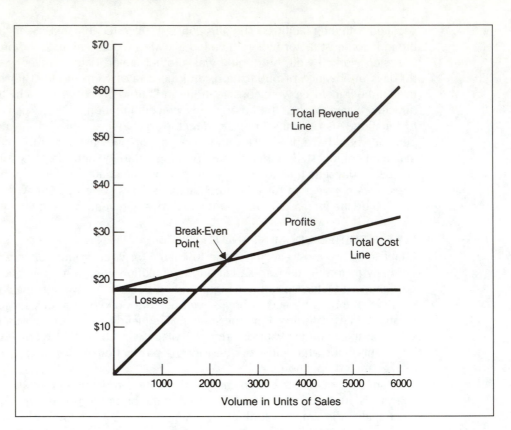

**Figure 14.1** Sample Break-even Chart (dollars in thousands)

$$\text{Break-even point in units} = \frac{\text{Total fixed costs}}{\text{Selling price per unit} - \text{variable cost per unit}}$$

To determine the break-even point in sales, divide the break-even point in units by the selling price.

$$\text{Break-even point in sales} = \frac{\text{Break-even point in units}}{\text{Selling price}}$$

Using the tools of the basic break-even chart and the sales and unit equations, you can use the break-even concept to establish profit objectives and the required sales revenue to meet these objectives. You arrive at this concept of the flexible break-even analysis by following these steps.

**STEP 1: Develop a Break-even Chart.**   Set up a chart with "$" on the vertical axis and "Occupancy" as a percentage on the horizontal axis. Plot total costs and fixed costs (as shown in Figure 14.2).

**STEP 2: Label the Chart.**   Select the point which corresponds to your current rate on the vertical axis and your current occupancy in percent on the horizontal axis. Label these as CR and CO. (In the example in Figure 14.3 we have assumed $50 and 70 percent.)

**STEP 3: Apply Intuitive Judgment.**   Using your knowledge of the local market and competition, make as many intuitive judgments as appropriate. Our example uses four intuitive judgments. We will start with the figures given in the example in Step 2, current rate of $50 and current occupancy at 70 percent.

Intuitive judgment 1: Assume a new rate is selected at $60, or an increase of $10 (labeled $NR_1$). What do you think will happen to your occupancy? Let's assume it will drop 11 percent (label new occupancy $NO_1$). (See Figure 14.4.)

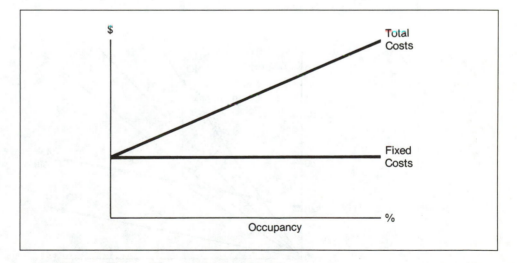

**Figure 14.2**   Break-even Chart Label Identification

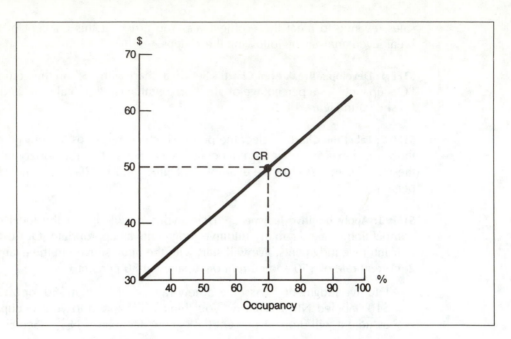

**Figure 14.3** Break-even Chart Judgment Estimates Applied for Occupancy

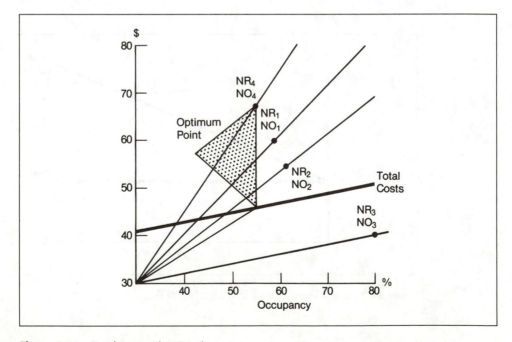

**Figure 14.4** Break-even Plot Graph

Intuitive judgment 2: Assume a rate increase of $5 is selected (labeled $NR_2$). What will happen to occupancy? Let's assume it will drop 7 percent (labeled $NO_2$).

Intuitive judgment 3: Assume you drop your rate $10 from $50 to $40 (labeled $NR_3$), what will happen to occupancy? Let's assume it will increase 80 percent (labeled $NO_3$).

Intuitive judgment 4: Assume you raise your rate $15 and occupancy declines 15 percent (labeled $NR_4$ and $NO_4$).

**STEP 4: Draw Projection Lines.**   Next, draw a straight line from the intersection of the axis to the projected new rates $NR_1$, $NR_2$, $NR_3$, and so on.

**STEP 5: Superimpose Total Costs Line.**   Now superimpose the total costs line from your break-even analysis.

**STEP 6: Determine the Optimum.**   Identify the farthest points in NR and NO from the total costs line. This should represent the optimum pricing line for the facility based on intuitive judgment. In this case, it is line $NR_4$ and $NO_4$, which represents the point farthest from the total costs line.

Let's look at the worksheet shown in Figure 14.5 to determine if this flexible break-even analysis employing intuitive judgment worked. For the purposes of our example we have filled in the numbers from our four assumptions. A word of caution is appropriate with respect to employing Key 6, the flexible break-even analysis and intuitive judgment. The technique assumes a thorough knowledge of competition and the marketplace. In addition, should you select lower occupancy and higher rates as the alternate course of action, you should also undertake additional analysis on the impact of this action on incremental revenue and profit centers. For example, while the profit figures from the calculations may increase, you must look at the "total picture." What is the impact on sales in the areas of food, beverages, gift shop purchases, and so forth? The flexible break-even analysis represents a key marketing weapon, which, like all of the pricing techniques suggested in this section, requires judgment prior to use.

**KEY 7:** RATE PYRAMIDING

This technique is a hybrid of key 1, offering a price range, and key 2, selling up. Rate pyramiding is segmenting or identifying the product or service by different characteristics or descriptions. The distinctions may be like those in the earlier Holiday Inns example in which rooms are categorized as "king leisure," "standard," and "special," or as simple as "mountain view" or "ocean view." For each categorization a rate or range of rates is specified. At the point of inquiry, the customer is offered a choice from the "pyramid." (See Figure 14.6.)

The technique now goes from "offering a price range" to "selling up," as follows:

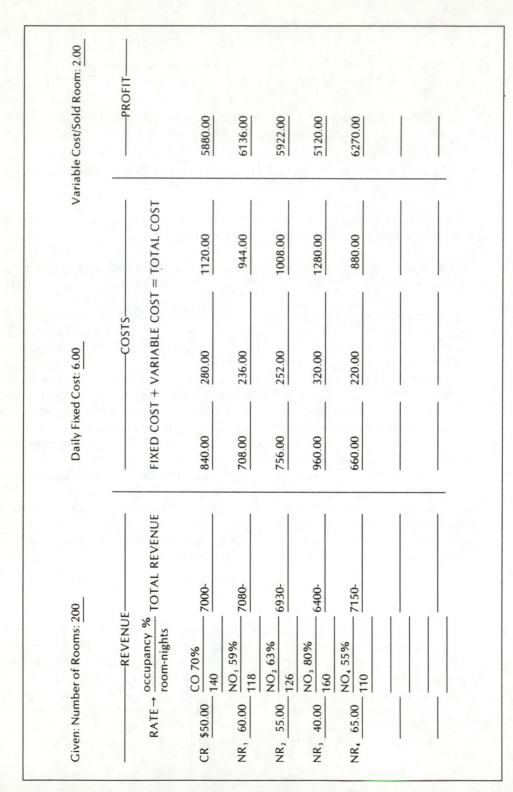

Given: Number of Rooms: 200    Daily Fixed Cost: 6.00    Variable Cost/Sold Room: 2.00

|  | ─────REVENUE───── |  | ─────COSTS───── |  |  | ──PROFIT── |
|---|---|---|---|---|---|---|
| RATE→ | occupancy % | TOTAL REVENUE | FIXED COST + | VARIABLE COST = | TOTAL COST |  |
|  | room-nights |  |  |  |  |  |
| CR  $50.00 | CO 70% | 7000- | 840.00 | 280.00 | 1120.00 | 5880.00 |
|  | 140 |  |  |  |  |  |
| NR₁  60.00 | NO₁ 59% | 7080- | 708.00 | 236.00 | 944.00 | 6136.00 |
|  | 118 |  |  |  |  |  |
| NR₂  55.00 | NO₂ 63% | 6930- | 756.00 | 252.00 | 1008.00 | 5922.00 |
|  | 126 |  |  |  |  |  |
| NR₃  40.00 | NO₃ 80% | 6400- | 960.00 | 320.00 | 1280.00 | 5120.00 |
|  | 160 |  |  |  |  |  |
| NR₄  65.00 | NO₄ 55% | 7150- | 660.00 | 220.00 | 880.00 | 6270.00 |
|  | 110 |  |  |  |  |  |

**Figure 14.5**  Flexible Break-even Rate-setting Worksheet

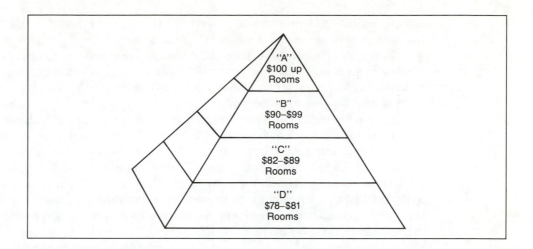

**Figure 14.6**  Rate Pyramid

"Welcome to the Clifton, Mr. Jones."

"What are your rates?"

"Our rates range from $78 for an economy room, from $82 for a standard room, from $90 for a deluxe, and $100 up for a suite."

"I'd like an economy room, please."

"Mr. Jones, we only have an $80 economy room available; however, I do have a very nice $82 standard room that I think you would like better."

If Mr. Jones opts for the $82 standard, he has been "pyramided" up $4 from the $78 economy room he wanted. If he opts for the $80 economy room he has been sold up $2. There are a good number of people who do not ask for an economy room simply because they do not want the cheapest, nor do they want the most expensive — this is human nature. By offering a pyramid rate structure you capitalize on this premise and can directly impact your revenue potential.

**KEY 8:** SEGMENTED ANALYSIS

Another way to view pricing or generating revenue is by the type of business. The mix or types of guests in a facility are not all the same in terms of their needs and desires and level of expenditures. Simply stated, kids may stay free, eat hot dogs, or not eat with you at all. On the other hand, a man attending a group meeting eats a banquet meal, drinks in your bar, and buys a gift for his children and spouse in your gift shop. Given a choice of to whom you should sell your room, the decision becomes clearer. Marriott has been a leader in food and beverage sales in its hotels. While it is true that Marriott creates restaurant concepts that appeal to the local market, it is also true that Marriott's mix of business is heavily oriented toward groups, executives, and corporate meetings. The result of this orientation is that it produces higher revenues throughout the properties.

You do not have to be as sophisticated as Marriott to analyze your market segments and go after the revenue producers. For example, let's take the case of a local restaurant called Nick's. The restaurant appeals to a broad spectrum of consumers ranging from families to office workers, to couples dining out. Nick's faced a choice — a local office supply company wanted the banquet room for Friday evening for 15 people for a sales achievement award dinner. At the same time, the River City Boys Baseball Champions requested the room for 23 boys and two adult coaches for a dinner. Nick's selected the office supply company with only 15 people instead of the baseball champions with the party of 25. The restaurant's analysis revealed that while both groups selected the same item (cost) from the banquet menu, the office supply group usually drank well into the night, which is more than enough to offset the reduced food revenue from 10 less people. The message is simple: Whether you're Marriott or Nick's, go after the high-volume/high-profit producers.

Pricing is a key marketing weapon that can maximize revenue and profit potential for your hospitality industry product or service offering. The techniques suggested in this chapter offer you a selection of weapons with which to better focus and maximize your marketing effort.

## KEY WORDS AND CONCEPTS

**Selling up** The concept of capitalizing on periods of high demand by charging a higher price, or *premium,* for your product or service offering.

**Cost-plus Theory** In periods of low demand, recognizing the need to price or sell the product or service offering by discounting the price (beyond fixed and variable cost levels) to stimulate sales.

**Inflation Rate–plus Concept** A method for increasing rates or prices that is based on the premise that increases in rates should be at the inflation rate plus a percent target.

**Rate Pyramiding** The concept of offering a variety of rates and/or ranges from which the consumer may select; also offers the opportunity to sell up.

## ASSIGNMENTS

1. Using the cost-plus theory, develop a program for a local establishment, demonstrating the positive effect of selling down. (Be sure to include the impact on average rate.)

2. Develop an analysis of revenue and profit per unit for a local establishment on a per-occupied room and a per-available room basis.

3. Analyze the directories and published rates of three chains or hotels and deter-

mine if a range is used, if rate pyramiding is applicable, and which appears to offer the greatest opportunity for selling up.

4. Work with a local establishment to identify the inflation factor and price increase history with the objective of applying the inflation rate–plus concept.

5. Select a local establishment and develop a flexible break-even analysis, and identify the optimum rate/occupancy mix for the facility.

6. Select an establishment that does not offer a rate pyramid, and develop a three- or four-tiered rate pyramid and related front-desk marketing program to sell up.

7. Analyze the mix of business in a local property or eating establishment, and determine the impact on revenues and profits of changing the mix. (A day of the week, a week, or an annual period may be selected.)

# The Total Corporate/ Multi-unit Marketing Plan 15

## PURPOSE

Up to this point we have presented what might be viewed as two phases of an overall marketing plan: the research phase and the application phase. In the first chapters of the book we have emphasized the importance of knowing your consumer from A to Z, and in subsequent chapters we discussed the direct application of the plethora of marketing tools to reach and sell to that consumer. The purpose of this chapter is to provide you with an outline for your marketing plan that ties it all together. We organized the book in this manner because we believe you cannot develop a marketing plan without the knowledge of your consumer and knowledge of each of the marketing weapons to sell that consumer.

Although this chapter addresses the lodging sector specifically, the issues and strategies can be applied, with some modification, to all sectors of the hospitality industry.

## OBJECTIVES

1. Provide a framework for a complete marketing planning process resulting in an efficient and factually based set of integrated marketing strategies.

2. Define and identify your objectives in priority order to maximize the return on your market dollar investment.

3. Focus on your problem areas and opportunities by methodically allocating your marketing resources to improve acceptance of your product or service.

4. Identify where and how much you should allocate to resolve your problem areas and how you should apply that allocation for measurable results.

Marketing tools can be very expensive, and with few exceptions there are never sufficient financial resources to support all the programs the marketer desires. If you approach your marketing plan in the traditional fashion, you sit down with last year's plan and apply what additional dollars you have, or you cut out certain programs as a result of budgetary constraints. If this is your approach, you are in trouble. You have completely ignored the basic premise of marketing — researching and knowing your consumer. You may say, "I've known my consumer for over 20 years." That's why you feel comfortable "ball-parking" the marketing budget allocations. We all need to know more about that — we need to know our consumer today and in which direction his or her needs are moving tomorrow. We must know the consumer's habits, preferences, and perceptions of our product or service as well as that of our competition. We must know our problem areas, be they markets, cities, specific properties, people, or whatever. Finally, we must know our strengths and related opportunities. Before committing one marketing dollar we must have exhaustive knowledge of all these areas. For planning purposes, one way to view this whole process is to begin with the *zero-based budgeting* concept.

## ZERO-BASED BUDGETING

At the outset, you must recognize that we are adapting and applying a broad concept to help us prioritize where we want to spend our limited resources. The *zero-based budgeting* concept states: no expenditure is justified just because it was made last year. Every expense is re-analyzed and justified each year on the basis that it will yield more favorable results than spending the same amount in another way.

One note of caution needs to be provided at this early juncture. Very enthusiastic and often naive proponents of the concept forget there is frequently a core, in other words, a vital element that must be maintained at a certain minimum level. For example, a product or service organization that relies on a sales force or reservation system should use extreme caution in applying this concept. In fact, one

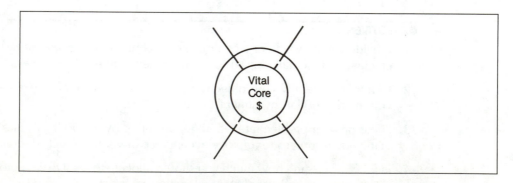

**Figure 15.1** Zero-based Budgeting Concept

approach is to subdivide the budget into a "vital core" and "all other" categories, and only apply the concept to the "all other" category. For some, this violates the principle of zero-based budgeting, while to others it is common sense. You are the best judge of your firm and the best qualified to determine which approach is most applicable. To apply both is often useful in helping focus on what areas other than the vital "core" may be more efficient or currently under-allocated. In essence, the pie is yours. How you slice it does make a difference (Figure 15.1).

## MARKETING PLAN DEFINITIONS

At this point we are intentionally deviating from format to suggest that you recap some key definitions; we want to ensure thorough comprehension before going into the structure of the marketing plan. These key definitions are found at the end of this chapter. Review them before reading any further.

## MARKETING PLAN STRUCTURE

The first major component of the complete marketing plan can be stated simply as "Research and Information Required." This component subdivides into four major items as outlined.

**MARKETING PLAN STRUCTURE**
RESEARCH AND INFORMATION REQUIRED

a. Market segmentation, need identification, and measurement of customer perceptions
b. Facts about competition
c. External facts
d. Internal facts

### MARKET SEGMENTATION, NEED IDENTIFICATION, AND MEASUREMENT OF CUSTOMER PERCEPTIONS

You may already know a great deal about your market and its segments; however, if you want to update your knowledge and maximize your marketing expenditures, there are nine basic areas you must research.

1. Identify the major geographic markets yielding the greatest number of travelers (both business and pleasure) to cities in which your facilities or services are located.

2. Using the major geographic markets (from step 1) for research sampling, determine the proper segmentation of the total market. This segmentation is to be done according to "need" segments, which was detailed in Chapters 2 and 3.

A brief listing of the segmentation process as applied to the lodging industry follows:

### End Users

Individual attending a group meeting or convention

Individual business person traveling on a relatively unrestricted expense account

Individual business person or sales representative traveling on a restricted expense account

Individual pleasure traveler without children

The family traveling for pleasure

The couple or family interested only in the essentials of lodging

The couple or family seeking to avoid the service, tipping, high costs, semi-rigidity, etc., of hotels, motels, and resorts

Banquet and local restaurant customer

### Intermediaries

The meeting planner

The travel agent

Traffic departments of major corporations

Secretaries

VIP clubs

Wholesalers

Airlines

Car rental companies

Reservations services

3. During the segmentation process, *roughly* determine the demographic characteristics of each of the segments. Research techniques are available to more accurately determine the demographics, but such attention to detail will probably add to the cost of the research. Estimate the demographics, to the degree that you are able, to determine the approximate size and trends of the segment. Then select appropriate media to promote your product or service to this segment. This approximate demographic definition should be adequate.

4. Quantify roughly the trends in the size of each of the demographic segments you want to reach. Fairly accurate quantification of these trends is possible through the use of a national probability sample. With the results of this sam-

pling technique, added to your knowledge of the market through examination of in-house demographic data, you can extrapolate meaningful trends. These will probably be sufficient for your initial efforts in marketing planning.

5. At this point you should make some major decisions regarding which segments you want to pursue and those you do not want to pursue. In making these decisions, you must consider such facts as:

Suitability of your own *existing* facilities to serve the needs of these segments

The trends in the size of the particular segment — is it growing or declining?

The profitability of the segment

For the most part, such decisions will not point your marketing approach in any new directions. However, for certain segments peripheral to your current business mix, these decisions will be very important, and you will need more information. You must have a better determination of the suitability of your product to the defined needs of these segments. Here, the marketing decision of whether to pursue the segment should be deferred until step 7.

6. Identify in greater detail the specific needs of each of the segments you hope to reach. Basically, you should be interested in identifying what factors are essential to people in each segment; you should get some feel for which items are most — and least — important. Trained interviewers can glean this information from *focus groups* — small representative groups of individuals from each segment you wish to pursue.

7. Analyze how well your existing product meets the needs of each segment. Determine where you fall short in providing the product or service required by each segment. Determine items in your own existing facilities that can be adapted to meet the needs of each segment. It is important to *objectively* determine how well your facilities meet the needs of the segments. Customers' views of your facilities and services often differ from yours. Some answers as to how well you satisfy customers' specific needs will have to come from further measurement of their attitudes toward you and your competition. This will be determined through measurement of customer perceptions in step 9. At this point, it is possible that additional segments will be eliminated from your potential market. Such will be the case if you simply do not provide facilities basically in concert with needs of the segments. (Note: It is possible that even though you may not fulfill the exact needs of the segment, you may still do so better than any competitor. This will be determined in step 9. If such is the case, you still may want to pursue that segment.)

8. Identify all major companies that serve your total market.

9. Measure customers' perceptions of both your products and those of all competitors serving the lodging market. This should be done in several steps:

With focus group interviews in each market segment, determine which particular lodging competitors the segment prefers. Determine what factors about each competitor are preferred by customers in each segment. Also determine the image (perception) of these competitors. You should be basically interested in determining which competitors relate best to each segment and why.

With focus group interviews in each market segment, determine the perceptions of each of the other lodging competitors. Determine negative as well as positive factors about all the other competitors (as perceived by the segment).

Again, with the same focus groups, determine how each competitor is perceived in relation to each item that was found to be most important to each segment (determined in step 6).

In all of these interviews, be sure your company is considered equally with other competitors. You want an objective measurement of how the different market segments view each of their alternatives.

Throughout all the research in step 9, the perceptions of each lodging competitor will be the result of the quality of the lodging facilities and how they are operated, and also of advertising and promotion schemes. Likewise, the solutions to making any changes in your image will lie equally in operations and facilities and in marketing.

The information obtained in this research will not be entirely new to you. However, information on how we relate to competition will probably be more objective than you have obtained before and, therefore, more useful to you. What you are really searching for are the refinements. For example: Where do we have a real advantage over competition? What are our weak spots? What are the weak spots of our competitors? Into which new segments can we expand our market? Which segments (if any) absolutely don't want our products?

With the preceding information you are able to more accurately position your company or product in the marketplace. We are almost ready to begin developing longer term objectives and marketing strategies, but we must first gather a few more facts about competition, ourselves, and industry trends.

In summary, we have now determined:

The market's segments as classified by needs plus very rough demographics.

The size of the market segment and its growth trends — which segments are growing and which are declining.

The specific needs of each segment and the relative importance of these needs.

An objective measurement of how well your firm and product or service is perceived to fulfill these needs in relation to competition.

An identification of which lodging companies best relate to each segment — and why.

## FACTS ABOUT COMPETITION

On occasion you may have a tendency to dismiss the effects of competition on your business. The philosophy of capitalizing on your strengths has some admirable traits. However, with the attitude that you don't need to worry about the competition, you may be overlooking several aspects relevant to marketing planning. Focusing solely on your present strengths is also somewhat naive in situations involving increasing competition, especially in a given market segment.

The philosophy assumes you are all things to all people (all market segments), when, in fact, your product may vary in quality and type to the extent you have confused some market segments. While you view your business as growing with additional or new facilities or upgraded older facilities, the guest has little or no appreciation of these factors. He or she sees you as a bed, a courteous (or discourteous) employee, a smoothly handled (or fouled-up) reservation, and so on. It is most important to know how you stack up against your competitors in these areas.

Although you regard all the things you do as important, the consumer does not always agree with you. He or she may have different priorities than you. Furthermore, consumers in different segments have priorities. Price, service level, and an overall good experience (lodging, food and beverage, and service) are extremely important.

The information you need to gather includes market share data, competitive marketing strategies and practices, and occupancy detail by city.

**Market Share Data.**   This information is very important to providing an overview of how you are generally faring over the long range in relation to your major competitors. Many times there is a problem in the industry in that good figures on the size of the total market are unavailable.

You can obtain a fairly useful measurement by comparing your own figures against the total of the group(s) of your major competitors. This can be accomplished on a local, regional, and national level.

**Competitive Marketing Strategies and Practices.**   It will be helpful in formulating your own marketing strategies to have a better appreciation of your competitors' marketing programs. This awareness should be developed methodically and be based on their current marketing program. The most effective way to get this information is to clip all advertising from magazines and newspapers for a period of several months. A clipping service can do this for you, or perhaps your advertising agency may be of help.

It would also be desirable to get a fix on competitors' activities in other marketing media and methods, including:

Radio and TV

Outdoor and airport advertising

Direct mail

Direct solicitation

Travel agent solicitation

Publicity

Sales promotion

This information will be more difficult to obtain, but there may be ways to learn more about these areas.

In this area, it is *not* important that the information be precise or detailed. You are only interested in:

1. What segments are your competitors pursuing?

2. What are their strategies in terms of image-building?

3. What media or marketing methods are they using?

4. How successful do their marketing programs seem to be?

After gathering this information over a period of time, you will be able to detect shifts in competitive marketing strategies of importance to you.

In your initial efforts at marketing planning, clipping the ads from magazines and newspapers will probably give you enough of a feel in this area.

**Occupancy Detail by City.** In some cases this may be difficult to obtain, but you should apply the data you are already accumulating to a comparison of your own occupancy and its trends with those of each competitive hotel or motel in each major metro area. This occupancy data should include all major competition, including hotels and motels that meet recreational and family travel needs as well as business-oriented hotels.

## EXTERNAL FACTS

External data on market and industry trends and travel patterns will be useful when you are ready to develop your own strategies.

**Trends in the Overall Travel and Lodging Market.** You should include an overview of the major trends, mainly an indication of the growth in pleasure travel versus business travel and any better information you can obtain regarding growth trends of the other market segments. This information will be of a very general nature, but the broad overview will be helpful in determining strategy.

**Feeder City Data.** This information will have obvious benefit when it comes to the planning of advertising. Much of this data may already be available and be used in determining placement of advertising. It must be included here in developing the total marketing program.

It is important to consider that there *may* be differences in feeder city data for pleasure and for business travel. You must consider both markets.

The scope of this category is very broad and may sound overly ambitious. Some information probably cannot be determined. However, in certain areas it may prove beneficial to gather facts regarding (1) when certain types of group customers historically have met, and (2) when certain industries put their sales people on the road, and other similar information which may help determine specific strategies designed to plug certain holes in your sales patterns.

## INTERNAL FACTS

**Marketing Expenditures.**   You should probably look at your marketing costs in a more objective framework (what they really are) to detect any trends. To determine the real situation, you should define marketing costs as "that amount which is necessary to procure the sale." Using this definition, you must include all the following expenses and reductions to income:

1. Sales people and administrative expenses

2. Advertising expenditures

3. Public relations expenditures

4. Travel relations expenditures

5. Coupon discounts

6. Reservation systems

7. Credit card

8. Others

This definition may not conform to a uniform system of accounts, but it will give you a truer picture of what is really happening.

Using this overview and the trend analysis, you should be able to determine more objectively the proper allocation of funds among these categories to carry out the marketing strategies you develop.

**Trends in Your Mix of Business.**   To get an adequate feel for the internal situation, get a measure of trends in rooms sales by the following segments:

1. Family and pleasure

2. Commercial (sales people, trade, etc.)

3. Executives

4. Groups (corporate and association)

This information — for a single hotel, on a geographical area basis, or chain-wide — will give you continual knowledge of what is really happening when sales are going up or down. You are interested in knowing how effective your efforts are in building business in a particular segment. When you have a sales problem, you must know in what segment the problem lies so that you may take more speedy and focused corrective action.

In short, this is your monitoring system — the indicator of what is happening and how well you are going in your marketing planning and execution.

## OTHER HOSPITALITY INDUSTRY SECTOR APPLICATIONS

The marketing planning process outlined in this chapter for lodging can be directly applied, with some tailoring, to other hospitality industry sectors. The *four major* items under research and information required apply to restaurant chains, airlines, car rental firms, cruise companies, and any other major entity serving the away-from-home market. The steps and questions listed within each research phase are, to some extent, applicable to your market and product or service. How you apply these, answer the questions, and analyze the data is up to you. The better your effort, the better your marketing and competitive edge.

## *MARKETING PLAN*

Now that we have examined the first part of the total marketing plan structure, asked the right questions, and obtained factual answers, let's get to the actual *marketing plan*. The following outline graphically displays the next phase of the total marketing plan.

### MARKETING PLAN STRUCTURE
MARKETING PLAN

a. Analysis of research and information
b. Objectives
c. Marketing program
d. Marketing appropriations (the marketing budget)
e. Sales goals
f. Action programs
g. Communication of assigned responsibilities
h. Monitoring of action programs

The marketing plan is really the document that analyzes what you have learned about your business, and translates it into action programs. By combining all this information into one document, you force yourself to see how (and whether) everything you are doing actually fits together, whether it is logical and sound, and whether, in total, it is possible to accomplish with the manpower and money available. It also clearly establishes guidelines for daily use so that day-to-day matters are handled in a manner consistent with your longer range objectives.

## ANALYSIS OF RESEARCH AND INFORMATION

Answers to the following questions will come from the market segmentation, need identification, and customer perceptions research discussed earlier. These questions will clearly spell out specific steps to include in the marketing program.

### Customer Needs, Preferences, and Perceptions

1. Which market segments relate best to your product or service?

2. In which areas of need is your product or service perceived by its current market segments to be strong? In which areas is it weak?

3. In which areas of need of each market segment do your strengths (as perceived by the segment) correspond to the first priority needs of the segment?

4. In each weak area of need are there operational weaknesses that contribute to the perceived weakness, or is it purely an image or awareness problem?

5. In each market segment with which you presently best identify, who is your major competition and what are their major strengths and weaknesses (as perceived by the segment)?

6. Are your main markets presently within the segments that identify best with your product or service, and are there any areas of need wherein competition is perceived as doing a superior job?

7. Which market segments relate least to your product or service? Does this lack of relating stem from your own past marketing programs whose thrust has been in other directions, or does it stem from an inaccurate or inadequate awareness of the product or service itself?

8. In each market segment wherein an opportunity is offered for you to broaden your market, define your major competition and related major strengths and weaknesses (as perceived by the segment).

### You Versus Competitive Trends

1. How have you fared against competitive lodging chains in recent years?

2. What are the major directions of your major competition?

3. What are the major competitive threats facing you now or in the near future?

### Immediate Problems

What are the immediate problems that *must* be corrected this year? The following list suggests examples of problems that must be addressed immediately.

Specific hotel with sales problems

Declining volumes of business in particular market segments

Quality and service problems

Pricing problems

New competitive lodging facilities that are expected to have an adverse effect upon a particular market or property

Existing marketing strategies that are unsuccessful

### Longer Range Major Problems

What are the major marketing problems you face that must be solved if you are to achieve greater success over the next five years?

Change of image required

Declining volumes of business in particular market segments being experienced industry-wide

Increasing successes of a particular competitor (in hotel facility design, in quality and service, in marketing, in overall results, or in combinations of these items)

Changes in preferences and needs of a particular market segment

Pricing

Adverse trends or yields in marketing expenditures

### Opportunities and Alternatives

1. What are the major competitive weaknesses that could be exploited more fully by your firm?

2. What needs have been identified in your present market segments that no one is really doing a very good job of satisfying? Is it possible to provide a service or product that will satisfy this need?

3. What market segments peripheral to your current marketing thrust offer opportunities for you to broaden your market?

## OBJECTIVES

What are the overall objectives of your marketing program? These objectives should be determined on the basis of your analysis of research and information in the prior section. Your setting of objectives should correspond to the areas listed in that section, as follows:

Marketing objectives resulting from the identification of customer preferences and the desire to change customers' perceptions of your product or service

Changes in marketing direction desired after comparing your present markets with shifts in the total market

Defensive or offensive marketing moves dictated by competitive successes and new competitive directions

Objectives of solving immediate problems

Objectives of solving major longer range problems

Objectives of taking advantage of opportunities open to you

In order to make the marketing program as effective as possible, you should restrict the number of marketing objectives to the major items of the highest relative priority. The whole purpose of the marketing planning process is to separate the "wheat from the chaff" and to identify those items that will yield the greatest results. Attempting to identify everything that must be done will result in more work and greater expenditures than will ever be possible; the result will be frustration for all and minimal results. By separating priority from nonpriority objectives, however, you can achieve positive results; hence, it is desirable to limit the number of objectives to be established.

## MARKETING PROGRAM

This section suggests an approach for your total marketing program for the next several years, with particular emphasis on the first year. This section, like the whole marketing plan, is updated each year.

### OVERALL STRATEGY

**The Proposition.**   You should define, in fairly general terms, what you are attempting to provide and sell to your markets. The proposition should be the strongest promise that can be made to the customers on behalf of your product that will have maximum appeal to the customers' own self-interests. It should be based on the facts gathered during the research steps of this marketing planning process. It must be truthful, possible to achieve, and unique. It must clearly distinguish you over the competition.

The possibility exists that multiple propositions will be required — a different proposition for each market segment. You must be careful to eliminate any inconsistencies between propositions.

**The Platform.**   You must spell out, item by item, all the claims you plan to make to your customers. This is not another general statement; it is the detail that supports the proposition. It is the list of advantages (of your firm's products to the customer) over competition upon which your promotion and advertising will be based.

### MEDIA STRATEGY

You must identify precise target markets at which to aim the media. Use the preceding established objectives to identify these markets. Establish specific advertising, public relations, and direct mail programs, and clearly determine the intent of the program, media selection, dates, and dollars for each.

Each of the advertising, public relations, and direct mail programs should be compared with previous media programs. Changes in thinking should be supported on the basis of how the new program will achieve the desired objectives and results better than did the old program. These media programs should also be compared against competitors' media programs and any obvious deficiencies corrected.

### SELLING STRATEGY

Specific sales strategies should be developed with regard to sales and promotion to associations, commercial groups, single commercial travelers, travel agents, and other market segments. Development of selling strategy must be accomplished at two levels:

**Corporate Level.** Activities should be identified that will be carried out by the marketing and national sales departments' marketing staffs. Overall sales strategies for implementation by individual or regional sales teams (where applicable) should also be identified.

**Property Level.** Specific sales targets and strategies should be developed for each property. (Again, the emphasis must be placed on identifying a few major strategies rather than attempting all the possible ways of building sales.)

These sales strategies should be compared with competitors' sales programs and any obvious deficiencies should be corrected. These sales strategies should also be compared with previous sales strategies to determine if there are sufficient differences to achieve your desired changes.

You must also identify new staffing requirements and the difference in cost from the preceding program.

### OPERATIONS CHANGES

You must identify the changes required in operating methodology or procedures to achieve the desired marketing objectives and establish timing costs.

## MARKETING APPROPRIATIONS

**Amount.** You must determine how much is needed to achieve the agreed-upon marketing objectives and supporting programs. What is the difference between the amount needed and available funds? Ultimately, a final amount of funds should be determined, keeping in mind if incremental funding is opted for, there should be an expected offset in incremental revenue.

**Allocation.** You must determine the allocation of available marketing funds among the various functions of marketing: advertising, publicity, sales force, travel agents' commissions, discount coupons, pre-opening campaigns, and research. Use the zero-based budgeting concept, wherein all expenditures must be fully analyzed and their justifications verified each year. This approach may aid in re-allocating resources from year to year into areas where they will do the most good.

Since there will probably never be sufficient funds available to execute all the programs needed, available funds should be apportioned, keeping in mind costs and benefits.

**Justification.**   The justification for the marketing budget is the research and analysis of the first half of this plan. If you have done your homework in approaching the marketing planning process in an analytical and pragmatic way, then the argument will have been well presented. If management does not allocate sufficient funds to achieve the necessary results, or if these funds are not efficiently spent, then something less than the desired objectives must be accepted.

## SALES GOALS

1. What is the total sales goal for all properties (as a group) that this marketing program is designed to achieve?
2. What is the average occupancy goal for all properties?
3. What is the average room rate goal for all properties?
4. What are the goals for room sales in each major business segment? Determine the percent for each segment.

Family and pleasure _____ %

Commercial (sales people/trade) _____ %

Executive _____ %

Groups (corporate and associations) _____ %

5. How much additional sales will be generated this year (over last year) for the increase in marketing expenditures over those of last year? Estimate the increase in dollars.

Increase in marketing expenditures $ _____

Goal for increased sales $ _____

Yield $ _____

## ACTION PROGRAMS

List in chronological order all the specific action steps listed under "Marketing Program" that survived the allocation of available marketing funds. Identify specific target dates, responsibility, and budgeted-approved expenditures. In Table 15.1 we suggest one way of organizing this information.

**Table 15.1**    Marketing Program Organization Chart

| | Item | Target Date | Approved Expenditure | Responsibility |
|---|---|---|---|---|
| Media Plan | | | | |
| Selling Plan | | | | |

## COMMUNICATION OF ASSIGNED RESPONSIBILITIES

Proper steps must be taken to ensure that the most important aspects of this plan, particularly the action program, are thoroughly communicated to those individuals responsible for its implementation.

## MONITORING OF ACTION PROGRAM

You must institute adequate follow-up to properly monitor progress on the action program. Figure 15.2 is a simple worksheet to help you in allocating the marketing budget by expenditure and by market segment. The worksheet is of particular value if you modify and apply it at the individual-property level.

     The first cut at completing a marketing planning process of this nature is always the most difficult. Updating and scheduling of periodic research data will help provide you with an ongoing flow of relevant and applicable information. You must be careful to make sound judgments at stages before the research is completed. However, depending on management's judgment, knowledge, and expertise, some of the data may have immediate application and be beneficial to your marketing programs.

## KEY WORDS AND CONCEPTS

**Marketing Planning** The organized process of studying the market, identifying and measuring its trends, developing major marketing objectives and supporting programs, and using the available facts in combination with the experienced judgments of the top marketing team. The process includes the development of targets (timing, costs, results expected) and the monitoring of actual achievement against these targets. Its purpose is the achievement of maximum desired results, through the efficient application of effort and resources.

**Objectives** Objectives are *what* you want to achieve. (Example: Increase our business in the pleasure travel market.)

## Marketing Budget (Zero-Based Concept)

| | Int'l | Resort | Family | Singles | Family Escape | Children's Escape | Other | Comp. | Assoc. | Executives | Exp. Acct. | Per Diem | Other |
|---|---|---|---|---|---|---|---|---|---|---|---|---|---|
| **MARKET SEGMENTS** | | | | | | | | | | | | | |
| | | | Pleasure | | | | | | | Business | | | |
| | | | | | Weekend | | Other | Group | | Executives | Commercial | | Other |
| **National** | | | | | | | | | | | | | |
| Advertising | | | | | | | | | | | | | |
| Consumer | | | | | | | | | | | | | |
| Trade | | | | | | | | | | | | | |
| Sports | | | | | | | | | | | | | |
| Directories | | | | | | | | | | | | | |
| Yellow Pages | | | | | | | | | | | | | |
| Airport Display | | | | | | | | | | | | | |
| **Local Advertising** | | | | | | | | | | | | | |
| **Production** | | | | | | | | | | | | | |
| Advertisements & Commercials | | | | | | | | | | | | | |
| Agency Fees | | | | | | | | | | | | | |
| Agency Travel | | | | | | | | | | | | | |
| **National Public Relations** | | | | | | | | | | | | | |
| Fees | | | | | | | | | | | | | |
| Expenses | | | | | | | | | | | | | |
| T.V. | | | | | | | | | | | | | |
| Participations | | | | | | | | | | | | | |
| **National Direct Mail** | | | | | | | | | | | | | |
| Mailings | | | | | | | | | | | | | |
| Listings | | | | | | | | | | | | | |
| **Brochures** | | | | | | | | | | | | | |
| **Research** (Advertising & Marketing) | | | | | | | | | | | | | |
| Projects/Internal Promotion/Mini Markets | | | | | | | | | | | | | |
| Advertising Administration | | | | | | | | | | | | | |
| **Local Public Relations** | | | | | | | | | | | | | |
| **Local Tie-Ins & Contests** | | | | | | | | | | | | | |
| **Direct Selling** Local Sales Departments | | | | | | | | | | | | | |

**Figure 15.2** Zero-based Budgeting Worksheet

| | | | | | MARKET SEGMENTS | | | | | | | |
| --- | --- | --- | --- | --- | --- | --- | --- | --- | --- | --- | --- | --- |
| | Pleasure | | | | | | Business | | | | | |
| Int'l | Resort | Family | Singles | Weekend | | Other | Group | | Executives | Commercial | | Other |
| | | | | Family Escape | Children's Escape | | Comp. | Assoc. | | Exp. Acct. | Per Diem | |

Row labels (left side):
- National Sales Departments Special Intermediary
- Trade Shows (Exhibitions)
- Familiarization Trips
- Promotional Parties
- Department
- TOTAL

**Figure 15.2** Zero-based Budgeting Worksheet (*continued*)

**Strategy** A strategy is the method by which you plan to achieve the objectives you have set. (Example: To increase our business in the pleasure travel market, we will: (1) increase outdoor advertising, (2) shift some of our advertising to family magazines.

**Customer Needs** A customer's needs are what he or she is really looking for in a product. They are the things he or she hopes the product will satisfy.

**Customer Perceptions** Perceptions are the way in which the customer, *in his or her own mind,* looks at a product. They include the customer's image of the product. These are very important because they almost always differ from management's beliefs and perceptions.

**Market Segment** A segment is a portion of the total market wherein all of those particular customers have something in common. There are several ways of segmenting a market. The most widely used is by *demographics;* i.e., age, income, sex, education, etc. A second method is by *psychographics,* wherein the market is segmented by needs or psychological motivation. Hence, people in a particular "need" segment share a common desire or interest. These needs or interests do not always follow demographic lines.

**Competition** Any business concern, product, or concept that competes for customers in your own market. It may be a product or concept completely different from that of your own.

**Zero-based Budgeting** The premise of this concept is that no expenditure is justified just because it was expended last year. Every expense is re-analyzed and justified each year on the basis that it will yield more favorable results than spending the same amount in another way.

**Action Program** That portion of the plan that lists specific things to be done. It includes target dates, approved expenditures (as differentiated from unapproved estimated costs), and the person(s) responsible for implementation.

## ASSIGNMENTS

1. Review an existing marketing budget and place it in a market segment/market method grid.

2. Develop a proposition and the supporting platform for a local hospitality business and then clearly spell out the advantages of the product or service.

3. Identify a hotel or motel and analyze the occupancy mix and market. Then develop specific sales goals for each segment in the mix.

4. Write a sample media plan for a lodging facility pursuing group business for its new convention complex.

5. Do a detailed comparative analysis of a local food and beverage operation and its top three competitors.

# The Total Hotel/Unit Marketing Plan

# 16

## PURPOSE

This section provides a complete outline of instructions, sample forms, and an actual workable marketing plan for an individual hotel or unit. Its purpose is to walk the user through the complete process of preparing an annual marketing plan. Examples are provided in selected sections. Just as in the preparation of a Total Corporate/Multi-Unit Marketing Plan (Chapter 15), the successful completion of this plan requires detailed self-analysis of your product, your market, and your competition.

## OBJECTIVES

1. Provide the user with a step-by-step instruction and approach to completing an annual marketing plan.

2. Ensure that the tools previously provided and described within this text are applied; these tools include rate analysis, pricing, competitive and market grid analyses.

3. Provide a focus for the individual on key product, market, and competitive trends that must be addressed.

4. Identify, address, and utilize key market segment analyses and related strategies.

## WHERE TO BEGIN

One of the best ways to begin is to establish a timetable for completion of key plan components. Here is an example.

### Marketing Plan Timetable

| | |
|---|---|
| July 15 | Instructions |
| September 1 | Completion of mission statement<br>Objectives and strategies<br>Competitive and market analysis |
| September 15 | Completion of preliminary advertising plan<br>Preliminary expense budget summary |
| October 1 | Final detailed budget<br>Completed advertising plan |
| November 15 | First quarter chronological plan |
| January 15 | Second quarter chronological plan |
| April 15 | Third quarter chronological plan |
| July 15 | Fourth quarter chronological plan |

## MARKETING PLAN OUTLINE AND INSTRUCTIONS

The first step is to set forth all the items and information required to produce a complete plan. In the pages which follow, an actual detailed package of hotel marketing plan instructions/outline is reproduced. Included are step-by-step instructions and definitions of what is to be completed and what is to be presented.

### MARKETING PLAN
#### OUTLINE AND INSTRUCTIONS

**I.** *Mission Statement — due September 1, 19__*
Provide a concise statement on your hotel to include the following:
a. Desired position and perception in the marketplace
b. Targeted business mix (transient percentage versus group percentage)
c. Targeted mix of weekday (Sunday through Thursday) and weekend (Friday and Saturday) transient rooms; i.e., weekday percentage versus weekend percentage
d. Goals for occupancy, average transient rate (ATR), total room revenue, group rooms, average group rate (AGR), group room revenue, gross operating revenue (GOR), and gross operating profit (GOP)

II. *Objectives and Strategies — due September 1, 19__*
   *Using Brief Statements,* list the key objectives (what you wish to achieve, quantified by dollar or percent if volume-related) you have set which, when achieved, will result in the fulfillment of the mission statement. For each objective, list the strategies (*how* you plan to achieve the objective; i.e., action steps) you will implement. Objectives should include, but not be limited to:
   a. *Business Mix.* Identify the objective and strategies planned to achieve the group/transient business mix goal you have set for 19__.
   b. *Pricing Philosophy.* State your objective pertaining to room rate and positioning. List strategies for achieving your targeted ATR. Include a competitive rate survey in the appendix.
   c. *Transient Market.* State your objective for weekday/weekend transient rooms mix. List major strategies planned to achieve desired results. List major strategies for travel industry sales and corporate transient sales.
   d. *Group Market.* State your objectives for group business as they pertain to group room nights, rate and group revenue. List your strategies. Include a summary of your group room night targets by market segment (including travel industry sales) in the appendix, using the form provided (Group Rooms Market Mix). Also include a list of sales staff market assignments.
   e. *Low Occupancy Periods.* Provide specific strategies aimed at solving low occupancy periods, be they weekends, summer, off-season, holiday, etc. Include results expected.
   f. *Community Awareness.* List strategies planned to increase your hotel visibility and enhance its reputation in the marketplace. In the appendix, include a list of professional and civic organization memberships maintained by the management staff.

III. *Competition and Market Analysis — due September 1, 19__*
   In this section of the marketing plan you are to give a very brief overview of market conditions and trends; then identify your hotel's position in the marketplace as it relates to your competitors. Be concise.
   a. *Economic Conditions.* Describe how the prevailing local economic conditions will affect your transient and group business. Information should include average occupancy for the marketplace during the past 12 months (if available). (Bullet [short/abbreviated] statement)
   b. *Opportunities/Concerns.* List any known or anticipated changes in your marketplace which would positively or negatively affect your hotel during this plan year.
   c. *Business Trends.* Briefly describe any trends exhibited during the past 2½ years with regard to transient demands (weekday and weekend), business mix, and valley periods. Complete the Group Rooms Market Mix forms and include in the appendix.
   d. *Product and Competitive Analysis.* Complete the fact sheets on your hotel and your three major competitors, listing all advantages and disadvantages.

e. *Competitive/Market Positioning Grid.* Using the forms provided, denote your hotel's position by placing an ''X'' in the most appropriate box. Do the same for your three major competitors on separate grids.

IV. *Summary Work Plan by Segment — due November 15, 19___*
*Using Brief Statements,* for each market, including travel industry sales and corporate transient sales, outline your specific planned activities under the categories of:
a. Direct sales and promotions (fams [familiarization trips], trade shows, etc.)
b. Direct mail (local and regional only)
c. Advertising (due November 15, 19___ in final form)
d. Public relations

Activities are to be tied to a targeted month and assigned to a salesperson. Ongoing activities are not to be listed. All work plans are to follow the sample format.

V. *Quarterly Chronological Plans (first quarter due November 15, 19___)*
The chronological work plan for January–March will be *due* by November 15. Activities should be listed in the date order by month (see sample). The chronological plan for March–June is due January 15.

VI. *Appendix — due September 1, 19___*
a. *Marketing Budget Estimates.* Using the summary form provided, outline your actual expenses for the past year, your estimated expenses for the current year and your projections for the plan year ahead.
b. *Room Rate Survey.* Complete a rate survey of your competitors using the sample format.
c. *Business Mix Trends.* Complete the Transient Rooms Mix versus Group Market Mix forms.
d. *Transient Market Segment Prioritization.* List all transient market segments you will address in the plan year and prioritize them according to their profitability to your hotel (see sample).
e. *Group Market Segment Prioritization.* List all group market segments you will address in the plan year and prioritize them according to their profitability to your hotel (see sample).
f. *Sales Staff Market Assignments.* Listing of how market solicitation responsibilities have been assigned within the sales department (see Figure 16.1).

## COMPETITIVE/MARKET POSITIONING GRID

A property's operating success is a major factor in determining an appropriate future action plan for that property. The operating success of a lodging facility is a function of both the potential of the market sector in which it is located and its competitive positioning within that market sector.

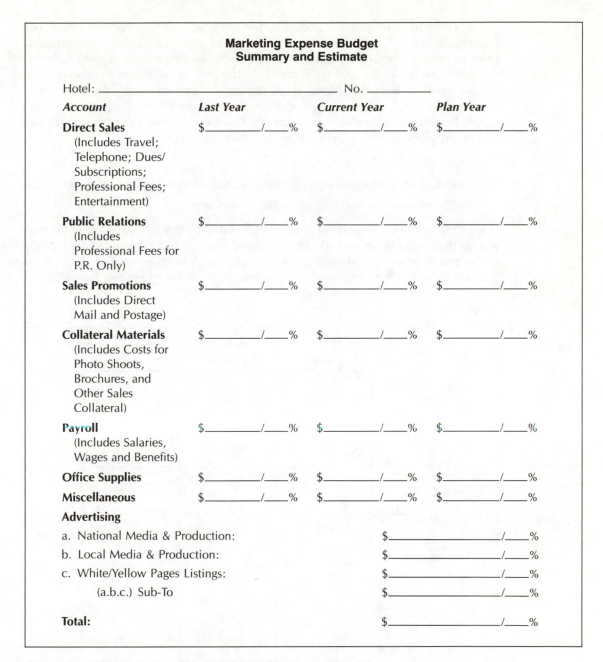

**Marketing Expense Budget
Summary and Estimate**

Hotel: _____ No. _____

| Account | Last Year | Current Year | Plan Year |
|---|---|---|---|
| **Direct Sales**<br>(Includes Travel;<br>Telephone; Dues/<br>Subscriptions;<br>Professional Fees;<br>Entertainment) | $_____/___% | $_____/___% | $_____/___% |
| **Public Relations**<br>(Includes<br>Professional Fees for<br>P.R. Only) | $_____/___% | $_____/___% | $_____/___% |
| **Sales Promotions**<br>(Includes Direct<br>Mail and Postage) | $_____/___% | $_____/___% | $_____/___% |
| **Collateral Materials**<br>(Includes Costs for<br>Photo Shoots,<br>Brochures, and<br>Other Sales<br>Collateral) | $_____/___% | $_____/___% | $_____/___% |
| **Payroll**<br>(Includes Salaries,<br>Wages and Benefits) | $_____/___% | $_____/___% | $_____/___% |
| **Office Supplies** | $_____/___% | $_____/___% | $_____/___% |
| **Miscellaneous** | $_____/___% | $_____/___% | $_____/___% |

**Advertising**

a. National Media & Production:           $_____/___%

b. Local Media & Production:               $_____/___%

c. White/Yellow Pages Listings:         $_____/___%

       (a.b.c.) Sub-To                    $_____/___%

**Total:**                                   $_____/___%

**Figure 16.1**   Marketing Expense Budget: Summary and Estimate

In order to develop an action plan, use the *grid concept*. We first introduced the grid concept in Chapter 6; we will use it here to relate the market sector potential to an estimate of the competitive position of each property within its market sector.

We have set up the grid in Figure 16.2. The horizontal axis of the grid denotes the potential of the market sector, while the vertical axis represents the competitive position of the specific property within that market sector. Ranking on both axes ranges from strong to weak. Competitive position is a function of both quantitative and qualitative considerations such as the following:

Amount and quality of competition

Competitive advantages as to location, access, image, facilities, size, rate, etc.

Ability to meet the needs of available market segments

Consider the present competitive position input on this evaluation with the plan year as the period under consideration. Obviously, there is a meaning to the position of the grid in which a particular property is placed. A hotel in position 1, 2, or 3 is the *best* show in town, or there is no discernable difference between the number 1

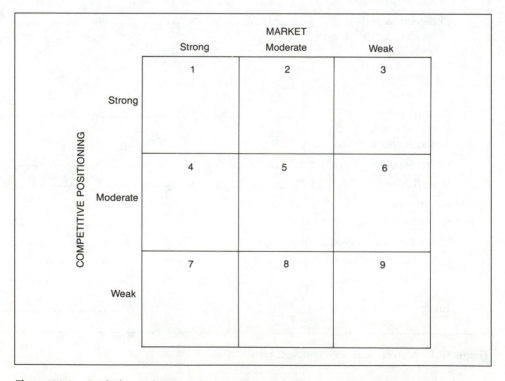

**Figure 16.2**  Grid That Relates Market Sector Potential to Competitive Position

and number 2 competitors. A hotel in position 4, 5, or 6 is not number 1 or number 2 in town. It is of *average* quality, and its competitive facilities are discernibly better. A hotel in position 7, 8, or 9 is of relatively *poor* quality when compared to competition. This hotel is in a discernibly disadvantageous position.

The optimum position on the grid is number 1 in the upper left corner, where a strong market sector potential combines with a strong competitive position within the market sector. The worst position on the grid is number 9 in the bottom right corner, where a weak market sector potential combines with a weak competitive position within the market sector.

For each hotel you must complete four positioning grids, one for each of the four major markets:

Business Travel — Group

Business Travel — Transient

Leisure Travel — Weekend

Leisure Travel — Vacation

Consider your property's position for each of these consumer targets. For example, a number 1 position means you have the best hotel in a strong market; that is, you have an 80 percent occupancy market. A number 3 position means you have a weak market — an occupancy market of 40 percent.

To utilize the grid shown in Figure 16-2, denote your hotel's position on the grid by placing an "X" in the most appropriate box. Do the same on separate forms for each of your *three* major competitors.

## WORK PLAN EXAMPLE

The following is an example of a work plan for group business from the corporate market. We also give examples of a chronological work plan, hotel check list, objectives and strategies, a rate survey table, a group market segment prioritization, and market assignments and goals.

**Table 16.1** Example of a Work Plan for Group Business from the Corporate Market
*(Objective: To generate 36,300 group rooms for the plan average rate of $86.00 or higher)*

|  | **Responsibility** | **Due Date** |
|---|---|---|
| **Action Plans** | | |
| *Direct Sales and Promotions* | | |
| 1. Schedule sales solicitation trips to call on key accounts in: | | |
| New York | Smith | Jan./Sept. |
| Dallas/Fort Worth | Carney | February |
| Detroit | Patton | March |
| Boston | Patton | April |
| St. Louis | Wallace | May |
| Kansas City | Carney | June |
| Minneapolis | Marshall | September |
| San Francisco/San Jose | Smith | October |
| 2. Attend national corporate business-related meetings for: | | |
| Meeting Planners Intern'l. | Smith | June/Dec. |
| Dialogue in Dallas | Carney | February |
| Dialogue in Chicago | Smith | June |
| Dialogue in New York | Smith | September |
| Meeting World in NY | Smith | July |
| Participate in Midwest Business Travel Assn. Annual Mtg. | Patton | May |
| 3. Participate in the following blitzes: | | |
| Boston | Patton | April |
| St. Louis | Wallace | May |
| Minneapolis | Marshall | September |
| San Francisco/San Jose | Smith | October |
| Host a Friends-of-the-Family account appreciation function | Staff | May |
| St. Louis corporate executives fam trip | Wallace | March |

**Table 16.1** *(continued)*

| Action Plans | Responsibility | Due Date |
|---|---|---|
| *Direct Mail* | | |
| 1. Include all Illinois corporate clients in quarterly activity schedule mailing | Staff | December<br>March<br>June<br>September<br>December |
| 2. Schedule a mailing to all corporate accounts promoting our "meetings package" to generate business for July, August, November, and December | Staff | April<br>October |
| 3. Develop a meetings brochure and mail to Chicago-area corporate accounts not currently on file | Wallace | March |
| *Advertising (local/regional media only)* | | |
| Heavy emphasis to be placed on advertising to the corporate group market. The following publications have been selected for local/regional placement:<br>　Chicago Tribune/Business Section<br>　Crains Chicago Business | Carney | Ongoing |
| *Public Relations* | | |
| 1. Releases to St. Louis media on Corp. Execs. Fam Trip | Carney | March |
| 2. Releases to trade publications on meetings package | Carney<br>Carney | April<br>October |
| 3. Releases to local media on Friends-of-the Family party | Carney | May |
| 4. General releases on newsworthy events relating to corporate meetings in the hotel | Carney | Ongoing |

**CHRONOLOGICAL WORK PLAN — EXAMPLE**
HOSPITALITY HOTEL, HEAVENLY, MARYLAND
JULY 19_____

*Week One: Monday, June 27 – Friday, July 1, 19__*

| | |
|---|---|
| Association sales calls in Washington, D.C. (two days) | J. Smith |
| Summertime government rate mailer to Annapolis | M. Patton |
| Local sales calls in Towson with G.M. | B. Wallace |
| Begin to prepare for August corporate phone blitz | D. Carney |

*Week Two: Monday, July 4 – Friday, July 8, 19__*

| | |
|---|---|
| Attend Meeting World in New York City | P. Johnson |
| RSVP Quarterly Newsletter mailed | B. Wallace |
| Research reunion leads from VFW magazine | J. Smith |
| Update DVSAE list | M. Patton |

*Week Three: Monday, July 11 – Friday, July 15, 19__*

| | |
|---|---|
| Sales calls on state associations (two days) | M. Patton |
| Brainstorming session on marketing plan | All staff |
| Deliver mailer for wedding rooms to local country clubs | B. Wallace |
| Attend counselor selling class in Houston | J. Smith |

*Week Four: Monday, July 18 – Friday, July 22, 19__*

| | |
|---|---|
| Local sales calls in Reistertown | B. Wallace |
| Follow-up calls to summertime government rate mailer | M. Patton |
| Sales calls in Philadelphia (two days) | P. Johnson |
| Finalize lists for August phone blitz | D. Carney |

## HOTEL CHECK LIST

*Name* of hotel.

*Location,* including street address, distance from airport and attractions.

*Physical structure:* Design, number of floors, and number of rooms per floor.

*Number and type of rooms:* Number of guest rooms and description of the bed types and decor of the rooms.

*Number and type of suites:* Same information for suites as given for standard rooms.

*Club floor:* If hotel offers "concierge" level, description of accommodations and services.

*Function space:* Location and number of meeting rooms, including dimensions and capacity for each (a capacity chart may be used).

*Food and beverage outlets:* Names and descriptions of each food and beverage outlet including type of cuisine, seating capacity, price range, and hours of operation.

*Recreation:* A list of all recreational facilities.

*Amenities:* A list of all other hotel amenities such as turndown service, complimentary *Wall Street Journal,* shoe shine, barber/beauty shop, etc.

*Parking:* Description of facilities and cost.

*Transportation:* Description of transportation service to the airport and area with accompanying cost. Does hotel provide complimentary van or limo service?

*Secretaries club:* If it exists at the hotel, description of the program.

*Frequent guest program:* If offered by the hotel, a brief description of its advantages and disadvantages in relation to your hotel.

## OBJECTIVES AND STRATEGIES

**OBJECTIVE 1:** BUSINESS MIX

Increase the group segment from 35 percent to 40 percent of the hotel's business mix.

### Strategies

Raise group room allotment to 250 rooms Monday to Thursday nights.

Raise sales goal for staff.

Increase number of sales trips to New York and Washington, D.C.

Increase advertising and direct mail to corporate group meetings planners.

**OBJECTIVE 2:** PRICING PHILOSOPHY

Become the price leader in the city, maintaining a $10 margin over the competition. Achieve an ATR of $82.

### Strategies

Increase rates $2 every two months or as needed to maintain the number 1 position.

Conduct a monthly rate survey.

Maintain a $60 average rate for packages June to September; $64 October to December.

Raise suite prices 10 percent in January.

Do not book groups below $50 average rate on weekends without approval of general manager.

Rate Survey

| | Hospitality Hotel | Hyatt | Hilton | Marriott | Holiday Inn | Sheraton | Radisson |
|---|---|---|---|---|---|---|---|
| No. of Rooms | 318 | 305 | 170 | 308 | 522 | 300 | 249 |
| Single Rack Range | 75/85/95 | 65/70/75 | 41/48/53 | 60/67/75 | 49/52 | 63/73/78 | 48 |
| Extra Person | 10 | 15 | 10 | 12 | 8 | 10 | 10 |
| Corporate Rate Preferred | 63 S/D | 63S;78D | 46S;56D | 60S;72D | 49S;57D | 70 S/D | 52S;62D |
|   Corporate Rate | 59 S/D | 58S;68D | 43S;53D | 60S;72D | 44S;52D | 58 S/D | 44S;54D |
| Secretary's | 63 S/D | 58S;68D | NA | 60S;72D | NA | NA | NA |
| Club Level | 15 extra | 85–100 | 66–76 | NA | NA | NA | 70S;90D |
| Government Rate | 44 | 45 S/D | 29–40 | 35 | 10% off Rack | 40 S/D | 39 S/D |
| Weekend Package | | | | | | | |
|   Room Only | 44 | 39 | 37 | 39 | NA | NA | 35 |
| Weekend Package | | | | | | | |
|   Room, B&D | 125/Couple | NA | NA | 80 | NA | NA | NA |
| Suite Range | 115–269 | 200–300 | 85–200 | 150–185 | 75–220 | NA | 225–400 |

| Group Rooms Market Mix (trends and forecast) | Hotel:_____ No:_____ | | | | | | | | |
|---|---|---|---|---|---|---|---|---|---|
| | 19xx Total | | 19xx Total | | 19xx Total | | 19xx Total | | 19xx Total | |
| Market | Total | % | Total | % | Total | % | Total | % | Total | % |
| Corporate | | | | | | | | | | |
| State/Reg Assn | | | | | | | | | | |
| National Assn | | | | | | | | | | |
| Travel Agent | | | | | | | | | | |
| Motor Coach | | | | | | | | | | |
| Sports | | | | | | | | | | |
| Gov't | | | | | | | | | | |
| | | | | | | | | | | |
| | | | | | | | | | | |
| | | | | | | | | | | |
| | | | | | | | | | | |
| | | | | | | | | | | |
| | | | | | | | | | | |
| Total (%) | | 100 | | 100 | | 100 | | 100 | | 100 |

**Figure 16.3**   Group Rooms Market Mix

## HOSPITALITY HOTEL
### GROUP MARKET SEGMENT PRIORITIZATION

| *Segment A* | *Segment B* | *Segment C* |
|---|---|---|
| Local corporate | National associations | Fraternities / sororities |
| State associations | Motorcoach tours | Military reunions |
| Corporate transient (RSVP) | Sports teams | Social rooms |
| Weekend packages | Relocation / long-term stays | Airline crews |
| | Government | Special events |
| | Travel agents | |

## HOSPITALITY HOTEL
### MARKET ASSIGNMENTS AND GOALS

*Sales Manager:* Jim Smith

| | |
|---|---|
| Primary markets: | Washington, D.C. national associations |
| Primary accounts: | All major associations |
| Secondary markets: | Government groups; Baltimore corporations |
| Secondary accounts: | IBM; Ernst & Whinney; Star Shipping Lines; Baltimore Port Authority |
| Geographic area: | Washington, D.C.; Maryland; Virginia (Washington NSO) |
| Room nights: | 250 per week |
| Outside calls: | 8 per week |
| Steam leads: | 1 per week |
| In-house entertainment: | 3 per week |

*Note:*Use this format, but include *all* sales people on one or two pages.

## USING THE PLAN

If you have religiously completed this plan outline for your hotel, you should have a useful working document. The plan must be reviewed, the progress assessed, and appropriate adjustments made on a periodic basis. For example, a chronological sales plan may be adjusted to reflect more productive potential customers, or an advertising plan expanded to adjust for new competiton. The plan is your hotel's blueprint to market share and success.

## KEY WORDS AND CONCEPTS

**Business Mix** The major market segments from which your guest come; for instance 30 percent group, 60 percent transient, and 10 percent leisure.

**Chronological Work Plan** A listing of action steps to be taken in date order with identification of responsibility.

**Club Floor** Usually a separate floor of upgraded rooms and services in a major hotel.

**Function Space** The actual meeting room space in a hotel (pre-function space is the area for socializing, breaks, etc., outside the meeting rooms).

## ASSIGNMENTS

1. Identify three competitive hotels and complete the market/competitive positioning grids. What strategies should each take to be more competitive?

2. Develop a quarter-by-quarter chronological work plan for a hotel which addresses at least three target markets.

3. Fill out a complete hotel fact sheet analyzing the strengths and weaknesses of the facility.

4. State your three primary strategies (or your major market thrust objective; for example, "Achieve a 60 percent transient, 40 percent group mix"), then develop a theoretical budget to support your objectives.

5. Complete a rate survey of three competitive hotels. Then select one and develop a rate change plan or recommendations.

# Marketing, Operations, and Research

# 17

**PURPOSE**

Employing every marketing weapon and adhering to an organized marketing plan will not, in themselves, be enough to succeed. Unless your marketing weapons are based on sound research and aimed directly at the target by your operating team, they will be less than fully effective. Market research can identify the consumers' needs, and marketing can then relate the product or service to those needs, but operations is responsible for seeing that those needs are satisfactorily fulfilled. This chapter focuses on the interrelationships of research, marketing, and operations. Special attention is given to tying the three together so that they support each other.

**OBJECTIVES**

1. Understand that research supports both marketing and operations and is vital to the marketing planning process.

2. Focus on the interrelationship between operations and marketing and on their impact on the consumer.

3. Relate the vital importance of all customer contact areas to marketing and fulfillment of your sales promises.

4. Apply training and operational techniques to directly increase revenues and profits.

5. Develop an operational organization that fulfills the level of expectation your customers have of your product or service.

6. Bring back repeat business through your operational efforts.

7. Tie your marketing and operational techniques together to have the strongest possible effort of any organization in the hospitality industry.

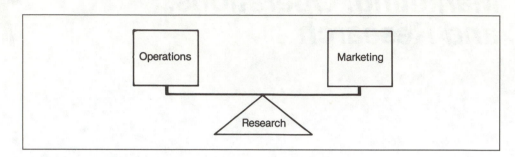

**Figure 17.1**    Research Support

*Research* can, and should, play a major role for both operations and marketing. The first four chapters of this text focused on understanding the market, consumer needs and preferences, and so on. The marketing plan presented in Chapter 14 is also heavily based on the information that research provides. Whereas research does *not* provide the strategies, it *does identify the issues* both marketing and operations need to adddress. In a very real sense, research is the balance and support to both marketing and operations (see Figure 17.1).

## RESEARCH

This text is not intended to dwell on research; however, it is important to understand a number of the roles that research should play as it relates to both marketing and operations. Research supports the overall marketing effort by helping to identify: (1) *what* is occurring within the market (customer perceptions, needs, etc.); (2) *who* is having an impact on the market (competitive strategy assessment); (3) *what* is likely to happen to the market (environmental forecast); and (4) *how* the product or service firm is performing within the market against the competition (see Figure 17.2).

The end result of research efforts should be factual parameters within which marketing, operations, and development can function. These parameters include identifying key market trends, competitive strategies, industry trends, and drawing implications upon which strategies may be developed.

Another role research should play in the overall marketing planning process is that of a *measurement* process. Research should provide a scorecard upon which you and your competition are graded, ranked, profiled, and compared. This measurement proccess tells marketing and operations *how* their strategy selection and fulfillment process is working; the focal point of the research can be measurement of performancce, strategy execution, and consumer response and preference. Regardless of how the scorecard reads (share of market, occupancy, average rate, covers, check averages, load factors), one of the roles of research is to objectively measure and compare the results of strategy execution. These results, no matter how

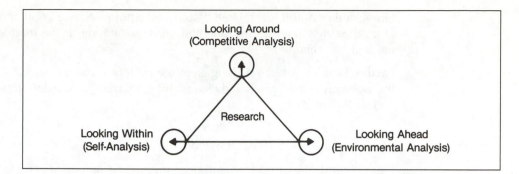

**Figure 17.2**  Focal Points of Research

they are expressed quantitatively, reflect the consumer's reaction to the marketing message or promise, and operations' fulfillment of that promise.

## OPERATIONS

Analysis of consumer needs and preferences needs to go beyond the research identification stage. Marketing's role cannot be executed successfully until operations is ready to fulfill the delivery of a product or service that meets the needs and expectations of the consumer. Research must convey an accurate assessment of consumer expectations to both marketing and operations. In order to ensure *customer satisfaction*, operations must adjust its perspective and methods to meet the consumer needs being promised in the marketing messages. One achieves customer satisfaction by meeting the identified needs of the consumer with a level of service or product quality that is in line with the expectation conveyed by the marketing message and related pricing.

Given the assumption that research, marketing, and operations are talking, listening, and acting as a team, a number of practical steps can be taken to see that consumers' expectations are being satisfactorily met. One approach that is particularly adaptable to the hospitality industry lodging sector is the use of an operations checklist based on the *consumers' perspective*. The checklist can be adapted for most hospitality industry service organizations or products offered. The emphasis is on the consumers' assessments and not on the viewpoints of marketing and operations.

***Operations Checklist (from the consumer's perspective)***

*Preliminary contact points*

\_\_\_\_ Advertising Display Board. Are they clean and up to date? Do they have the correct telephone number and clear directions?

____ Limousine or Auto Driver. Do the auto and employee have good appearances? Does the driver have a sales-oriented, positive attitude? Is the service convenient and on schedule?

____ Facility Exterior. Are the parking areas fee of debris, the bushes clean of paper; the walkways well lighted and clean, and the parking and exterior areas secure and well lighted?

*Major contact points (front desk/lobby)*

____ Front Desk. Is the area clean and does it project a feeling of activity? Does the desk clerk give a friendly, positive greeting, with efficiency in checking in (and checking out) the guest? Does the clerk ask about a future reservation? Are promotional materials visible and readily available without cluttering the counter?

____ Telephone Operators. Are they polite, courteous, and well trained? And most important, is there an adequate staff? How many rings before an answer?

____ Bellstaff. Is the bellman courteous and helpful? Does he have a good appearance and some ''hustle'' in his manner? Is he informative and sales-oriented without talking too much?

____ Bath Lounges. Do lounges near the public areas have adequate supplies? Are the floors cleaned prior to and after meeting breaks? Are the countertops wiped prior to and after breaks?

*Food and beverage areas*

____ Breakfast Service. Is it fast? Is coffee always refilled? Is a morning paper available? Is personnel attitude warm and friendly?

____ Attitude and Appearance. Are all guest-contact and guest-visible employees (employees who bus tables, etc.) trained to convey a friendly and helpful attitude? Is their appearance clean? Are they efficient?

____ Food Quality/Presentation. Does the food quality convey value? Does the presentation of the food convey quality and quantity, and is it attractive?

____ Menus and Promotional Materials. Are they on the tables or presented to the guest quickly? Are they accurate? Clean?

____ Floors/Windows. Are they clean?

____ Table Tops. Are all utensils, linens, glassware present, in their proper place, and clean?

____ Check Presentation. Is the customer's check quickly presented when requested? Is the customer told how and whom to pay at that time?

*Other areas*

\_\_\_\_ Gift Shop. Is it well stocked with current issues of reading material? Do the gift items relate to the traveler's needs, such as gifts for women and children? If credit cards are accepted (and they should be), is this information adequately displayed?

\_\_\_\_ Recreational Amenities Area. Are there towels available at poolside? Are supplies, such as rackets and balls, available for sports and game area? Are the recreational amenities clearly promoted and are directions to the facilities clearly visible?

These checklist items are what the guest or consumer has contact with, and the manner in which they are presented determines the consumer's perception of your operation. Addressing each of the preceding items will result in customer satisfaction with the marketing message and fulfillment of the operational expectations. *Always remember the perspectives of the customer!*

Recognizing we cannot be on target 100 percent of the time, it is important that both marketing and operations are thoroughly trained to handle the adversities when they occur. Some key questions to answer in this respect are:

\_\_\_\_ Is there a clear refund procedure and guidelines for dealing with dissatisfied customers?

\_\_\_\_ Is there a guest comment card and a number or person a guest can call to have a complaint resolved?

\_\_\_\_ Are the staff members trained to respond to and take care of the problem immediately?

\_\_\_\_ Is a management person informed of all such problems?

Adherence to the procedures identified in the four questions can result in keeping the customer and repeat business. One way to ensure that these procedures work is to develop a "listen and tell" system. Simply stated, each employee is trained to listen to guests' comments and conversations and to pick up comments such as, "The light bulb doesn't work," or "The faucet leaks," and to pass the information along to the appropriate person or department to ensure the problem is promptly corrected — if possible, before the guest even returns to his or her room. This approach results in satisfying the customer, and preempts the need to placate the complainer.

Thus, marketing does not drive operations nor does operations drive marketing. The consumer drives both, and research is one way to determine consumers' needs and how to best relate to these needs. Marketing cannot work without researched information and operational fulfillment. It is a mutually beneficial support system with research as a base, marketing as a communication, and operations as fulfillment; the result is customer satisfaction.

## KEY WORDS AND CONCEPTS

**Customer Satisfaction** Meeting the identified needs of the consumer with a level of service and product quality that is in line with the expectation conveyed by the marketing message and related pricing.

**Consumer Perspective** The views of the consumer of your product or service offering — *not* the views of marketing or operations on the product or service offering!

## ASSIGNMENTS

1. As a customer, what do you look for in a product or service of the hospitality industry? Are your needs perceived and addressed? Select a local firm, service, or product, and record your observations on the items presented in the checklist.

2. Visit a property and use the consumer-oriented checklist presented in this chapter to evaluate your satisfaction as a potential customer.

3. Analyze a local facility's advertising message, and then observe the actual operations to determine if the level of expectation of the marketing message and actual operational fulfillment are resulting in customer satisfaction. If not, identify what is wrong and why you believe it is wrong.

# Practical Steps to Maximize Marketing

# 18

## PURPOSE

This chapter will discuss and provide examples of many additional steps you can take to creatively improve the marketing of your product or service. The chapter is intended as a challenge to you, to make you ask yourself and answer many questions. Your success in responding can be measured in increased sales and profits. It is important to recognize that these tools, examples, and techniques are concepts that must be used within the total marketing plan framework to be most effective. Additional procedures and guidelines are provided so you can make sure you are using all your marketing weapons flawlessly. We will discuss some common faults and oversights and will provide you with some checklists for success. Finally, we examine a key step for all marketing personnel in the hospitality industry — *change*. We look at how to identify the time to change your marketing message and the related techniques to execute that message.

## OBJECTIVES

1. Use your marketing savvy to sell beyond the normal expectations.

2. Learn methods to make money out of what you have — and sometimes out of what you don't realize you have.

3. Develop new marketing *profit centers* within your product or service line.

4. Take advantage of the psychological motivations and feelings of your consumers to maximize profits.

5. Develop your own insurance policy and guidelines to ensure your marketing dollars are not wasted.

6. Identify those items to look for and at through checklist systems.

7. Understand when your marketing program, message, or techniques need to change.

8. Know when to respond to change and what to do to keep on track.

Marketing weapons need not all be cannons or tanks; sometimes rifles can produce effective results. There are many practical steps to increasing revenues and profits that include not only marketing, but capitalizing on what already exists within your hotel, restaurant, or customer base. The ideas expressed within this chapter will not be applicable to everyone, but will produce results in many instances.

## REVENUE AND PROFIT PRODUCTION IDEAS

### IN-HOUSE PROFIT CENTERS

Viewing your establishment as a place through which consumers pass, and recognizing that even the smallest service you can provide and from which you can profit will help you meet some need of the consumer is a major step in recognizing the potential of *in-house profit centers*. A hotel can traditionally be viewed as having revenue and profit centers in the major areas of rooms, food, and beverage; some even have banquet sales and gift shops. Each should be viewed as a profit center with target, sales goals, and profit margin objectives. How many other profit centers can be identified within a property? Is there a game room, a gift shop, lobby displays (space leased from the hotel for display purposes), a health club, a barber/beauty shop, or a lobby bar? Does the property have an infrequently used storage room that should be cleaned out and used in some manner to generate revenue and profit? Would a coin-operated copy center be useful? How about secretarial services? Laundromat? Bookstand? Wall art display sales? Think about the opportunity to generate the maximum amount of revenue and profit per room and apply your creative marketing ability to "sell that guest" when he or she is on your premises.

Restaurants frequently have an antiquated display case with mints, gum, and cigars visible through dirty glass; this is their one method of increasing revenue through sales at the cashier's stand. What else can be done to generate incremental revenue and profit out of the already purchasing customer? Does volume and space merit a gift shop? Do the restrooms lend themselves to vending necessity items? Does the display case have items presented in an attractive manner to encourage sales? Is there one or possibly two dessert items or specialty items that can be packaged and sold to the departing customer? Are there any items that appeal to children? (Even if children are not your clientele, many away-from-home parents will buy on whim.) Would a dessert cart improve the merchandising and volume of dessert sales? The point is to maximize merchandising with revenue and profit production items that *fulfill the customer's needs* while he or she is in "your house." Finally, do you monitor sales and set goals for each profit-making opportunity?

### REDUCE GUILT AND EARN MONEY

Research has proven that humans have guilt complexes. You can seize the opportunity to help your guests resolve guilt feelings and earn money. For a long time the telephone company, postal service, and greeting card companies have played on our minds by suggesting "How nice it would be to call home," or "Aren't you rotten for not thinking of grandma and sending her a card or letter?'' So, why shouldn't hotels — through marketing — simply say, ''Remember your wife (or husband) and children: try our gift stand.''

One large hotel chain with primarily male clientele recently tripled its gift shop sales by recognizing this marketing opportunity. The chain took a bold step and stocked its gift shops with transportable (fit within a suitcase or travel bag) items for women and children, and reallocated its shelf space from 80 percent men's items to 80 percent women's and children's items. Sales of these items, such as quality trinket jewelry and sturdy high mark-up children's toys, helped the male guests feel better by reducing their guilt. For the hotels it meant sizable incremental revenues and profits. In addition, the female guests found the women's items attractive and also made purchases from the gift shop. The merchandising was skillful, and the marketing message was subtle. The in-room merchandiser simply stated, ''We have a well-stocked gift shop, including a fine selection of women's and children's items, open from 6 a.m. to 1 a.m.'' Not coincidentally, the gift shop remained open another 30 minutes after the bar and lounge closed, and the gift shop was located between the bar and the elevator. A small poster-picture was visible through the glass window of the gift shop of a child with a tear in his eye. The caption, ''Did You Remember Me, Daddy?'' was clearly visible even to the blurry eye. (An interesting postscript to this tale is that the period one hour before closing was the period of highest volume revenue and profit for gift shop sales.)

## MAKE A KID HAPPY AND EARN MONEY

Casinos have a huge ability to generate income. In the casino are slot machines into which adults insert coins and pull levers at a rate of speed that frequently defies measurement. Well, kids are people too, and we are in an electronic age. Do you have electronic games or a game room? You may not only make the child happy by having something for him or her to do, but you may very well make the parents happy by providing a place for the children to go (with a pocket full of quarters). Marketing this revenue and profit-generating opportunity can be achieved through in-room merchandising. One entrepreneurial hotel owner goes one step further by providing one free game token to all children.

## INVEST $0 AND EARN MONEY

If you have the space, there are many ways to invest nothing and make something. Consider the game room as one opportunity. You can make a deal with a reliable distributor to set up your game room in the space you provide and collect a percentage of the profits (up to 50 percent). The same concept applies to vending, although the percentages may be lower. Earlier we mentioned dressing up your property with a display of perhaps art work or glassware. Other take-offs may include flower carts, plant displays, and paperback racks. Now think about a percentage of the sales! The key is to meet needs of your customers, enhance your property, and generate incremental revenues and profits with little or no investment!

## SOOTHING PAIN OR INFLICTING PAIN AND EARNING MONEY

Keeping in shape and relaxing have become major psychological desires of our population. Are you taking advantage of this fact? If your property has the space (one large room, a rooftop, or a parking lot perimeter), you should consider the possibilities of an exercise room, sauna, or jogging course. Obviously, you cannot expect to charge for such amenities, but that does not mean you cannot earn money. Many promotions and tie-ins can be designed to stimulate sales. In-room materials can promote a "health cocktail of the month" or a "special high-protein dinner." Tie-ins to the property's amenities are logical. For example, one hotel's promotion program lays out the jogging course and tells the guest to pick up his or her "time card" which, when submitted to the hostess in the lounge, will provide the "second health cocktail on us." In addition, the hotel has three menu items (good profit margins on all three) promoted as the "lo-cal," "high-pro," and "dieter's delight." The results have been excellent — guests are satisfied because their needs are being recognized, and the hotel is realizing increased beverage sales and food profits.

## EARN MONEY ON YOUR CASH FLOW

Do you want to improve your earnings and simplify your banking? Many restaurant owners, motel owners, and others who offer travel services and products can improve their cash management program. Keeping cash on the premises is hazardous, so let's assume we are all avoiding this problem. Checking accounts *cost* money (for checks, fees, services, etc.) — they don't *earn* money. Savings accounts and NOW accounts earn money but lose to inflation. Most people cannot tie up their cash flow in long-term savings certificates. So where do you turn? Money market funds are one place to look. Interest rates generally exceed most local rates offered by savings and loans institutions, and liquidity (the ability to use your cash when needed) is the same as a checking account. Most money market funds also provide free checks. Consider this approach: Use a NOW account (where allowed) for general disbursements, and use a money market fund to channel your cash through on a regular basis. Consider these results to your bottom line as shown in Table 18.1.

There are obviously more sophisticated cash management techniques for larger sums of money. Rates will change for all types of investments, but unless there is a radical change that closes the gap between the traditional savings and checking accounts and money market funds, you are the loser. (A list of the money market funds and prevailing rates is published daily in the *Wall Street Journal.*) Money market funds also represent a good resting place for advance deposits — why not earn money on someone else's money?

## PRODUCTIVITY

Good workers are increasingly difficult to find. Consider two juxtaposed approaches to increasing your operation's productivity. Approach 1 is a "see-what-happens" approach called "Let Someone Go" or "Don't Fill It." It has special applicability where a sizable staff in involved. Someone leaves your sales staff or is released by

**Table 18.1**  Financial Management: Comparison of Types of Accounts

| Type of Account | On $1,000,000 in Average Cash Flow Available for Investment | On $100,000 in Average Cash Flow Available for Investment |
|---|---|---|
| Standard checking account | Costs you money | Costs you money |
| Savings account/NOW checking account | Earns 4–6% interest | Earns 4–6% interest |
| Certificates of deposit | Earns 7–16% interest (Ties up your cash) | Earns 7–16% interest (Ties up your cash) |
| Money market fund | Earns 5–15% interest or $75,000–$150,000 | Earns 5–15% or $5,000–$15,000 |

you. What happens to your overall sales (and more important, your overall profits) if you do not fill the position? A number of things can happen, such as a decrease in costs per sale, an increase in productivity per remaining employee, or the worst — a decline in sales, which, to be of concern to you, has to be greater than the total cost for the person who left the operation.

Approach 2, called "Bring Someone In," sets a reasonable production target; this target may equal total costs for the new person times nine or ten, or a dollar amount in sales. A variation on this approach is to perhaps offer an attractive incentive to the travel agent producing a specific multiple of the incentive cost in sales for your product or service. The advantage to this alternative is that you have no additional overhead, yet you have effectively extended your sales force. One hotel chain recently offered an expensive sports car to the travel agency that produced the greatest sales increase over a base figure (four times the recovery cost of the car). The results were dramatic — agency sales quadrupled and the winning firm produced enough incremental sales to award a fleet of vehicles!

## METHODS TO DISTINGUISH YOUR OPERATIONS

Increasing revenue and profits from your operations may involve more than applying a marketing strategy. Frequently operational, physical, and even attitudinal changes may be required. Let's briefly look at some ideas that may help you distinguish your operations, product, or service, and then at some psychological keys to building repeat business.

Marketing your product or service may extend beyond the traditional sales, advertising, and promotional techniques we have discussed. There are a number of methods that can add to the *marketing attractiveness* of what you offer. These suggestions may not work for everyone, but they might stimulate your thinking about what else you can do to improve the marketability of your hospitality product or service.

## SELECTION BUT PERFECTION

Offering a good selection (in price and variety) in your food and beverage operation or restaurant will aid in your attempt to meet broad customer needs. However, you should further identify at least two items that you can offer to *perfection*. The items should be those upon which you can build your reputation as being the best place to have the items; you should also achieve such perfection in these areas that you bring back repeat visitors. Perfection applies to many things, including, but not limited to, quality, preparation, presentation, promotion, and perception as a real value. The items may be specialty dishes, main entrees, or unique desserts. The key is that they have broad appeal and that they be consistently perfect. *Consistency* in the preparation and presentation is imperative.

## DO SOMETHING UNIQUE

This method of distinguishing your operations may take on an infinite variety. For example, one hotel restaurant/lounge in the Midwest offers a unique "English Bloody Mary." The drink is served in a large, frosted, bowl-shaped glass, dressed with a salt coating, and garnished with a celery stick and parsley. In addition, a four-ounce cold beer chaser is set next to the mildly spicy drink. The marketing of the beverage offering extends beyond the tent card and well-trained waitresses who suggest you buy this unique beverage. The pricing is two-tiered; $2.25 for the English Bloody Mary and the first beer chaser. The four-ounce refill of the chaser, which is served by the alert and well-trained waitress who has a small 16-ounce frosted pitcher of cold brew, is priced at $1.50. Needless to say, many patrons end up consuming six or seven dollars worth of drink consisting of one large well-presented Bloody Mary and many four-ounce chasers. The beverage offering has developed its own following, thus encouraging repeat business, and it is also an excellent trial item for the new patron. The end result is higher profits, more volume, and a unique identity for the restaurant.

## THE UP-FRONT SIGNALS

What is first perceived is what may be believed. This phrase can be applied not only to helping the marketability of your product or service offering, but it can also add to your bottom line. Perceptions and first impressions are important; the more visible the better. A hotel in western United States has taken this "up-front signals" method to heart and to the bank — here's how!

The hotel (we'll call it Classic Hotel) was a first-class hotel although it was more than 40 years old. The owners were concerned about competition from a new Hilton highrise with a magnificent black glass exterior. The new Hilton looked good — it had marketability from the outside appearance; however, the older hotel's service levels and quality were better. What could the older facility do to distinguish itself and retain its status that would give an immediate "up-front" perception equal to or better than the "black glass special" without spending millions? A consultant came up with a very practical and inexpensive "up-front signal." He suggested that the owners of the older brownish stone building add a door-to-streetside gold-colored canopy and an appropriate plush sidewalk covering. The consultant also suggested a few additional "investments" be made. One was to add the word *"The"* before the hotel's name on the canopy in script writing: *The Classic Hotel*. Next, he helped the owners recruit a local college basketball player (over six feet, four inches tall) to work in a luxurious doorman's suit and top hat (also gold and brown) from 4:00 p.m. to 9:00 p.m. only. Finally, to recover the return on these investments, he suggested that the older hotel *raise its rates* slightly in excess of the new Hilton's. The owners went along with the recommendations. Here are the results.

First, the canopy and tall doorman were the most visible sights when coming down Main Street. So eye-alluring were the canopy and doorman that the "black glass special" just faded into the skyscape. First-class guests coming to this western city would receive only one reply when inquiring about the best place to say — *"The Classic Hotel* is the classiest place in town, and it is only one or two dollars a night more than the Hilton." (Postscript: This same concept has worked well for a number of restaurants trying to upgrade their images!)

## THE INSIDE SIGNALS

Improving the marketability of your product or service to the consumer can be achieved in ways other than upgrading the outside wrapper or packaging. There are a number of highly visible interior areas where simply changing the lighting or adding a mirror can achieve wonders. Recently, a major luxury hotel chain discovered it had a small operational problem: occasionally, because of poor planning, its elevators provided slow service during high occupancy periods. In addition, the windows at the end of the corridors where the elevators were located looked out onto the heating and ventilation equipment clustered on the roofs below. It was physically impossible to add elevators. The solution to keeping the guests occupied during their wait was very simple. The hotel installed full-length mirrors on the walls near the elevators. The mirrors provided a perfect distraction for the guests, who could view themselves and their appearance. By indulging their guests' vanity, the hotel diverted attention from a potential annoyance and enhanced the appearance of its interior.

Complaints virtually ceased and the idea was soon adopted by other hotels in the chain with similar elevator problems. The guests' dissatisfaction and negative viewpoints turned into satisfaction when they viewed themselves in those wonderful mirrors by the elevators!

Another general manager knew his rooms were not due for refurbishing but were at the stage of just not appearing competitive. His approach was to compensate through a technique of substitution. He decided to identify about 20 percent of his rooms as intended for women travelers, and another large percentage for men only. In the rooms for women, he added a fresh flower in a clearly visible bureau-top vase, new and softer color towels, new colored shower curtains, a skirt hanger, and a new double dead-bolt lock. In the rooms for men, he placed a current issue of *Sports Illustrated, Time, Newsweek,* or *U.S. News,* the latest edition newspaper, and a complimentary pen and pencil set. While the hotel incurred small costs, it regained guest satisfaction and business stayed; the hotel's slightly worn rooms remained competitive. In essence, his inside signals were compensating for an aging problem.

### "CAN OF PAINT" TECHNIQUE

The least expensive way to change the appearance of something old or dirty is to paint it. The "can of paint" technique can work for you! Walk around the outside of your property. Look for the most visible aging signals. It may be a dirt-stained wall near the lobby entrance, striping on the parking lot surface, or deteriorating signage. Invest in the "can of paint" — a signal to the consumer that you have changed from dirty or old to fresh, clean, and well kept.

This brings us to the point of suggesting that there really are signals or keys that can help bring consumers to you and even bring them back as repeat visitors. Let's look at 10 keys for repeat business, greater marketability, and improving the consumer's perception of the product or service you offer.

## TEN KEYS TO POSITIVE CONSUMER REACTION

### KEY 1: THE FRESH AND NEW SIGNAL

"Fresh" and "new" are positive signs to most consumers. Whether it be the can of paint or the replacement of tablecloths, napkins, towels, uniforms, or menus, you need signals that clearly convey that your product or service has the appeal of being fresh or new. Take a good look at your facility or operation and identify what you can do to provide the strongest "fresh and new" signal to your market.

### KEY 2: THE NEAT AND CLEAN TEST

Your product or service need not be "brand new" to convey positive signals. Cleanliness is another very strong desire on the part of the lodger, diner, and traveler. Rooms (especially bathrooms), lounges, restaurant floors, and even airline seats should pass your cleanliness inspection. Even new facilities will lose out if they are sloppy or dirty. Guests emphasize this point regularly when they are surveyed about hotels, restaurants, and public travel-oriented facilities. Check it out: Are the lounges cleaned prior to and after meeting breaks or large volumes of traffic? Are the carpets clean and vacuumed? Is everyone a member of the "paper patrol"? (This means that if, for instance discarded paper is on the floor or room service trays are in the hall-ways, does your entire staff — including you — clearly understand it is their job to pick it up or move it from the consumer's view?)

### KEY 3: EFFICIENCY AND HUSTLE

For many travelers time is of the essence. Fast check-in and check-out, and an impression of efficiency at the front desk are essential to ensure a positive customer reaction. While it is important that front-desk personnel display a warm, friendly attitude, a pleasant face is no substitute for efficiency to the busy executive. You can smile all you want, but if the customer has been waiting for 10 minutes you can bet he or she won't be smiling back. An efficient check-in and check-out, coupled with that smile, will be the winning combination for pleasing your customers.

### KEY 4: RELIABILITY

The obvious place to start with reliability is ensuring the customer's reservation is there and correct when he or she arrives; but this is certainly not where reliability should end. A guest is always relieved to know his or her reservation is there and that it is for the right night, the name is correct, and the room or table is ready. Some other key factors include, but are not limited to, a television that works, adequate lighting (especially in work or reading areas), towels and tissues, and an accurate and prompt message service system. Reliability means that when room service says "It will be up in fifteen minutes," the tray arrives in 10 to 12 minutes — not 30 or 45. Reliability means that when someone calls a guest, the message is taken and delivered. Reliability is the combination of all these factors to give the guest a com-fortable feeling that "this place works."

### KEY 5: ACCEPTABILITY

People like to be accepted. Does your operation convey that feeling or do your guests feel as though they are processed. Are they viewed as outsiders instead of customers? Does the word *welcome* still exist in all your people-contact personnel? Are the employees also "acceptable" to your customers? Rude attitudes, shabby appearances, and so on can take a perfectly reliable operation and turn it into a very unacceptable environment for your customers. Make sure your customers feel ac-cepted.

### KEY 6: RECOGNITION — SELF AND PLIGHT

Not all your customers will arrive at the front desk and express joy. In fact, almost everyone has a slightly different plight or frame of mind. Be sure your personnel are trained to deal with different attitudes and are capable of recognizing those who might have just been through a trying experience. The importance of *acceptability* and *recognition* can be related in the following true story.

I was recently invited to give a presentation at a distant resort area. Having had other commitments, it was necessary for me to take a very late flight, and there was no time to shave or clean up. Arriving at the resort after a six-hour flight, unshaven and having had the two drinks on board, I wanted to check in quickly and get some rest before the early morning presentation. Unfortunately, my suitcase had been lost by the airline, and by the time the lost-bag forms were completed, it was after 1:00 a.m. when I entered the hotel. Walking up to the front desk proved an interesting experience in this first-class resort.

A night auditor, who was busy sorting through index cards, peered over his bifocals. The look was easily readable: "If I ignore him (me, the customer), I'm sure he'll leave." After all, I was unshaven and had no suitcase. The auditor, now making his appearance as a front-desk clerk, continued to sort his little cards and mumbled, "I'll be with you in a minute. I want to finish this batch." Feeling not particularly "accepted" at this point was only the beginning. After a brief exchange, in which I indicated that I would appreciate an expeditious check-in, the night auditor asked, "Do *you* have a reservation?" My response was, "Yes, it was guaranteed by both my host (the resort's owner) and my American Express card." The auditor's response was, "I don't see it — are you sure you had a reservation for the 29th?" By now, a full 10 minutes had passed and still no registration card, no key, no room — from no "acceptability" to no "reliability."

I won't go into the details of how Mr. Night Auditor learned empathy or how to hustle, but I will tell you he is no longer with that resort! Acceptability and reliability are two keys to positive customer reactions — use them!

### KEY 7: UNIQUENESS

Because you so often hear the expression "They are all about the same," wouldn't offering some uniqueness make sense? It does not have to be totally different (like a double-decker London bus for a limo), but you should have something that tells your market (your potential customers): This is the place that has "great food," or "hustling personnel," or "a good piano bar," or "the six-foot, four-inch doorman." Being unique with the idea of offering the customer something that can be identified with you will give your product or service a recognizable edge.

### KEY 8: CLASS

Class has many definitions, but perhaps one of the most applicable to the service industry is *the ability to function with grace under pressure*. The handling of an irritated executive by an experienced front-office clerk can be a demonstration in class for all to observe. Class is also an air or feeling within the property or operation that is established as a result of the employees' overall esprit de corps. Class is *not* an arrogant general manager or director of food and beverage who is unable to extend a helping hand to a lower level employee. Class is an attitude that you and your people convey to the customer in combination with your physical product or service offering. If you have class, your customers will know and react positively.

### KEY 9: BEAT-THE-SYSTEM OFFER

Survey after survey indicates that most people do not like a regimented environment, or what "the system" offers. One technique in obtaining positive customer reactions is to ensure your customers have at least one opportunity to "beat the system" (your system) during their visit with you. The opportunity may be nothing more than "free after-dinner mints" or "the second drink on the house," or a "discount."

### KEY 10: VALUE

Throughout this book we have defined value as *quality at a fair price.* Just as most people want to believe they have "beat the system," no one wants to feel cheated. Over-pricing, poor quality products, and inadequate service levels are "rip-off" signals that destroy the opportunity to offer the consumer the strongest reason to be your customer — value. Today, more than ever, the public is demanding quality at a fair price yet finding it increasingly difficult to obtain. Offer value and you will be successful. You will have given the customer the strongest possible reason and signal that will result in the most positive reaction — purchase and repeat purchase of your product or service.

## FIVE STEPS TO MORE COMPETITIVE MARKETING

*Go out and look* at your strongest competitor's operation. That means looking at more than the rates and facility. Look at the competitor's staff — their level of desire, competency, enthusiasm, courteousness, and thoughtfulness. Set some stringent performance objectives.

*Make more (even if only one more) sales calls.* Go after revenue and customers as the number one priority. All else flows from revenue.

*Make deals.* Today you need them. Maximize revenue; unless every room is occupied, you are losing revenue.

*Change strategy.* You can do whatever you need to do in order to beat your competition. So don't hesitate to change strategy if it makes sense. If it doesn't cost you anything to offer it, do so. Even if it does, it will be less costly than losing the business. For example, shop your competition and find out the rates they are quoting in your valley periods, then adjust accordingly. Go after — and *steal* the business.

*Select and inspect.* Check a sales file *daily* and discuss it with the responsible employee. Everyday observe the front desk at check-in and the cashier at check-out. Be sure *your* guests are being handled properly. You work hard to sell them; make sure others are working hard to keep them coming back.

## KEY WORDS AND CONCEPTS

**In-house Profit Centers** An area within a hotel, restaurant, or any operation that has revenue and profit production potential and is identified as a profit center unto itself.

## ASSIGNMENTS

**1.** Identify a local operation and determine how the management views the operation in terms of profit centers. How many are there? What others can be identified?

**2.** Select one of the ideas or concepts presented within this chapter and develop an implementation plan (including costs and expected results where applicable) for an appropriate local entity.

**3.** Make your own audit checklist of the "10 Keys to Positive Customer Reaction" and see if you can find a local hospitality industry operation that ranks a "10."

**4.** Find an opportunity to distinguish an operation either by employing one of the suggestions within this chapter or creating a concept of your own.

# Travel Purchasing Systems: Automation and Beyond

# 19

## PURPOSE

At the very outset of this book we made the point that the hospitality business is not driven by operations or marketing, but rather by the consumer. As a result of automation the consumer has come to expect ever more from marketing. The advances in computer applications in travel transactions, the purchase of travel, reservations services, front-office systems, guest history and relations, customer service, and research analysis are all changing the game called marketing in our industry. In fact, these applications will, in all likelihood, cause a revolution in the hospitality industry. This chapter reviews these trends and predicts what the future will hold.

## OBJECTIVES

1. Explain the significance and importance of automation as it becomes an even greater part of marketing.

2. Identify the major areas of marketing affected by these technological developments.

3. Provide a brief review of each area within the industry and travel purchasing processes where automation will affect the consumer.

4. Paint a likely scenario of the emerging forces within and servicing the hospitality industry for the years ahead.

## AUTOMATION

The hospitality industry is no exception to worldwide industrial trends when it comes to automation: the replacement of manual or personally performed functions by automated equipment such as computers. Granted that the industry is one of the lag-behind business segments to be engulfed in automation, but the impact is likely to be of great importance. Just as computer-driven assembly lines and robotics transformed the automobile and other heavy manufacturing industries, automation is likely to have a dramatic impact on the hospitality industry. In fact, the impact will be in the very area that opponents of automation claimed to be sacred in the services industries, the people-contact area. Automation will have one of its greatest impacts on the hospitality industry in the expediting of the purchasing decision, change of the purchasing behavior, and providing of new services to the guest and traveler.

Traditionally, automation was narrowly perceived as a tool for producing and analyzing budgets, reports, statistics, and accounts. These largely financial applications crept into other areas of application such as sales reporting, rooms inventory control, and timekeeping. As telecommunications and computer technology grew, so did reservation systems and their ability to handle transactions. This, in turn, led to further analytical applications of captured data, thus providing marketing information. The further applications of automation and computer technology resulted in front-office systems which provided such marketing data as customer histories, patterns of use and customer preferences. It became very clear that automation had entered the world of marketing in the hospitality industry.

## THE RELATIONSHIP TO MARKETING AND THE CUSTOMER

These technological advances in computers, system development, and telecommunications continue to result in many different relationships to marketing and to the consumer. For marketing, automation has provided the valuable tool of guest histories, customer preferences, demographic and psychographic profiles, and the resulting improvement of services and delivery of such services to the consumer. For consumers, their very purchasing behavior has been affected by 800 numbers, central reservations offices, pricing based on statistical analyses of supply and demand periods/ratios, and a plethora of conveniences. These conveniences include the presentation of multiple choices instantly displayed on CRTs, express/automated ticket purchasing, express check-in and check-out, automatic traveler check and cash dispensing machines linked nationwide, and one-stop trip purchasing, to cite just a few. Today, the consumer can simply dial an 800 number or even access their own CRT and do all the travel/trip purchasing in one call — hotel room, car rental, airline ticket, events tickets, etc. How these conveniences are delivered to the marketplace and which players are alert enough to recognize the advantage in doing so are things to watch for as this industry makes exciting advances in the years ahead. For those who recognize the trends and invest and adjust, it will mean success. Failure to recognize these trends will likely result in losing touch with the consumer and declining sales. Think about it. Today, consumers opt for the convenience of an automated teller machine to access their cash. Why shouldn't they expect the same convenience when checking in or out of a hotel, buying an airline ticket or renting a car?

## *RESERVATION SYSTEMS*

Airline, car rental, and hotel reservation systems all have evolved into performing much broader functions than their original functions of enabling a consumer to make a purchase or a rental. Today, airline systems have become travel purchasing systems with immense capabilities. Car rental systems have evolved into highly sophisticated data banks which generate everything from car preference to purchase preference histories on sophisticated lists. And, perhaps the laggard in the development cycle, the hotel reservation system, has turned into a system for storing customer history and preference records as well as marketing and management information systems.

Before we look at specific reservation systems as they have evolved into travel purchasing systems, let's put the reservation system into perspective and provide some logic to a very sophisticated process and outcome. Basically, the reservation system has become the collector or gathering point of vast amounts of consumer, product, and market data. Figure 19.1 depicts the reservations system in this collector or gathering role.

It is suggested that one of the first phases in the evolution of reservations systems was simply the *purchase facilitator* phase often associated with an 800 number and central reservations facility. The second phase was an expansionary one which might

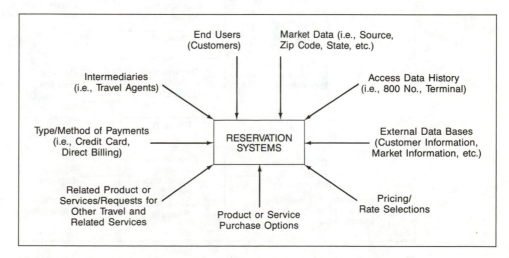

**Figure 19.1** Reservations Systems as Collectors

be termed the *data collector* phase. The third phase was the organized process of recasting this data into usable marketing and operations data — what is often referred to as the *management information* phase. This, in essence, is depicted in Figure 19.2.

Many expansions of system capabilities paralleled the development of computer hardware and software. Today, one could argue that the ability to interface external data bases with reservation systems, thus providing data back to consumers, is the fourth phase of system development. The instantaneous or simultaneous relationship of data in all transaction outlets and locations may be thought of as another key phase or breakthrough — call it phase five. Regardless of terminology or the number

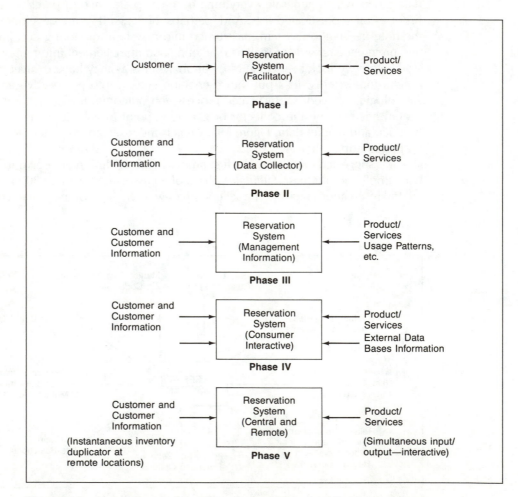

**Figure 19.2** Major Phases of Development and Growth of Reservation Systems

of phases involved, these developments were, and are, major changes to what was originally a simple purchase facilitator.

There are many different reservation systems and associated names and acronyms. One often hears about Westron in the hotel industry. This hotel-related system was one of the pioneers. Its capabilities were often used as a model for the development of many other hotel reservations systems. Today, Holiday Corp. has the Holidex system, Hilton the Hiltron system. The same is true in the rental car area, with the "Wizard of Avis" and the "Hertz System." Likewise, the airlines reservations systems, which, in reality, were the first of these three travel components, for years were dominated by American Airlines' associated SABRE system and United's Associated APOLLO system. We will discuss these systems and others to have emerged and which promise to have a major impact on how travel is marketed in the years to come.

## PROPERTY MANAGEMENT SYSTEMS

Just as automation has influenced the purchasing process, so too is it influencing how the product or service is operated. Property management systems, front-office systems, and "back of the house" automation can be complex subjects in themselves. This section is intended to simply relate the relationship of property management systems to marketing. There are literally dozens of property management systems and firms in the business. There are dozens of hardware and software suppliers. Our concern is their significance to marketing and the consumer.

Marketing directly benefits through applications of data that come from property management systems. Revenue maximization can be the big payoff from knowing a property management system with related software technology to provide accurate forecasting. The ability to make rate adjustments daily and hourly based on historic profiles, resulting in incremental revenues, is one of the benefits of such systems. Knowing when to sell up or when to discount can be invaluable to maximizing revenue. Other benefits include better rooms inventory control, more accurate management of room blocks, and yield management capabilities.

The importance to marketing and the consumer also includes better service through guest histories and related recognition programs. Today, a consumer often can count on the same room, same seat, and same car preference as a result of guest or user history and preference systems. Property management systems have also enhanced the ability to offer express check-in, express check-out, and even automated check-in and check-out. This same technology has allowed for automated ticketing and car rentals. The significance of all this technology to marketing centers around understanding and closely monitoring the consumers acceptance, use and related behavioral changes. If the consumer puts a high value on any particular aspect, marketing and operations must respond. The analogy is simple. The banks that don't offer 24-hour access through automatic teller machines found customers deserted their fine "personal" service for convenience, an overriding need. Hoteliers, especially those of the old school, will need to open their minds and be flexible in their attitudes in order to reach their customers. In essence, automation at the property level dispels the myths that operations is sacred and marketing is almighty. For, in reality, it is the consumer and his desires that are the true driving force today in the hospitality industry.

## MARKETING INFORMATION SYSTEMS

Automation has also spurred numerous varied applications of data and information for marketing purposes. Today, the sales department in a hotel can act with some sophistication in profiling customer behavior, analyzing meetings patterns, prioritizing accounts, lead generation, and overall productivity. Marketing can assess promotions by tracking patterns of response: identifying geographic and demographic types who respond and why, where, and how they actually responded. Selection of media based on key feeder market data and selection of the creative approach based on identifiable potential customer likes and dislikes is now at our finger tips and demanding to be used and applied. Marketing partners such as travel agents and tour operators can be selected and evaluated based on automated records of performance, market preferences, and even clientele profiles based on demographics and psychographics. The influence of automation continues in virtually every aspect of marketing from research sampling to media selection.

The elements of a marketing information system include key group trends such as location preference and history, frequency of use, type and number of rooms, and spending patterns. For corporate accounts these can be established by dollar volume, market, size, or other measurement. Promotional programs and travel agency productivity can also be included as part of the detailed data output. Again, the purpose of all these applications is simply to be better in marketing your product or service and, most important of all, to keep up with and understand how to reach the consumer.

## TRAVEL PURCHASING SYSTEMS AND BEYOND

All the pieces are identified and the major players are emerging for what many believe will be a revolution in the marketing of travel. The technological developments in hardware and software have evolved to a remarkable level of sophistication. In this section, we will identify the most likely major players, the directions their developmental activities may take us, and some of the exciting ways marketing and the consumer may respond. So, let's begin with the players in the lead at the present time.

**SABRE.**  The renowned reservations system of American Airlines has spawned a separate subsidiary called AMR Information Systems, Inc. This group appears to have a substantial lead in the application of sophisticated reservations system technology, software applications, and technical skills to develop multiple new products and services. This group has also acquired the technology for video home banking, bill payment and processing, and a full gamut of financial services. AMR is developing technological applications for hotel, car rental, and other non-air suppliers to improve their ability to sell products and services electronically. The AMR subsidiary also offers a multihost system in which other airlines can use SABRE as their reservations system. It is very likely that it is now technologically possible to offer a complete at-home or at-office "travel purchasing system." In fact, IBM now has available an IBM PC travel agency system which provides the programming necessary to host airline reservation systems with SABRE as one of its first such systems. DEC and others are also in the marketplace. The obvious significance is the potential at-home and at-office marketing implications as the hardware and software become readily available directly to the consumer.

**APOLLO.**   United Airlines also created a venture with its APOLLO airline system referred to as COVIA. This group is moving into areas of telemarketing and into servicing other industries outside of travel services. Should COVIA focus on the consumer — as does AMR— a competitive travel purchasing system will emerge. Imagine the convenience of one-stop shopping at home or at the office for everything: airline ticket and seat reservation, hotel room, rent-a-car, dinner and entertainment reservations, and cash or travelers checks to boot!

**PARS.**   In 1986 TWA sold part of its PARS reservation system to Northwest. This sale enabled the PARS marketing system to receive a substantial financial base of support and to accelerate its developmental efforts. PARS marketings' initial focus was on preparing advertising and brochures, providing seminars for travel agents, and training to the airlines' sales staffs. The PARS reservations computer system and PARS marketing have the capability to provide enhanced marketing services to the travel intermediary. Should these technologies be channeled to the end user, one could expect a strong competitor to SABRE and APOLLO.

**SystemOne.**   Also in 1986, Texas Air Corp. absorbed Eastern's SystemOne reservations technology. Now SystemOne Direct Access, Inc. is part of the holding company System One Corp. Coming under this umbrella corporation are Eastern Automated Services, Inc., the Eastern Airlines reservations system computer, CCS Automation Systems, the Continental reservations computer, and SystemOne Travel Resources, Inc., a back-office automation vendor. Initial developmental activity concentrated on enhancements from merging the entities. Texas Air Corp. also has been a leader in automated point-of-purchase ticketing machines and in credit card tie-ins. The future may well see these various components merge into an integrated travel purchasing system available directly to the consumer.

**Table 19.1** Potential Major Players in Travel Purchasing Systems and Related Services

| Name | Origin |
|------|--------|
| SABRE | American Airlines' reservations system |
| APOLLO | Unitied Airlines' reservations system |
| SystemOne | Eastern's reservations system (SODA) absorbed by Texas Air Corp. |
| PARS | TWA's reservation system expanded via acquisition by Northwest |
| DATIS | Delta Airlines' reservation system |
| RESERVEC | Air Canada's reservation system |

**DATAS.** Delta's DATAS reservations system is another source that may develop into a travel purchasing system. Delta has the expertise and financial strength that would support expansion into this area. Delta has made excellent use of yield management techniques, developed good packaging capabilities, and, with its 1987 absorption of Western Airlines, truly developed a nationwide base from which to grow. The question of venturing out into travel purchasing systems remains to be answered.

**RESERVEC.** Air Canada has also been a leader with its powerful RESERVEC system. Its expertise in packaging capabilities and future applications and enhancements could result in another travel purchasing system.

These six systems listed in Table 19.1 are likely to emerge as dominant factors in the purchasing of travel services. The focus, be it on the end-user — the consumer, — or the travel intermediary (agent, in-plant, etc.) will result in a major impact on the marketing of all the components within the hospitality industry. Airlines, hotels, car rental services, destination services, financial services, insurance, and even hard goods purchasing — all of these services might be offered directly to the consumer in the home or office through simple access of a personal computer.

## SUMMARY

Going beyond the traditional boundaries of airline automation is fast becoming a reality. The linking of consumer-related services, hospitality industry services, home banking systems, and even manufactured travel-related products is not only technologically feasible but in progress today. Because of the interest of IBM, DIGITAL, WANG, and other computer giants who sell hardware and software, the technological expertise of the world is dreaming up ideas for how we will purchase and market the hospitality industry's products and services. One can foresee many scenarios for these applications. Imagine sitting in your own family room or office and, via a PC and television monitor, being able to select everything from your airline seat to the view desired from your resort room. You press a button and receive your tickets and travelers checks — not to mention the cab that will take you to the airport which may automatically call for you an hour before flight time.

Yes, today's technology is well on its way to revolutionizing the purchasing process for travel. You will hear more and more about SABRE, APOLLO, PARS, DATAS, SystemOne, and RESERVEC as these airline reservations systems become much more than computerized timetables. Advancements in technology, the lack of a "total" travel purchasing system (TPS), and fair trade and deregulation all point to the emergence of one or more of the above as the total system of the future. The total system will encompass more than imagined, as the technologies of reservations systems, automated banking, fiber-optics, and telecommunications are linked with new micropressing technologies to form the super TPS capable of providing everything from your boarding passes to your banking travel advance, your room key code to your car access code, and even your "buy" and "sell" order for your stock transactions. The future is now — the pieces just need to be put together.

## KEY WORDS AND CONCEPTS

**ATM** Automated transaction or teller machines or ticketing machines, etc.

**Automation** The computerization of manual functions.

**Front Office Systems** The computerization of front office functions including items such as rooms management, housekeeping, rooms availabilities, rates, etc.

**Guest History** A record of a customer's purchase patterns and preferences.

**Property Management Systems (PMS)** Property Management Systems are computer-automated systems for a variety of management tasks including room inventory, control, guest histories, and rate management.

## ASSIGNMENTS

1. Interview a travel agent who uses a SABRE or APOLLO terminal for booking reservations, and identify the number of hospitality industry components, such as airline ticket, hotel, etc., which can be directly accessed by the agent.

2. Identify the areas of a nearby hotel which are currently automated through an interview with the manager.

3. Call an airline, car rental service, and hotel 800 number, and determine the ability of each to book the others' services.

# From Seed to Sequoia: Corporate Strategy Within the Hospitality Industry

# 20

## PURPOSE

Many forces, including external trends and internal industry occurrences, shape a marketing strategy. Knowledge of these trends and the direction of the overall marketplace can be critical to everything from a promotional program to carrier selection. The focus of this analysis is to identify from where the industry has come and in which direction it appears to be headed and to draw selected implications for marketing in the future.

## OBJECTIVES

1. Understand the historical base as the rationale for the future.

2. Identify internal as well as external industry forces.

3. Dissect current corporate strategy(ies) as it relates to the marketplace and related forces.

4. Examine how such strategies relate to products in the hospitality industry.

5. Present some key trends and likely scenarios for the years ahead.

Understanding corporate strategy within the hospitality industry requires an insight into both internal (within the corporations themselves) and external (macro sociodemographic and psychographic trends) factors. Fundamental causes of the strategies are as varied as the propagation of segmented product, service levels, and development approaches existing today. In some instances these fundamental causes disappear almost as rapidly as a chameleon changes its appearance. In fact, use of the analogy of a chameleon changing its appearance to reflect threats and changes to its environment is also appropriate for many corporations in today's hospitality industry.

## HISTORIC BASE

A brief historical review is essential to understanding the evolution of most corporate strategies in this industry that are based on internal factors. Historically, the hotel was a product that served the person traveling to urban centers. Synonymous with the word "hotel" was the name Hilton. In the 1950s one of the very first alternative corporate strategies to hotels was the invention of the roadside motel product by Kemmons Wilson. His concept translated itself into Holiday Inns, which quickly became synonymous with the word "motel." Thus, two major product segments emerged in the hospitality industry: the hotel, a downtown product; and the motel, a highway or roadside product. One was geared for business travelers; the other aimed at the family market. With this emergence came the beginning of large-scale market segmentation in the hospitality industry.

Before we examine the evolution of these product and market segmentation strategies from their embryonic state to today's levels, it is important to also note one additional historic root of the hospitality industry and its strategic thrusts. Just as Hilton and "hotels" were historic synonyms, Marriott, Stouffer, and others were companies that had emerged from root beer stands, ice cream shops, and coffee shops into legitimate restaurant companies. The evolutionary strategy that took both William Marriott and Vernon Stouffer from one simple small food establishment into the full gamut of food service facilities and preparation processes continued until it manifested itself in the next logical service — providing beds. Thus, added to the single-product strategy and the market-segment strategy is the third strategic corporate thrust — multiple service with integrated, generally related, products. I am sure there are other historic or fundamental reasons for strategies — but these three represent what has emerged as the base from which many of today's corporate strategic thrusts have been launched. Before we look at the emergency of these and at their proliferation, there is yet another fundamental base we must touch upon — it is called *resources*.

The entrepreneurs who built the hospitality industry were not the wealthy computer-age geniuses we see as today's entrepreneurs. These were hard-working men and women whose primary resources were their own skills, personal friendships, and, often, borrowed money. As they began to succeed, demand for their "concept" or "opportunity" outstripped the availability of resources for expansion. The answer for bringing more of their product or service to the market was quickly found in another pioneering corporate strategy called *franchising*. Holiday Inns' phenomenal growth best exemplifies franchising in its heyday. One need only look at McDonalds' and Wendy's to see its application in the fast food industry to further underscore franchising as a strategy for growth.

These basic product, market, and expansionary strategies nurtured the growth from the seed to the tree, and eventually, to a forest of hybrid strategies. Placing these in a neat logically ordered structure is not an easy task, especially if it includes an audit trail that leads us to today's corporate strategy in the hospitality industry. I will attempt to do this categorization a little bit later, but first I must comment upon what forces make these strategies dynamic rather than static. There are two such forces — the internally driven and the externally reactive.

## INTERNALLY DRIVEN FORCES

The very early strategy of today's corporations was truly internally driven. Simply stated, it was the driving force of entrepreneurs, the desire to see their businesses grow, and new ideas that were the principle corporate strategy. This occurred during an age in which quantitative units and growth rates were the only buzz words known in hospitality companies. In fact, not until the early 1970s did "strategic planning" even become a part of the vocabulary of hospitality corporations. This internal strategic drive resulted in further market and product segmentation. It took on different meanings for different companies. For Holiday Inns it meant locations that were at logical stopping points along the highway. Later, for Hilton and others, it meant entering the marketplace with an "inn" product and expanding this product through franchising. For the hospitality industry it meant the birth and emergence of what would, one day, be known as the age of brand proliferation — the 1980s. For the seed had now proliferated and grown and become a forest with new growth; there emerged Ramada Inns, Quality Inns, Sheraton, and Hilton Inns. There were also larger trees such as Sheraton Hotels, Hilton Hotels, and Inter-Continental Hotels.

It is evident that a dual strategic thrust existed — internally driven product diversification and externally demanded market segmentation. However, in the 1950s and early 1960s the motivator or cause was internal, and growth in the number of units was the game.

## EXTERNALLY DRIVEN FORCES

Long before John Naisbitt wrote or even conceived of *Megatrends,* major external forces were in place that would have a lasting strategic impact on the thought processes of corporations in the hospitality industry. These external forces were categorized as quantitative and qualitative trends of a magnitude to influence and shape corporate strategy as it related to markets, products, quality, levels of services, pricing strategies and so on. Those who stayed in step with these trends would later emerge as the industry leaders and growth companies of the 1980s. Key external forces can be succinctly listed.

1. Population trends (growth, mix, and movement)
2. Growth of affluence (wealth, discretionary income, etc.)
3. Emergence of classes (low, middle, upper-middle, upper)
4. Development of transportation systems (interstates, airports, "hubs," etc.)
5. Tier qualitative segmentation of values, tastes, and psychographics
6. Internationalism of commerce; global perspective versus national isolationism

What is significant is not the importance of each of these individual factors, but the fact that components of each (a wealthier America, an older population, the emergence of "yuppies," etc.) were strong enough forces to cause everything from today's increasing supply of luxury accommodations to a surge in the budget motel lodging segment.

## CORPORATE STRATEGIES

Thus, in examining corporate strategies, one finds that there is no one overriding factor. Rather, that multiple internally driven and externally driven forces combined with a specific company's historic roots to determine the strategies espoused today.

Earlier I said we would attempt to provide some logical categorization of strategies being employed today and explain how they had evolved. There are as many ways to categorize as there are corporate strategists in the industry. The perspective which follows is based on participation in planning processes within several of the companies used as examples, and from 20 years of study and observation of other corporations in the industry. We have already discussed some of those whose hospitality businesses expanded from some type of food concept to encompass lodging (Howard Johnson's, Marriott, Stouffer) Therefore, the first categorization might simply be termed *horizontal expansions.*

### CORPORATE STRATEGY I: HORIZONTAL EXPANSION

Taking the perspective that the hospitality business encompasses food, beverage, lodging, travel-related services, horizontal expansion simply means expanding from one line of hospitality product or service — for example, food — to another — for example, lodging. This was, and still is, a strategy of today's corporations. As an example, Marriott now encompasses many away-from-home, or hospitality, services: food, lodging, entertainment, cruise ships, in-flight feeding (airline catering). Holiday Corporation now includes multiple lodging companies (more on this later), restaurant chains, and gaming or casino operations. Ramada is now in lodging, restaurants, and casinos. And there are many other examples of horizontal expansions. This is but one form of the dynamics of the hospitality industry strategies.

## CORPORATE STRATEGY II: GEOGRAPHIC EXPANSIONS

The hospitality industry, by nature, has capitalized on geographic demand. At first, companies developed within a relatively small radius of the origin base. Marriott was known as a Washington, D.C.–area company right up to the 1970s. In fact, it was its rapid growth in lodging west of the Mississippi that helped it develop into a national brand. Holiday Inns was a mid-south company, Ramada a southwestern company, LaQuinta a Texas company. A combination of factors — the market growth opportunities, sales of franchises, and unit growth mentality of the 1960s and 1970s — caused the local and regional hospitality firms to emerge with national, and ultimately international, status. The same is true of restaurant firms, such as Denny's, Wendy's, Brown Derby, and Arby's. For airlines, mergers and route system expansions created regional and then national carriers. Southern, Mohawk, Northeast with its yellow birds, and Hughes AirWest all were absorbed into larger carriers. Now, this trend has accelerated due to not only geographic expansion, but also due to economics of this industry segment.

## CORPORATE STRATEGY III: PRODUCT HYBRID

Perhaps because of Holiday Inns' phenomenal growth and the entry of other motel developers into the marketplace, it wasn't long before traditional high-rise hotel companies entered franchising and began developing low-rise "inns." Hilton Inns and Sheraton Inns are two examples of product hybrids that emerged in the late 1960s and early 1970s. Product hybrids also were natural strategies for those who started out with motels; soon there were high-rise motels called Holiday Inns, Ramada Inns, Marriott Inns. In fact, at one point in many of these companies' histories, their actual names were Marriott *Inns,* Stouffer *Inns,* Quality *Inns,* and so on. Product hybrids continued to emerge as high-rise and mid-rise facilities offering more services than had the traditional motel. Marriott's lodging operations, for example, at one point actually changed its name to Marriott Motor Hotels, and there were Sheraton Motor Inns. There are also Holiday Inn Hotels and Marriott Hotels, products designed and developed to offer "hotel" services and amenities. Product hybrids were but the seed of a much larger and complex segmentation strategy that would fully bloom in the late 1970s and 1980s.

## CORPORATE STRATEGY IV: SPECIALIZATION

Just as Holiday Inns began with the idea of offering families affordable accommodations, other entrants into the marketplace began as specialists categorized by price or service levels. For example, Motel "6", Days Inns, LaQuinta, and Budget Inns began with a specialized product offering limited facilities — essentially a room with virtually no services. In the food segment of our industry came fast food, salad bars, pizza parlors, specialty restaurants, steak houses, and seafood eateries. Specialization also went upscale in both pricing and services offered. Today there are Guest Quarters, Embassy Suites, and a plethora of luxury hotel chains. Interestingly enough, some of these specialized products and services were the result of what is, perhaps, one of the most commented-upon corporate strategies: product "tiering."

## CORPORATE STRATEGY V: PRODUCT TIERING

Product tiering was an initial corporate response to limitations of growth or the aging of its prevalent product. These limitations could have resulted from market saturation or occurred when the actual economics of the original concept no longer worked or were not as lucrative as an alternative approach. Ramada Inns developed a three-tiered approach in the early 1980s: Ramada Inns, Ramada Hotels, and Ramada Renaissance Hotels. Each of these product tiers reflects pricing, levels of service, and operational variations. Holiday Inns, Holiday Inn Hotels, and Holiday Inn Crown Plazas represented Holiday's original product tiering. Other companies soon followed with various forms of product tiering, manifested in an upscale movement from inn to hotel to super hotel. Product tiering also touched those such as Marriott, which deemphasized inns and franchising, and opted to go in other directions: hotels and mega-hotels (1,000 rooms plus) called Marriott Marquis, followed by a low-rise lodging product, Courtyards by Marriott, and most recently to an all-suites product. Radisson, Howard Johnson's, Quality International, Hyatt, and other lodging chains all placed product-tiering designators on lodging facilities which offered varying levels of services, amenities, and pricing structures. This was simply the lodging industry's response to the mega-forces of population, demographic, economic, and psychographic segmentation. Product tiering was rampant in the industry by the early 1980s.

## CORPORATE STRATEGY VI: PRODUCT BRANDING

The most recent corporate strategy to emerge might best be labeled *product branding*. This was a result in part of the proliferation of tiering and the subsequent consumer and franchise confusion it caused. The confusion was the result of a whole lot of product relabeling mixed in with some genuine product tiering. An establishment looked like a motel, smelled like a motel, but often had another name. As a result of this confusion and of an even stronger force or marketplace dynamic known as consumer awareness, product branding emerged. Ironically, the hospitality industry, one of the world's oldest, was just entering the product development era of brand identification. The focus of product branding is clearly delineating what that product or service is in terms of price, level and quality of service, location, and other key consumer-oriented factors such as the psychographic appeal of "prestige" or "thrift." There are a number of clear examples of today's product branding. To understand these one might think of the hospitality corporation as analogous to General Motors or Mercedes. For example, Holiday Corporation has followed the General Motors product branding concept and new offers Holiday Inns, Hampton Inns, Holiday Inns Crown Plaza Hotels, Embassy Suites, and Harrah's Casinos. Everything from a Chevrolet to a Cadillac. Marriott has adopted a similar strategy, choosing to keep the "Marriott" label on all its products: Marriott Hotels, Marriott Resorts, Marriott Marquis, and Courtyards by Marriott. Others have elected to utilize what might be analogous to the Mercedes, Porsche, or Jaguar concept: one product of high quality — one brand, no variations. Examples include Four Seasons, Stouffer Hotels, Ritz Carlton, and Westin, to name a few. These firms have room to grow within their brand and currently do not need to adopt an alternate strategy.

## OTHER TYPES OF CORPORATE STRATEGIES

There are other corporate strategies that transcend product, brand, and market. These are the financial/developmental approaches of today's hospitality firms. They can be oversimplified into the following categories.

**Nonfranchising Corporations.**   Usually, product quality control, ownership, and management control are the motivators behind firms that do not franchise, and often these firms have strong enough financial resources or can obtain such. Examples of lodging chains that do not franchise are few. Stouffer Hotels (parent Nestle), Westin Hotels, LaQuinta, and Motel "6" are such examples.

**Restricted Franchising: Predominant Control Corporation.**   Marriott Hotels is perhaps a good example of one such corporation. It is primarily a hotel management and operating company; however, it does have a few selective franchise operators with hotels carrying the Marriott banner. These are limited in number and usually are viewed as offering quality of service and adherence to standards that would be found in a parent-owned and-operated facility.

**Franchising Corporations.**   These are more prevalent; Holiday Corporation, Ramada Inc., Quality International, and Howard Johnson's are examples of lodging firms that are large franchisers. McDonald's, Wendy's, Dunkin' Donuts', and Arby's are leaders in the fast-food area. Today it is possible to purchase a franchise for virtually everything from a travel agency to a destination resort.

In addition to these developmental/financial growth strategies there are additional emerging corporate strategies increasingly visible in today's hospitality industry. These are juxtaposed in that one incorporates vertical and horizontal integration of various or all components of the hospitality industry, while the other focuses on singleness or simplicity.

**Vertical and Horizontal Integration Strategy.**   This is a corporate strategy which is premised on involvement in more than one component of the hospitality business. One example is the Carlson Companies. Carlson is the parent of Radisson and its line of lodging products; "Ask Mr. Foster," a large travel agency group; and TGI Friday, a restaurant company. Unlike in the pre-1980s when integration in the hospitality business might have consisted of a firm with hotels and restaurants or a firm with an airline and hotel chain, deregulation has provided the opportunity to gain competitive edges by owning or investing in multiple components of the industry.

**Singleness Strategies.**    Some industry firms have opted to concentrate on one product or service and to develop that specific component solely, forgoing product segmentation, tiering, and vertical and horizontal integration strategies. Stouffer Hotels, for example, has opted for a single product of all first-class hotels with ownership and management control. Four Seasons is another lodging firm following this strategy.

Finally, I would be remiss if a number of other specific corporate strategies and trends were not highlighted. Granted, these are at random, much like the development of our industry — growth-oriented and in natural evolution.

**Values-Related Products/Services.**    Residence Inns, Compri by Doubletree, and Embassy Suites exemplify concepts developed to respond to specific value and psychographic trends. The residential approach, social environments, and suite concept are all aimed at specifically expressed needs of today's consumer. As the sophistication of the consumer continues to develop with expressed demands and product service desires, corporations will identify and fulfill these with appropriate and timely strategies. These are but three of many examples available from within the hospitality industry. Others include the variety of credit cards and services, such as gold cards, platinum cards, etc.; the variety of air travel options, such as all first class, or budget fares, and new airline brands.

**Global Product Strategies.**    Today the oceans, to some extent political ideologies, and other traditional trade barriers no longer seem insurmountable hurdles for the hospitality industry. Lodging firms have no imposed boundaries. Holiday, Westin, Marriott, Ramada, Sheraton, and others have products throughout the world. As the United States–based firms expand globally, foreign companies have entered our market — Meridian, Trusthouse Forte, Sofitel, New Otani, and others. The brands and signs of fast food chains can be seen in most international cities and airports. Investment reasons, risk levels, growth strategies, reasons for expansion all vary by corporation and by market. These are influenced by many different social, economic, and political trends and events. These corporations' perspectives are as varied as the products, services, and markets they serve. An Arizona-based firm like Ramada Inc. had products in Europe and Asia. Memphis-based Holiday Inns has products virtually surrounding the globe. Yet Stouffer Hotels, whose parent is the global Nestle company, opts for only the U.S. market. And a French lodging chain, Meridian, begins to emerge in the United States. United Airlines affiliates with Swissaire and Delta with JAL to have more competitive frequent traveler programs.

## SORTING OUT POTENTIAL WINNING AND LOSING STRATEGIES

In a dynamic environment and industry, change becomes the only sure bet. To pick winners and losers is virtually impossible. There are, however, some winning characteristics to look for in making your own judgments. These include financial strength, quality control, ability to change, brand identity, broad-based and strategic orientation. A close look at some emerging trends and likely scenarios will reveal just how *key* each of these will be in our industry.

**Trend 1: Overbuilding in Luxury Lodging Segments from Full Service Hotels and Suite Concepts to Resorts.**  The likely survivors will be those with the deepest financial resources, the best quality and concept, and brand identity of critical mass. The strong will absorb the small and weak. Supply and demand will be more in line as affluence increases.

**Trend 2: Population Bulges in Older Age Groups.**  This trend means a strong demand for lower-priced budget facilities, which is likely to be the next overbuilt category. While market demand is strong, aggressive development will occur in the next five years. The longer term market will demand upgraded lodging and dining experiences. Inexpensively constructed facilities will be converted to other uses.

**Trend 3: Mega-companies Emerge.**  Marriott, AMR, Holiday, Carlson, and some others all continue to accelerate their growth through acquisitions and new product development, and are emerging as true giants with a distinctly competitive edge. Only those who are specialized, have singleness of strategy, and are strong financially will be able to carve their own niche and prosper.

**Trend 4: Concept Sort-out.**  Surprisingly, very few of the new concepts will survive. All-suites without all services will appeal to some, but not big spenders. Trends away from socializing may hamper social or residential concepts that are banking too heavily on the club environment. Likely successors will have "social/secure" environment.

**Trend 5: Loss Through Lack of Understanding.**  As the population mix changes, there will be an emergence of strong value orientations and psychographic trends. It will be increasingly important for the employer to understand these trends in order to attract and keep employees. The old guard must recognize new ways to survive and relate to the customer and to the employee.

**Trend 6: Complexities Beginning.**  The complexity of marketing one's product or service is about to explode. Incentives, promotions, tie-ins, media, technology, and consumer types are also becoming increasingly complex. Those who are asleep or are banking on the old image may as well lower the flag. The game of bringing the consumer in will be equally as important as the service, value, and quality-level offerings for encouraging their return.

**Trend 7: Critical Mass Gets More Critical.**  Competition will require that the baseline for survival become larger with an increasing size and number of locations and units needed over past years for market and brand awareness. This suggests incentives to merge, franchise, create joint ventures, and joint market. The brand proliferation of the mid-1980s (over 50 new brands in the 1984–1985 24-month period) resulted in consolidation in the late 1980s. The strong swallow the weak and go for mass.

These trends and corporate strategies combine to provide for a fast moving, exciting period in the hospitality industry. Those who have been in this business and are amazed at how it has grown over the past 20 years, will be equally astounded by the next two decades.

For, it is just the beginning of one of the world's fastest growing and largest industries — the hospitality industry. The one industry whose corporate strategies as a whole result in bringing people together, in caring for others, and ultimately building a better world.

## KEY WORDS AND CONCEPTS

**Product Hybrid** A variation on a base product, such as a high-rise inn or motel.

**Product Tiering** A variation in degree of product quality and/or level of services, such as Ramada Inn, Ramada Hotel, and Ramada Renaissance Hotel.

**Product Branding** Labeling a product with a name by which or upon which it is marketed and identified, such as Embassy Suites or Residence Inns.

**Megatrend** A massive qualitative or quantitative trend which has a substantial impact on an enterprise or society.

## ASSIGNMENTS

1. Select a demographic, psychographic, or social trend, and explain its likely impact on lodging or food and beverage.

2. Identify a brand in the hospitality industry, and discuss what you perceive to be its positioning or image objective.

3. Select one company with multiple products or concepts in the food service or lodging area, and provide what you believe is their rationale for multiple concepts.

4. Pick one brand or firm mentioned in this chapter which has been acquired, dissolved, or merged with another. Identify which trend was the likely cause, and state whether or not you believe this was a good or bad strategic marketing move.

# *Epilogue*

*T*he "weapons" are available for your selection. Load them up and get firing! Use your creativity and the practical "keys" to go after the market and each key segment. The results will be most satisfying both to you and your customers!

# Bibliography

Abbey, Dr. James R., and Milton T. Astroff, **Convention Sales and Service.** Dubuque, Iowa: Wm. C. Brown Co., 1983.

American Hotel and Motel Association and School of Hotel, Restaurant, and Institutional Management. **Commercial Lodging Market, Phase Two.** East Lansing: Michigan State University, 1968.

Aronin, Robert A., "U.S. Travel Industry." Unpublished Manuscript, 1976.

Bogart, Leo. **Strategy in Advertising.** New York: Harcourt, Brace and World, 1967.

Boone, Louis E., and David L. Kurtz, **Contemporary Marketing.** Hinsdale, Ill.: The Dryden Press, 1967.

Boyd, Harper, William and Massy. **Marketing Management.** New York: Harcourt Brace Jovanovich, 1972.

Chase, Cochrane, and Kenneth L. Barasch. **Marketing Problem Solver.** Radnor, Pa.: Chilton Book Company, 1977.

Coffman, C. DeWitt. **Hospitality For Sale.** East Lansing, Mich.: The Educational Institute, American Hotel and Motel Association, 1980.

**Cornell Hotel and Restaurant Administration, Quarterly.** School of Hotel Administration, Cornell University, Ithaca, N. Y.

Drucker, Peter. **Management — Tasks, Responsibilities, Practices.** New York: Heineman, 1974.

Holloway, Robert, and Robert Hancock, eds. **The Environment of Marketing Behavior.** 2d ed. New York: John Wiley and Sons, 1969.

Kotler, Philip. **Marketing Management.** Englewood Cliffs, N.J.: Prentice Hall, 1972.

Laventhol & Horwath. **Financing the Lodging Industry: A Survey of Lender Attitudes.** New York, 1975.

Laventhol & Horwath. **Hotel Operations in 1979.** New York, 1979.

Laventhol & Horwath. **U.S. Lodging Industry.** New York, 1980.

Lundberg, Ronald E. **The Hotel and Restaurant Business.** 3d ed. Boston: CBI Publishing, 1979.

McIntosh, Robert. **Tourism — Principles, Practices, Philosophies.** Columbus, Ohio: Grid, 1972.

Myers, James H., and Edward Tauber. **Market Structure Analysis.** Chicago: American Marketing Association, 1977.

Nykiel, R. A. "The Incentive Travel Market." Washington, D.C.: Marriott Corporation, 1972, 1973.

Nykiel, R. A. "Away from Home Eating Trends." Washington, D.C.: Marriott Corporation, 1973.

Nykiel, R. A. "The Japanese Travel Market — Outbound." Washington, D.C.: Marriott Corporation, 1973.

Nykiel, R. A. "Market Segmentation and its Applications to Sales and Advertising." Washington, D.C.: Marriott Corporation, 1973.

Nykiel, R. A. "Marketing Planning Process." Washington, D.C.: Marriott Corporation, 1973.

Nykiel, R. A. "The Next Thirty Years — A Study of Significant Quantitative and Qualitative Trends Affecting the Business Climate and Lifestyle in America." Washington, D.C.: Marriott Corporation, 1972, 1973.

Nykiel, R. A. "The Prospects for Future Growth in International Pleasure Travel." Washington, D.C.: Marriott Corporation, 1973.

Nykiel, R. A. "A Qualitative Study of the Domestic Lodging Market Needs by Segment." Washington, D.C.: Marriott Corporation, 1973.

Nykiel, R. A. "The Vacation Market's Preferences and Needs." Washington, D.C.: Marriott Corporation, 1973.

Nykiel, R. A. "Cruise Market Trends." Washington, D.C.: Marriott Corporation, 1974.

Nykiel, R. A. "Vertical and Horizontal Integration of the Travel Business." Washington, D.C.: Marriott Corporation, 1974.

Nykiel, R. A. "Factors Influencing the Domestic and International Hotel Development Process." Paper and speech to the Business and Economics Graduate Program, Industrial College of Armed Forces, Washington, D.C., 1975.

Powers, Thomas F. "The Competitive Structure of the Hotel/Motel Market." A paper presented to the Council on Hotel, Restaurant and Institutional Education, 1969.

Reis, Al, and Jack Trout. **Marketing Warfare.** New York: McGraw Hill Book Co., 1986.

Reis, Al, and Jack Trout. **Positioning: The Battle For Your Mind.** New York: McGraw Hill Book Co., 1981.

Russell, Thomas, and Glenn Verrill. **Otto Kleppmer's Advertising Procedure.** Englewood Cliffs, N.J.: Prentice Hall.

Summer, Prof. J. R. **Improve Your Marketing Techniques: A Guide for Hotel Managers and Caterers.** London: Northwood Books, 1985.

U.S. Government Printing Office. **Directory of National Trade Associations of Businessmen.** Washington, D.C., 1980.

U.S. Travel Data Center. **The Importance of Tourism to the U.S. Economy.** Washington, D.C., 1975.

Wahab, S., L. J. Crampon, and L. M. Rothfield. **Tourism Marketing.** London: Tourism International Press, 1976.

# Glossary

**a la Carte** According to the bill of fare; with a separate price for each item on the menu. (See **Prix Fixe** and **Table d'Hote**)

**Action Program** That portion of the plan that lists specific things to be done. It includes target dates, approved expenditures (as differentiated from unapproved estimated costs), and the person responsible for implementation.

**Add-On** A supplement. For example, an air/sea package may feature different airfare add-ons to the cruise fare depending on the city of departure.

**Adjoining Rooms** Two or more hotel rooms located side by side but without private connecting doors. Rooms may be adjoining without connecting.

**Advance Purchase** A general term used to define a variety of types of discounted fares and rates. Some of the more common are 30-, 14-, and 7-day advance purchase periods.

**Aft** Near or at the rear of a ship. Also means towards the rear, or in that general direction but not necessarily right at the rear. An aft cabin is not necessarily at the very back of the ship.

**Agent** Broadly, one who acts or has the power to act; more often, one who acts for or as the representative of another. Most frequently in travel, a specific kind of agent, such as: (1) a retail travel agent; (2) a carrier employee who sells tickets, a counter agent, or ticket agent; (3) one with broad powers to act for a principal, a general agent; or (4) (usually outside the United States and Canada) anyone in the travel business other than a principal, such as a retail travel agent, receiving agent, local operator or wholesaler.

**Air/Sea** Special arrangements combining air transportation to and from the port of embarkation with the cruise itself, sometimes called fly/cruise.

**Alcove** An area, usually for sleeping, set off from a larger room.

**All-expense Tour** A tour offering all or most services (transportation, lodging, meals, porterage, sightseeing, etc.) for a pre-established price. The terms *all-expense* and *all-inclusive* are misused. Virtually no tour rate covers everything. The terms and conditions of a tour contract should specify exactly what is covered.

**American Automobile Association** An organization that provides its members with a variety of services (travel information, highway and legal services, insurance, etc.)

related to owning and operating automobiles. AAA also operates AAA Worldwide Travel, a multibranch retail travel agency organization.

**American Hotel and Motel Association** A federation of state and regional lodging industry trade associations covering the United States, Canada, Mexico, and Central and South America.

**American Plan** A hotel rate that includes a bed and three meals. (See **Modified American Plan**)

**American Sightseeing Association** An international trade association of local tour operators. American Sightseeing International (ASI) is a promotional and business name owned by the parent association.

**American Society of Travel Agents** The leading trade association of U.S. and Canadian travel agents and tour operators.

**Amtrak** The name under which the National Railroad Passenger Corporation operates virtually all U.S. intercity passenger trains, excluding commuter trains, under contract with individual railroads.

**APEX** Advance Purchase Excursion Fare (airline).

**Association of British Travel Agents** The principal trade association of travel agents and tour operators in the United Kingdom.

**Association of Caribbean Tour Operators** A trade association.

**Atlantic Passenger Steamship Conference** A rate-making conference of shiplines operating on the North Atlantic. Recently dissolved with the formation of the International Passenger Ship Association.

**Auditorium Style** Rows of chairs, with aisle(s), facing the speaker or stage. (Also called **Theater Style**)

**Auditorium Style, Semi-Circular** A variation with the rows of chairs in an arc, facing the speaker. (Also called **Senate Style**)

**Auditorium Style, V-Shape or Herringbone** The rows of chairs are angled so that the base of the V is at the center aisle.

**Australian Federation of Travel Agents** A trade association of travel agents in Australia.

**Automation** A general term used to define the computerization of travel-related information. Automation has been applied to reservations systems, front office systems, telephone systems, and a variety of management information systems and techniques.

**Available** (or **Availability**) Connotes a conditional status: "space available," for example, means "if the space is available."

**B and B** Bed and breakfast. A sleeping room rate, often in a guest house, or in Europe in a private home, which includes a full breakfast. In hotels often called BP (Bermuda Plan).

**Back-to-Back** Describing a program of multiple air charters between two or more points with arrivals and departures coordinated to eliminate aircraft deadheading and waiting. For example, when one group is delivered at a destination, another is ready to depart from that point.

**Banquet Business** Group of guests or people served in a separate room from the regular dining room with food service preselected at a flat price per person.

**Benefit Needs Segmentation** The dissection of the market into smaller segments based on the benefits sought, needs fulfilled, and, in some instances, things to be avoided.

**Bermuda Plan** Hotel accommodation with full American-style breakfast included in the rate.

**Berth** A bed on a ship or railroad car, often, but not necessarily, built in. A space at a wharf for a ship to dock or anchor.

**Best Available** A reservation pledging a principal to provide some sort of accommodation and to upgrade the client if possible. A request for a reservation meaning, "I'll take anything you have, but I'm willing to pay for your best."

**Blocked Space** Reservations, often subject to deposit forfeiture, made with suppliers by wholesalers of travel agents in anticipation of resale.

**Board of Directors Style** A long table or series of tables set in a long rectangular shape, with chairs on both sides and ends. Ends may be oval or squared off.

**Boarding Pass** A permit to board a ship, plane, train, or other form of transportation.

**Bonding** The purchase, for a premium, of a guarantee of protection for a supplier or a customer. In the travel industry, certain bonding programs are mandatory. ATC insists that travel agents be bonded to protect the airlines against defaults; the CAB forces the operators of inclusive tour charters to carry bonds to protect their customers against default. Some operators and agents buy bonds voluntarily to protect their clients and for promotional purposes.

**Booking Form** A document that purchasers of tours must complete to give the operator full particulars about who is buying the tour. It states exactly what is being purchased (including options) and it must be signed as acknowledgment that the liability clause has been read and understood.

**Bow** The very front of the ship, also called the prow.

**Breakdown Time** The time needed after an event or function to rearrange the setups.

**British Tourist Authority** The official government travel promotion agency of Great Britain.

**Brochure** A printed folder describing a tour or a package and specifying the conditions of the offering.

**Bulk Fare** A net fare contract for a certain number of seats. Similar to blocked space except that the tour operator, wholesaler, or travel agent usually contracts for airline seats at a net price without the option of releasing space back to the airline. Thus the operator/wholesaler/agent acquires inventory.

**Bump** To displace a passenger or guest by virtue of holding a reservation with a higher priority (regular fare passenger will bump a standby passenger) or by being sufficiently important (a Senator can usually bump an ordinary passenger, even in first class). A bumped passenger may or may not be entitled to denied boarding compensation depending on the sort of ticket he or she holds.

**Cabana** A room in a beach or pool area, with or without beds; usually separate from a hotel's main building.

**Cabin** A sleeping room on a ship; may imply less luxury than a stateroom.

**Cambio** An office where currencies may be exchanged. This Spanish word is used in many non-Spanish countries as well.

**Caribbean Cruise Association** A trade association of shiplines that operated Caribbean cruises; recently dissolved with the formation of the International Passenger Ship Association.

**Caribbean Travel Association** A cooperative promotional agency supported by Caribbean national governments.

**Carrier** Any organization that deals in transporting passengers or goods.

**Cash Bar** A bar setup where guests pay for drinks.

**Channels of Distribution** Vehicles through which travel-related products or services may be marketed by suppliers and/or purchased by consumers.

**Charter** To hire the exclusive use of any aircraft, vessel, or other vehicle.

**Charter Flight** A flight booked exclusively for the use of a specific group or groups of people who generally belong to the same organization(s), or who are guests of a single host, or who are traveling on an inclusive tour charter program. Charters are much cheaper than scheduled air services but are available to individuals and groups only under rigidly specified conditions. They may be carried out by scheduled or supplemental airlines. (See **Inclusive Tour Charter**)

**Check-in** The formalities attendant to arrival at a hotel, including signing the register.

**Check-in Time** Most hotel-days begin at 6:00 a.m. but an arriving guest may be unable to occupy his or her room until after the established check-out time, usually 1:00 p.m.

**Check-out Time** All hotels post a time (usually, but not necessarily, 1:00 p.m.) by which guest must vacate their rooms. Late checkouts are often permitted but must be approved by the hotel management.

**Child** In travel, the supplier defines the chronological limits of childhood. Fare structures and hotel rates often contain break points at which children are offered reduced rates, but these vary.

**City Pair** Two or more cities that share intercity travel to a major proportion of their total travels; for example, Boston and New York.

**City Terminal** An airline ticket office, not located at an airport, where a passenger may check in for a flight, check his or her baggage, receive a seat assignment, and secure ground transportation to the airport.

**City Ticket Office** A carrier ticket sales office or counter located outside a terminal.

**Civil Aeronautics Board** The federal agency that regulated domestic air commerce and international air commerce to and from the United States. The CAB had authority to license air carriers and exercised control over their routes, schedules, rates, and their dealings with one another, other travel industry segments, and the public. The CAB as an entity was abolished in the 1980s.

**Civil Aviation Authority** The agency that administers British civil aviation with responsibility for route licensing, safety standards, and traffic control.

**Client** A travel agent's customer.

**Coach Service** U.S. domestic passenger carriage at the international equivalent of Economy.

**Collateral Materials** Print-based support materials that assist in the marketing of products and services. Included are brochures, tent cards, posters, directories, maps, guides, menu inserts, flyers, entertainment promotion pieces, etc.

**Commercial Rate** A special rate agreed upon by a company (or other multipurchaser) and a hotel. Usually the hotel agrees to supply rooms of a specified quality or better at a flat rate.

**Commitment** The detailed arrangement agreed to by both the meeting planner and the facility.

**Common Rated** Describing two or more relatively adjacent destinations for which the fare from a specific point of origin is identical.

**Compartment** In general, any section of a railroad coach.

**Competition** Any business concern, product, or concept that competes for customers in your own market. It may be a product or concept completely different from your own.

**Concierge** In virtually all European hotels (and elsewhere), the superintendent of minor services (porterage, mailing letters, making reservations, and the like) for guests. The concierge is often a guest's principal link with both the hotel and the city in which it is located.

**Conducted Tour** A prearranged travel program, usually for a group, escorted by a courier. In a fully conducted tour, escort and/or guide service is provided throughout. A sightseeing program conducted by a guide.

**Conference** An association of carriers formed to establish rules for the mutual benefit of its members. Among other things, a conference may establish rates; allocate routes; formulate and enforce safety, service, and ethical standards; and establish rules governing the conduct of others (for example, travel agents) who do business with its members.

**Configuration** The interior arrangement of a vehicle, particularly an airplane. The same aircraft, for example, might be configured for 190 coach passengers; for 12 first-class passengers and 170 coach passengers; for 12 first-class passengers, 100 coach passengers, and two cargo pallets; or for any other combination within its capacity.

**Confirmed Reservation** An oral or written statement by a supplier (a carrier, hotel, car rental company, etc.) that he or she has received and will honor a reservation. Oral confirmations have virtually no legal worth. Even written or telegraphed confirmations have specified or implied limitations. For example, a hotel is not obligated to honor a reservation if the guest arrives after 6:00 p.m., unless late arrival is specified.

**Connecting Flight** A segment of an ongoing journey that requires the passenger to change aircraft (but not necessarily carriers). Under IATA regulations, a flight connection becomes a stopover if the passenger is required to wait more than 24 hours for his or her next flight.

**Connecting Rooms** Two or more rooms with private doors, permitting access from one to the other without use of hotel corridor.

**Consumer Perspective** How the consumer of your product or service views that offering — *not* how marketing or operations views the product or service offering.

**Continental Breakfast** At a minimum, a beverage (coffee, tea, or milk) and rolls or toast. Sometimes includes fruit juice. In Holland and Norway, may include cheese, cold meat, or fish.

**Continental Plan** A hotel rate that includes bed and continental breakfast.

**Cooperative Promotion** A promotion involving two or more suppliers of services or products joined together in a common promotion for their mutual benefit.

**Co-oping** Joining together with others to advertise when dollar constraints would normally prohibit you from going it alone, or joining together to promote a common benefactor to all, such as the region or market.

**Core Market** Represents a core of consumers who are vital to your product or service and who form the consistent core of purchasers.

**Cost-Plus Theory** In periods of low demand, recognizing the need to price or sell the product or service offering by discounting the price (beyond fixed and variable cost levels) to stimulate sales.

**Coupon, Flight** The portion of a passenger ticket that indicates the route on which passage has been purchased.

**Coupon, Passenger** The portion of airline ticket that constitutes written evidence to the passenger of the contract of carriage.

**Creative** Indicates the production of new business, particularly for airlines. A creative travel agent presumably produces new business by inducing people to travel. Airline marketing personnel believe that agents who produce a high percentage of pleasure and group sales are more creative than those who produce business and point-to-point sales.

**CRT** Cathode Ray Tube. The screen linked to a computer which displays information for a travel supplier and permits direct communication with the computer's data base.

**CTC** The CTC designation is awarded by the Institute of Certified Travel Agents to travel professionals with five years or more industry experience who have completed a two-year, graduate-level travel management program.

**Customer Needs** A customer's needs are what he or she is really looking for in a product. They are the things he or she hopes the product will satisfy. These are the same as customer "wants," "desires," etc.

**Customer Perceptions** Perceptions are the way the customer, *in his or her own mind,* looks at a product. They include what the customer's image is of the product. This is very important because his or her image is almost always different than what management thinks it is.

**Customer Satisfaction** Meeting the identified needs of the consumer with a level of service and product quality that is in line with the expectation conveyed by the marketing message and related pricing.

**Customs** The federal agency charged with collecting duty (taxes) on specific items imported into the country and restricting the entry of forbidden items.

**Cutoff Date** Date when meeting planner must release or add to room requirements.

**Dais** A raised platform on which the head table is placed.

**Day Rate** A special rate for non-overnight use of a hotel room. Usually good only between 6:00 a.m. and 5:00 p.m.

**DBA** Doing business as (for example, the Doe Travel Co. might do business as D Travel Tours).

**Deadhead** A person traveling on a free pass; more specifically, an airline crew or crew member in transit. Any aircraft, ship, or vehicle in transit without a payload. To operate an empty vehicle.

**Delivering Airline** A carrier that is transporting a passenger to an interline point.

**Delivery Package** The essential tools, including required forms, copy, photos, fact sheets, and biographies, to ensure that you are ready to effectively execute public relations programs.

**Deluxe** In travel usage, presumably "of the highest standard." A much misused and, in many respects, meaningless term except where employed as part of an official rating system. (See **Hotel Classifications**)

**Demi-Pension** A hotel rate including bed, breakfast, and either lunch or dinner.

**Demographic Segmentation** The division of a market by like characteristics, such as age, sex, income, home ownership, marital status, occupation, education, etc.

**Deposit Reservation** A reservation for which the hotel has received cash payment for at least one night's lodging in advance and is obligated to hold the room regardless of the guest's arrival. Most commercial hotels do not feel obligated to refund deposits unless reservations are cancelled at least 48 hours in advance. Cancellation policies at resort hotels vary and should be verified in advance.

**Deregulation** In the 1980s the U.S. government sought to establish a more laissez-faire system for travel. This general movement became known as deregulation. Under deregulation, mergers, acquisitions, new fare and route structures, and considerable vertical and horizontal integration took place.

**Destination** The place to which a traveler is going. In the travel industry, any city, area, or country that can be marketed as a single entity to tourists.

**Direct Face-to-Face Sales** This is direct in-person or person-to-person selling.

**Direct Flight** A journey on which the passenger does not have to change planes.

**Direct Mail** Promotional letters, pieces, or any sales-oriented correspondence sent to prospective guests.

**Discount 50 Fares** Certain fares at 50 percent of normal rates offered to overseas visitors to North America.

**Discover America Fares** Air tariffs offering visitors to the United States unlimited travel within specified time limits on some airlines. Similar rates on some bus lines.

**Discover America Rates** Reduced rates offered to foreign visitors by some hotels and attractions in the United States.

**Discover America Travel Organizations** Former name of a large nonprofit association of companies and government organizations formed to promote travel to and within the United States. Now merged into TIA. (See **Travel Industry Association**)

**Discriminatory** In reference to fares, offering lower rates to certain people (servicemen and women, young people, old people, etc). Such promotional fares are under constant, and sometimes successful, attack on the grounds that they are unfair to those who are ineligible.

**Double** Loosely, any hotel room for two persons; more specifically, a room with a double bed. (A room with two smaller beds is a twin.)

**Double Bedroom** A bedroom suite.

**Double-Double** (See **Twin Double**)

**Double Occupancy Rate** The price *per person* for a room to be shared with another person. The rate most frequently quoted in tour brochures.

**Double Room Rate** The full price of a room for two people, but be careful — some people say "double" when they mean "double occupancy."

**Downgrade** To move to a lesser accommodation or class of service.

**DSM** District Sales Manager.

**Duplex** A two-story suite connected by a private stairway.

**Economy Fare** or **Service** In U.S. domestic airline operations passenger carriage at a level below coach service. In international operations, carriage at a level below first class.

**Efficiency** Any accommodation containing some sort of cooking facilities.

**English Breakfast** Generally served in the United Kingdom and Ireland. Usually includes fruit or fruit juice; hot or cold cereal; bacon, ham, sausages, or kippers; eggs; toast; butter; jam or marmalade; and tea or coffee.

**Eurailpass** A railroad pass sold for a flat rate for a specified number of days. It provides unlimited first-class travel through 13 European countries. Also available at student and children's rates.

**European Civil Aviation Conference** An association concerned with facilitating air commerce within Europe. Nations are represented by their civil aviation directors.

**European Plan** A hotel rate that includes bed only; any meals are extra.

**Excursion Fare** Any fare offering roundtrip transportation at a rate below the combined cost of the component one-way fares.

**Exposures** The number of consumers actually hearing or seeing your advertising. One ad may reach 100 million people if it is on national television at prime time, or provide you 100 million exposures.

**Extension** A fully arranged subtour offered optionally at extra cost to buyers of a tour or cruise. Extensions may occur before, during, or after the basic travel program.

**Familiarization Tour** A complimentary or reduced-rate travel program for travel agents and/or airline employees that is designed to acquaint them with a specific destination to stimulate the sale of travel.

**Family Plan** A discount schedule offered by carriers (and often hotels and resorts) to second and successive members of families who travel together.

**Feeder City** A city that generates major travel to another city; for example, Los Angeles to Las Vegas.

**First-class Fare** or **Service** In air, rail, and sea travel, the best and most expensive way to go.

**First-class Hotel** An average, comfortable hotel.

**FIT** (See **Foreign Independent Travel**)

**Flag Carrier** Any carrier designated by its government to operate international services.

**Flight** A scheduled air service, identified by a flight number, from departure point through any designated stops to destination point and operated as a single entity.

**Flyer** A printed advertisement intended for distribution to potential customers, usually by mail.

**Folder** Any travel supplier's printed advertisement. Technically, a folder is not a brochure.

**Foreign Independent Travel** An international, prepaid tour, usually unescorted, although guide service is often offered on some segments. An FIT is designed to the specifications of an individual client or clients.

**Foreign Independent Travel Operator** (or **Wholesaler**) A specialist in preparing and operating FITs at the request of retail travel agents.

**Forward** At or near the front part of a ship; toward or in the direction of the front. See **Aft**.

**French Service** Each food item is served by a waiter, as opposed to serving a completely setup plate.

**Frequent Traveler Programs** A type of promotion which blossomed in the 1980s rewarding a variety of incentives to frequent flyers and/or guests for their repeated use of the hospitality industry product or service. An attempt to build brand loyalty.

**Full Pension** Particularly in Europe, a hotel rate that includes three meals daily; an American Plan rate.

**Function Room** A room suitable for meetings, dining, exhibits, entertaining, etc., with no sleeping facilities.

**Garni** As applied to European hotels, without restaurant services except for continental breakfast.

**Geographic Segmentation** The arbitrary division of a market by region, state, zone, district, SMSA, city, sectional center, or zip codes.

**GIT** (See **Group Inclusive Tour**)

**Ground Services** Broadly defined as all the services received at a destination (excluding method of travel to the destination), such as rooms, food, beverage, local tours, etc.

**Group Inclusive Tour** A prepaid tour of specified minimum size, ingredients, and value. (See **Group Inclusive Tour Fare**)

**Group Inclusive Tour Fare** An airline fare applicable to a group inclusive tour.

**GSA** General sales agent.

**Guarantee** The figure given by the meeting planner to the hotel, usually 24 hours in advance of the event, of the number of persons to be served. Most hotels prepare for some additional people. Payment is made on the guaranteed number or the actual number, whichever is greater.

**Guaranteed Payment Reservation** A hotel reservation secured by the guest's agreement to pay for his or her room whether it is used or not. Payment is usually guaranteed by a company, travel agent, or tour wholesaler who has an established credit rating with the hotel.

**Guaranteed Tour** A tour guaranteed to operate unless cancelled before an established cutoff date (usually 60 days prior to departure). In the event of a cancellation after the deadline, full commission is paid on confirmed agency bookings.

**Head Tax** A fee which some countries charge each arriving or departing passenger.

**Heavy User Segmentation** A method of segmenting the market by identifying the most frequent customers of the production services.

**Hollow Circular Style** Like the square but curved tables form a circle.

**Hollow Square Style** Tables set in a square with hollow center. Chairs are placed on the outside of each table.

**Horseshoe Style** Tables set in a horseshoe shape. Chairs set up on the outside but may be set on the inside as well if space is needed.

**Hospitality** Hotel room used for entertaining, usually a function room or parlor.

**Hospitality Suite** A hotel suite, parlor, or studio engaged for the entertainment of those attending a convention or similar meeting.

**Hostel** An inexpensive, supervised lodging, particularly for young people.

**Hostelry** An inn; by extension, any accommodation that provides food and/or lodging to travelers.

**Hotel Classifications** The following designations are generally understood throughout Europe and, to an extent, the world, but it is sometimes difficult to know whether a hotel is being described by a reliable source or at the whim of a promoter. There is neither an official nor generally accepted rating system for U.S. hotels. **Deluxe** A top-grade hotel; all rooms have private baths, all the usual public rooms and services are provided, and a high standard of decor and services is maintained. **First Class** A medium-range hotel; at least some rooms have private bath, and most of the usual public rooms and services are provided. **Tourist (Economy** or **Second Class)** Budget operations; few or no private baths are available, and services may be very limited. The Official Hotel & Resort Guide further subdivides these three categories into three groups: superior, average, and moderate. Thus, a superior deluxe hotel rates with the best in the world and an average, first-class hotel is about in mid-range. OHRG says that hotels below its superior tourist rating should be used with caution by westerners. In addition, many governments rate their hotels according to the international five-star system, under which a five-star hotel is the best. Some countries are meticulous and generally current in their ratings; many are not. In general, three-star and better hotels (and a few two-star properties) are believed suitable for Western travelers.

**Hotel Package** A typical offering might include transportation and transfers plus room, board, and the use of sports facilities at a resort hotel. (See **Package**)

**Hotel Register** (or **Registry**) The permanent record maintained by all hotels of the arrival and departure of guests, all of whom must sign it on arrival.

**Hotel Representative** (or **Rep**) A person (or company) who offers hotel reservations to wholesalers, travel agents, and the public. He or she is paid by the represented hotels on a fee basis. Many hotel reps also offer marketing and other services.

**Hotel Sales Management Association** A professional society.

**Hotel & Travel Index** A Ziff-Davis quarterly directory covering rates, commission rates, capacity, services, location, and representation of more than 20,000 hotels and resorts throughout the world.

**Hotelier** A hotelkeeper.

**Housing Bureau** An organization, often government-sponsored, that acts as a clearing house for accommodations, particularly for conventions and other large meetings. Often established on an ad hoc basis during major touristic events to maintain a registry of private accommodations to supplement an area's regular lodging industry.

**HSMA** (See **Hotel Sales Management Association**)

**HTI** (See **Hotel & Travel Index**)

**Hubs** A term which emerged in the 1980s under the era of deregulation. The hub concept is as the word implies: a central point at which airline routes of the same carrier converged. Hubs resulted in major gains in individual market share plus competitive and noncompetitive pricing.

**IATA** (See **International Air Transport Association**)

**ICAO** (See **International Civil Aviation Organization**)

**Incentive Travel** A trip offered as a prize, particularly to stimulate the productivity of employees or sales agents; the business of operating such travel programs.

**Inclusive Tour** A tour in which specific elements (air fare, hotels, transfers, etc.) are offered for a flat rate. An inclusive tour rate does not necessarily cover all costs.

**Inclusive Tour Charter** An aircraft charter that carries an inclusive tour. By extension, an ITC is trade vernacular for a tour that may be sold to an individual, on which basic transportation is provided by chartered aircraft. Particularly from the United States, ITC itineraries, tour ingredients, and minimum rates are rigidly specified. ITC organizers must meet established financial standards.

**Inflation Rate Plus Concept** A method for increasing rates or prices that is based on the premise that increases in rates should be at the inflation rate plus a percent target.

**In-house Profit Centers** An area within a hotel or restaurant or any operation that has revenue and profit production potential and is identified as a profit center unto itself.

**In-plant Agency** A travel agent's sales outlet located on the premises of a company and confined to doing business for that company only. In-plant air commissions are lower than those paid regularly; at this writing, only a handful of agents maintained in-plant locations.

**In-room Merchandiser** A promotional device containing a single or various marketing and sales messages. The device may be laminated plastic, a leather folder, tent card, brochure, etc.

**Interchange Flight** A through flight which requires passengers to change planes en route.

**Intermediary** An individual or firm that comes between the consumer of the travel product or service and the supplier of these services. Intermediaries frequently make the decision for the consumer. There are two groups or types; commercial, those who earn a commission, and captive, those whose salaried job it is to make travel plans for others.

**International Air Transport Association** The world trade association of airlines that operate international services. IATA operates as a supranational organization, setting rates, conditions of service, safety standards, etc., and providing the machinery which makes the unified world system of air transportation possible.

**International Civil Aviation Organization** An organization of 124 governments that works in relationship with the United Nations to promote the safety of international civil aviation by standardizing technical equipment, services, and training. ICAO also provides economic and statistical services to airlines and governments and extends technical assistance to developing countries.

**International Hotel Association** A European-based trade association.

**International Union of Official Travel Organizations** A world association of national government agencies for the promotion of tourism.

**Interstate Commerce Commission** A federal agency for the regulation and supervision of interstate commerce. Of particular interest to travel because it licenses bus and motorcoach operators.

**Intrastructure** Loosely, anything that supports travel. Legally, the government and quasi-governmental machinery that regulates and/or promotes travel and related industries. Physically, in a developing area, the public utilities (highways, water supply, electric power, etc.) needed to support a tourist plant. In a developed area, the entire local transportation, lodging, restaurant, entertainment, and cultural establishment.

**Introductory Promotion** A promotion designed to introduce a new product or service to the market.

**ITC** (See **Inclusive Tour Charter**)

**Itinerary** The travel schedule provided by a travel agent or his or her client. A proposed or preliminary itinerary may be rather vague or very specific. A final itinerary, however, spells out all details (flight numbers, departure times, etc.) as well as describing planned activities. It should be delivered shortly before departure.

**ITX** Independent Tour Excursion Airfare. A fare which may be available to passengers who pay in advance for a land package at certain destinations. Unlike the ITC, passengers flying on ITX fares may travel independently.

**Japan Association of Travel Agents** A trade association.

**Joint Fare** A special through fare for travel on two or more airlines.

**Junior Suite** A large hotel room with a partition separating the bedroom and sitting areas.

**Lanai** Generally, a veranda. In travel, a room with a balcony or patio overlooking water or a garden, usually in a resort hotel.

**Leg** The portion of a journey between two scheduled stops.

**Letter of Agreement** Written confirmation by the meeting planner to the facility's proposal. Both sides should sign copies of both the proposal and letter of agreement.

**Level of Expectation** The basic premise of advertising that reflects the concept of never promising more than your product or service can actually fulfill in an advertisement.

**Lido** A swimming pool and the area surrounding it.

**Low Season** That time of the year at any given destination when tourist traffic (and often rates) is at its lowest.

**Market Segment** A segment is a portion of the total market all of whose customers have something in common. There are several ways of segmenting a market. The most widely used is by *demographics* (age, income, sex, education, etc.). A second method is by *psychographics,* where the market is segmented by "needs" or "psychological motivation." Hence, people in the "need" segment all share a common desire or interest. These needs or interests do not always follow demographic lines.

**Market Share** Your product's or service's piece of the total market for that product or service. Usually expressed in a percentage basis or on a point scale.

**Marketing Planning** The organized process of studying the market, identifying and measuring its trends, and developing major marketing objectives and supporting programs, utilizing the available facts in combination with the experienced judgments of the top marketing team. The process includes the development of targets (timing, costs, results expected) and the monitoring of actual achievement against these targets. Its purpose is the achievement of maximum desired results, with the minimum of effort and resources utilized in the most efficient manner.

**Marketing Position Strategy Grid** An analytical tool designed to help select strategies to improve your market share and gain on competition.

**Media** The vehicles by which you can advertise. Broadcast media include television and radio. Print media include magazines, newspapers, direct mail, brochures, yellow pages, outdoor advertising boards, etc.

**Mobil** A national rating system for lodging facilities utilizing a star concept ranging from one star (minimal rating) to five stars (top rating).

**Modified American Plan** A hotel room rate including breakfast and either lunch or dinner.

**Mom and Pop Shop** A small travel agency operated by a husband and wife. By extension, any independently owned small agency.

**Motel Association of America** A confederation of state trade associations of motel operators located in the continental United States.

**National Air Transport Conference** The trade association of U.S. intrastate, commuter, and scheduled air taxi and third-level airlines.

**National Tour Brokers Association** A trade association of U.S. tour brokers.

**National Transport Safety Board** The Department of Transportation agency that develops safety standards for all modes of public transportation and investigates accidents.

**Net Rate** A wholesale rate to be marked up for eventual resale to the consumer.

**No-show** A passenger or guest who fails either to use or to cancel his reservation. A reservation neither cancelled nor fulfilled.

**Objectives** Objectives are the identification of *what* you want to do; for example, "increase our business in the pleasure travel market."

**Occupancy Rate** The ratio, expressed as a percentage, of bed nights sold to the total offered for sale, by a hotel or group of hotels.

**Official Airline Guide** Any of the several passenger and cargo air service manuals published by the Reuben H. Donnelly Corporation and in general use throughout the world. There are two principal passenger OAGs — the North American Quick Reference Edition and the International Quick Reference Edition. Either may sometimes be referred to as a QRE.

**Official Hotel and Resort Guide** A Ziff-Davis directory that describes and rates 25,000 hotels, resorts, and motor hotels throughout the world. The OHRG is published in a loose-leaf format to permit both regular and extraordinary revisions on a continuous basis.

**Off-peak** In reference to a fare or a hotel rate, any period(s) other than the period(s) that is usually busiest.

**Open Bar** A bar setup where guests do not pay for drinks.

**Open Jaw** Any trip essentially of a round trip nature, but where the passenger returns to a different point from the point of origin or departs for the round trip from a point other than the original destination.

**Open Ticket** A ticket that is valid for transportation between certain points, but indicates no specific reservation.

**Option Date** Date agreed upon to make definite the tentative agreement between facility and meeting planner.

**Overbooking** The practice of confirming more seats, cabins, or rooms than are actually available to ensure against no-shows. Overbooking can be unintentional, too.

**Override** An extra commission; sometimes called an **overriding commission.** Airlines pay overrides on ticket sales made in conjunction with tour sales. Wholesalers pay them as bonuses for volume business. Suppliers pay them to provide a profit margin for wholesalers (who must themselves pay commissions). Hotel groups or governments pay them as a volume incentive to wholesalers.

**Pacific Area Travel Association** An organization of nations interested in promoting tourism throughout the Pacific and Indian Ocean areas.

**Package** Loosely, any advertised tour; often, however, a tour to a single destination that includes prepaid transportation, accommodations, and some combination of other tour elements (meals, transfers, sightseeing, car rental, etc.). A package may include more than one destination (for example, a cruise) but the term connotes an offering intended to provide a holiday rather than meet the cultural or other requirements of the more serious traveler.

**Packager** Anyone who organized and advertises a tour or a package; a wholesaler.

**Packaging** The combining of more than one hospitality product or service into a single purchase item for a single price.

**Paid Bar** A bar setup where drinks are prepaid, usually involving the use of tickets.

**Parlor** A living or sitting room not used as a bedroom. In some parts of Europe, called a **salon.**

**Parlor Car** A railroad car, and sometimes a motorcoach, with individual swivel seats, food, and bar service.

**Passenger Mile** One passenger carried one mile.

**Passenger Traffic Manager** An employee who makes travel arrangements for other employees of his or her company.

**Peak Fare, Peak Rate,** or **Peak Season** On many carriers and at many destinations, the highest level of charges assessed during the year.

**Pension** In Europe, a guest or boarding house.

**Pitch** (1) The distance between rows of seats on an aircraft. (2) The rise and fall of a ship at sea, with the bow rising as the stern falls, and vice versa.

**Placement** Where your advertising actually appears, be it a time slot on radio or in the January issue, page 6, upper right-hand corner.

**Platform** The item-by-item list of things that directly support your proposition.

**Plus-plus** The term used to indicate that taxes and gratuities must be added to the rate.

**Pool Route** An arrangement more common in Europe whereby two carriers, usually airlines, that fly the same route share equally their total revenues, borrow planes and crews from each other, and share check-in facilities.

**Porterage** Baggage-handling service. The client on a tour that includes porterage should neither have to carry luggage nor pay the person who does. Enlightened self-interest, however, might lead the traveler to offer an occasional nominal tip.

**Post-convention Tour** An extension designed to supplement the basic travel home from a convention.

**Pre-convention Tour** An extension designed to supplement the basic travel to a convention.

**Pre-registration** Room assignment and the filling out of registration cards prior to a guest's arrival. Often used for convention, meeting, and tour guests.

**Price Promotion** A promotion where the incentive to purchase is based on price.

**Principal** The dominant participant in any given situation; more specifically in travel: (1) the primary producer of any unit of travel merchandise (an airline, a hotel, shipline); (2) any person (or company) who assumes responsibility for a travel program; or (3) anyone who pays a commission to another for selling a travel program.

**Prix Fixe** The price at which a table d'hote meal is offered.

**Promotion** A creative idea that is aimed at providing business and supports the overall marketing efforts. It may be used to stimulate new, trial, repeat, or incremental sales.

**Proposal** Letter sent by a facility outlining the understanding between the facility and meeting planner.

**Proposition** The strongest factual statement you can make on behalf of your product or service.

**Protected** As in "commissions protected," "agent protected," or "all departures protected": a guarantee by a supplier or wholesaler to pay commissions, plus full refunds to clients, on prepaid, confirmed bookings regardless of subsequent cancellation of, for example, a tour of a cruise.

**Psychographic Segmentation** A method of subdividing the market based on like needs and psychological motivations and values of groups of consumers.

**PTM** (See **Passenger Traffic Manager**)

**Public Relations** A marketing weapon that is the communications vehicle between your firm and customers, potential customers, and the variety of audiences in the marketplace.

**Publicity** One facet of public relations; it is the mentions or exposures received from announcements, events, and releases.

**Pullman** Sleeping and parlor car service operated on Western Hemisphere railroads by the Pullman Company. An almost universal term for a sleeping car. A particular kind of reserved-seat car on some British railroads.

**QRE** (See **Official Airline Guide**)

**Rack Rate** The official tariff as established and posted by a principal.

**Rate Pyramiding** The concept of offering a variety of rates and/or ranges from which the consumer may select; also offers the opportunity to "sell up."

**Receiving Agent** A tour operator or travel agent who specializes in services for incoming visitors.

**Reconfirmation** A statement of intent to use a reservation. Under airline rules, reserved space may be resold unless the passenger reconfirms within specified time limits.

**Red Book** Official Registry (and directory) of the American Hotel & Motel Association.

**Rep** A representative, either an individual or a company, empowered to act for a principal, usually in a sales or reservation capacity.

**Res** (or **Rez**) **Agent** A person who takes reservations and/or sells tickets, usually for an airline.

**Reservationist** A carrier (usually airline) employee who accepts, verifies, and confirms reservations (often by telephone) but does not actually write tickets.

**Retail Agency** The business establishment of a retailer, a subdivision of a wholesale and retail travel organization.

**Retailing** The selling of a travel product or service directly to the consumer.

**Roll-away Bed** A mobile bed that may be added to any room to accommodate an additional person.

**Rooming List** Meeting planner's list of those who will occupy previously reserved accommodations.

**Roundtrip Fare** The rate charged for a trip to a destination and return by the same route to the point of embarkation.

**Run of the House Rate** A flat price at which a hotel agrees to offer any of its rooms to a group.

**Sales Blitz** A concentrated short-term series of sales calls by a number of sales representatives to obtain a large number of bookings or reservations.

**Sample Room** A room suitable for display of merchandise.

**Scheduled Airline** An air carrier that offers scheduled service for individuals.

**Schoolroom Style** Row of tables (6 feet X 18 inches) on either side of a center aisle. Chairs face speaker or stage.

**Schoolroom Style Variations** (**V-Shape** or **Herringbone**) Perpendicular. (Tables are perpendicular to stage with chairs on outside, only on both sides of tables.)

**Seat Rotation** A system used on motorcoach tours to ensure that passengers have an equal opportunity to sit up front. Passengers change seats frequently, usually after every stop, according to a set pattern.

**Sectional Centers** The first three digits of a zip code which signify a specific geographic area; used widely by the direct mail industry.

**Segment** In an air itinerary, a leg or group of legs from boarding to deplaning point on a given flight.

**Segmentation** A portion of the total market in which customers have something in common.

**Selling Up** The concept of capitalizing on periods of high demand by charging a higher price or "premium" for your product or service offering.

**Senior Citizen Fare** An airline promotional fare for older people, usually above 60 or 65 years old.

**Service Charge** A specified percentage of a hotel bill (usually 10 or 15 percent) assessed against a guest; in return, the guest presumably is relieved of the responsibility for tipping. A fee charged to a client by a travel agent in addition to the commissions paid to him or her by the principals.

**Setup Time** The time needed before an event or function to arrange the setups.

**Share Excursions** Land tours sold by cruise lines or tour operators to cruise passengers. Usually available at each port of call.

**Share Fare/Rate** Fares or rates given to single persons who indicate willingness to share accommodations with a member of the same sex, provided one can be found by the tour operator, carrier, or hotel.

**Shoulder** A season between high or peak and low or off-peak.

**Shoulder Fare, Rate,** or **Season** On some air routes and at a few hotels, a price level between that charged during the low season and the high season. In the Caribbean, however, rates during the shoulder seasons (spring and fall) have at times been at the year's lowest level.

**Single** Any facility or reservation to be used by one person.

**Single Supplement** An extra charge assessed to a tour purchaser for single accommodations.

**Skal Club** A local social organization of the travel industry (the International Federation of Skal Clubs; the worldwide organization of local Skal clubs).

**Sleeper** A railroad car with sleeping accommodations.

**SMSA** (See **Standard Metropolitan Statistical Area**)

**Space** Availability of seats or accommodations. Tour operators may or may not have space on a particular departure.

**Standard Metropolitan Statistical Area** A census definition for a large concentration of people.

**Standard Ticket** An air ticket issued by travel agents which can be valid for travel on any ARC-member airline and other designated airlines.

**Standby** A passenger on a waitlist who may actually appear at an air terminal, prepared to travel in the event of a cancellation or a no-show; in that circumstance, he or she may be called a **go-show.**

**Standby Fare** A promotional tariff based on a conditional reservation. The holder of a standby ticket is not eligible to board the flight until all passengers who have or want confirmed reservations have been accommodated.

**Star, One** (**Two, Three, Four,** or **Five**) A hotel rating.

**Starboard** The right side of a ship, if you are facing the bow.

**Stateroom** A sleeping room on a ship; may imply more luxury than a cabin.

**Stern** The very rear of the ship.

**Stiffing** Deliberately withholding a tip.

**Stock** The type of paper or material used for printed materials; usually defined by weight, grain, or texture.

**Stopover** An intentional interruption of a journey, which either prevents a continuous through fare, or is permitted by the carrier in conjunction with a through fare.

**Strategic Market** One of 24 major U.S. markets that generate, in total, over 50 percent of the overnight travel in the United States.

**Strategy** Strategies are the identification of *how* you plan to achieve the objectives you have set. (Example: To increase our business in the pleasure travel market, we will (1) increase outdoor advertising, (2) shift some of our advertising to family magazines, etc.)

**Studio** A hotel room with a couch (or couches) that converts into a bed. Thus, a studio may be used as a parlor or a bedroom.

**Suite** A parlor connected to one or more bedrooms. To avoid confusion, designate the kind of suite you want by the number of bedrooms; for instance, a one-bedroom suite.

**Supplemental** (or **Supplemental Airline or Carrier**) An airline certified to offer passenger and cargo charter services. Sometimes called a **charter airline** or a **non-sked.**

**Supplier** The actual producer of a unit of travel merchandise; a carrier, hotel, sightseeing operator,etc.

**Table d'Hote** A full-course meal served at a fixed price; may or may not offer alternatives.

**Tariff** Any individual fare or rate quoted by any supplier. Any class of fares or rates; for example, a youth tariff. Any published list of fares or rates established by any supplier. A published compendium of listed fares or rates for any category of supplier. An official publication containing all fares or rates, conditions of service, etc.; a legal tariff.

**Telephone Selling** Contact by telephone whose primary purpose is to obtain a reservation for a room or group commitment.

**Tender** A boat used when docking is not possible to transport passengers from ship to shore and back.

**Tent Card** An internal promotion tool that rests on the top of a table, desk, bureau, or other flat surface that offers a promotion. It may be more than a single fold or it may contain more than one promotion.

**TGV** Tres Grande Vitesse; high-speed French train.

**Third-class Fare** Cheapest transportation on some Far Eastern railroads.

**Third-class Hotel** A poor place to stay.

**TIA** Travel Industry Association; now includes DATO.

**Ticket** Written or printed evidence that an individual (or group of individuals) is entitled to transportation, entry, etc. The passenger ticket and baggage checks, including all flight, passenger, and other coupons therein issued by the carrier, which provide for the carriage of the passenger and his or her baggage.

**Ticket Agent** A carrier employee who takes reservations and sells tickets.

**Time Sharing** A condominium concept whereby clients purchase the use of an apartment for the same brief period each year.

**Tour** Any prearranged, but not necessarily prepaid, journey to one or more places and back to the point of origin.

**Tour Basing Fare** A reduced-rate excursion fare available only to those who buy prepaid tours or packages. Inclusive tour, group inclusive tour, incentive group, contract bulk inclusive tour, tour basing, and group roundtrip inclusive tour basing fares are all tour basing fares.

**Tour Broker** A person or company who holds an ICC license to organize and market motorcoach tours.

**Tour Departure** Related to the operation of any published tour; the date of the start by any individual or group of a particular travel program; by extension, the entire operation of that single tour. For example, a tour operator may schedule a European escorted group tour with 16 departures; that is, the same basic tour may be operated 16 times.

**Tour Escort** An individual who accompanies a tour throughout, and is responsible for its smooth operation and for assisting passengers.

**Tour Leader** Strictly speaking, a person with special qualifications to conduct a particular travel group; for example, a botanist who conducts a garden tour. Often used inaccurately to designate a courier.

**Tour Manager** A courier, especially one employed to conduct a prepaid tour from beginning to end, including any trans-ocean legs.

**Tour Operator** A company that creates and/or markets inclusive tours, performs tour services, and subcontracts their performance. Most tour operators sell through travel agents and directly to clients.

**Tour Organizer** An individual, sometimes a travel agent, who organizes a group of passengers to participate in a special, prepaid tour. An organizer does not necessarily have conference appointments, nor does he or she usually pay commissions.

**Tour Shells** Brochures containing artwork, graphics, and/or illustrations, but bare of copy, which are to be overprinted by tour operators or wholesalers.

**Tourism** The business of providing and marketing services and facilities for pleasure travelers. Thus, the concept of tourism is of direct concern to governments, carriers, and the lodging, restaurant, and entertainment industries, and of indirect concern to virtually every industry and business in the world.

**Tourist Card** A kind of visa issued to tourists before entering a country, required in addition to a passport or other proof of citizenship.

**Tourist Class** In general, accommodations or establishments somewhat below top grade. In shiplines, segregated, less than first-class service; in airlines, unofficial designation for economy or coach service.

**Trade Media** The group of publications and/or broadcast media that follow your specific industry and product or service; the travel trade/industry media.

**Trade-outs/Barter** Exchanging your product or service for advertising coverage in either the broadcast or print media.

**Traffic Conferences** Within IATA, the suborganizations of carriers that serve the three areas into which IATA has divided the world. Thus, TC1 sets rates and makes rules applicable to Area One; TC2, for Area Two; etc.

**Traffic Flow** A term used to describe the flow of travelers between destinations.

**Transatlantic Passenger Shipping Conference** The chief North American executives of the now dissolved Atlantic Passenger Shipping Conference members.

**Transfer** Local transportation and porterage from one carrier terminal to another, from a terminal to a hotel, or from a hotel to a theater. The conditions of a tour contract should specify whether transfers are by private car or motorcoach and whether escort service is provided.

**Transpacific Passenger Conference** The promotional and regulatory association of shipping companies which offer passenger services in the Pacific.

**Travel Agent Magazine** A twice-weekly U.S. trade publication.

**Travel Group Charter** The CAB's designation for a proposed class of regulated roundtrip charter programs for individual travelers. At publication, no travel group charter has ever been operated, and the concept appears likely to remain controversial for several years.

**Travel Industry Association of Canada** A trade association embracing the entire range of Canadian travel and transportation, as well as related industries and governmental organizations.

**Travel and Tourism Research Association** A professional society of travel industry market research specialists.

**Travel Trade Magazine** A U.S. weekly trade publication.

**Travel Weekly** A Ziff-Davis trade newspaper published twice each week and sold to the vast majority of U.S. and Canadian travel agents.

**Travel Wholesaler** Services retail travel agents in the preparation of tour packages, ordering, billing, and advertising. It is possible for a travel agent, travel wholesaler, or tour operator to perform each other's functions, as is true in any business. In practice (economic theory), the levels are retail travel agent, travel wholesalers, and tour operators. Sometimes travel wholesalers and tour operators have their own retail company.

**Travelage East** and **Travelage West** Weekly U.S. regional trade publications.

**T-shape Style** The tables form a T. Chairs are set on the outside of the crossbar and on both sides of each leg.

**Twin** Room for two guests with two single beds.

**Twin Double** Room for two, three, or four people with two double beds.

**United States Tour Operators Association** A recently formed trade association of West Coast tour operators.

**United States Travel Service** The official U.S. agency for the promotion of tourism.

**Universal Air Travel Plan** The credit card system originally organized by the U.S. domestic airlines but now recognized by all IATA airlines.

**Universal Federation of Travel Agents Associations** A world organization of national travel agents trade associations.

**Upgrade** To move to a better accommodation of class of service.

**Validation** Imprinting a piece of airplane ticket stock with the special stamp that makes it a legal ticket.

**Value** Quality at a fair price — both perceived by and delivered to the customer.

**Value Season** A term used by some suppliers to indicate times of the year which are not peak season when prices are lower.

**Visa** An official authorization appended to a passport permitting travel to and within a particular country or region.

**Vouchers, Tour** Documents issued by tour operators to be exchanged for accommodations, meals, sightseeing, and other services. Sometimes called **coupons.**

**Waitlist** A list established by a supplier, particularly an airline, of customers who seek space on a date or a time that is sold out.

**Wholesaler** A company that usually creates and certainly markets inclusive tours and FITs for sale through travel agents. Often used interchangeably with tour operator, but several distinctions might be drawn. (1) A wholesaler presumably sells nothing at retail; a tour operator often does both. (2) A wholesaler does not always create his or her own products; a tour operator virtually always does. (3) A wholesaler is less inclined than a tour operator to perform local services. Industry reportage often fails to make distinctions, and to confound things further, many travel companies perform any or all of the functions of a travel agent, contractor, tour operator, and wholesaler.

**Winter Fare** or **Rate** Either the most expensive or the least expensive level depending on the area under discussion. In the North Atlantic, air fares are lowest in winter; in the Caribbean, winter fares are highest.

**World Travel Directory** A Ziff-Davis annual worldwide reference for domestic and international travel planners. Includes pertinent data on the sales personnel and outlets of travel agents and tour operators; air, sea, and rail carriers; car rental and sightseeing firms; consulates, embassies, and national and state tourist offices; travel and hotel representatives; publications; schools and associations; and motel/hotel systems.

**Yield Analysis** Analysis of revenue and profit generated by each type of consumer and/or market segment for your product or service.

**Zero-based Budgeting** This concept says that no expenditure is justified just because it was spent last year. Every expense is reanalyzed and justified each year on the basis that its expenditure will yield more favorable results than spending the same amount in another way.

# Index